the ifilm
Digital Video
Filmmaker's Handbook

Maxie D. Collier

ifilm publishing

lone eagle

SON #1 MEDIA

The IFILM Digital Video Filmmaker's Handbook
Copyright ©2001 by Maxie D. Collier

LONE EAGLE PUBLISHING COMPANY™
1024 N. Orange Drive
Hollywood, California 90038
Phone 323.308.3400 or 800.815.0503
A division of IFILM℠ Corp., www.IFILM.com

Printed in the United States of America

Cover design by Ryder Booth
Book design by Carla Green
Edited by Scott Smith

Library of Congress Cataloging-in-Publication Data

Collier, Maxie D.
    The IFILM digital video filmmaker's handbook / Maxie D. Collier.
        p. cm.
    ISBN 1-58065-031-7
        1. Cinematography—Handbooks, manuals, etc. 2. Digital video—Handbooks, manuals, etc. I. Title

TR850 .C55 2000
778.5'3—dc21

00-046488

Books may be purchased in bulk at special discounts for promotional or educational purposes. Special editions can be created to specifications. Inquiries for sales and distribution, textbook adoption, foreign language translation, editorial, and rights and permissions inquiries should be addressed to: Jeff Black, IFILM Publishing, 1024 North Orange Drive, Hollywood, CA 90038 or send e-mail to: info@ifilm.com

Distributed to the trade by National Book Network, 800.462.6420

Lone Eagle Publishing Company™ is a registered trademark.
IFILM℠ is a registered service mark.

This book is dedicated to all of the artists daring to pursue grandiose artistic visions, even while fighting the battles of everyday life.

"Don't talk about it, be about it . . ."

■ ■ ■ ■ ■ Contents

■ ■ ■ ■ ■ Much Respect—
i.e. Acknowledgments

I'd like to give a heartfelt thanks to all of the family, friends, and associates who have contributed to this work directly or indirectly, especially: My mother, Dr. Betty Collier-Burston; Tenisha and Monica Holloway for the sacrifices they made by loving a filmmaker; Dr. Bruce Marshall, the person who opened the door for me; everyone who ever worked on any of my projects, especially the cast and crew of *Mind Games, Detention, Hacks, Unit 43* and *Paper Chasers*; all my folks at BET who patiently schooled me about the biz in the early days, and continue to support my works today; Peter Broderick and everyone at Next Wave Films for their encouragement; Scott Smith for his contribution to this revised edition; the staff of IFILM; and finally, Jeff Black, Lauren Rossini and Carla Green of Lone Eagle Publishing for working tenaciously to help push me through this revision.

■ ■ ■ ■ ■ Editor's Note

A recent technology discussion at the Directors Guild Association in Los Angeles featured among its panelists an almost perfect sampling of DV pioneers—from producers to equipment manufacturers—a group of experts so youthful that they exposed the infancy of the digital film-making revolution. The lone exception was Director of Photography Roger Deakins, who had just finished his first major digital post-production effort on the Coen brothers' feature film, *O Brother, Where Art Thou?*

When the forum got underway, Deakins confessed that he felt a bit "crusty" among the other panelists, a hive of fresh-faced videophiles donned almost entirely in sleek black clothing. But when one of the panelists explained the clever practice of using inexpensive Chinese lanterns for set lighting in DV productions, Deakins was quick to explain that documentarians and low budget independents had beat digital filmmakers to that trick thirty years earlier. As far as he was concerned, there was no difference between the moviemakers of the past and the generation just coming into the form. The tools may have changed, but the challenges are the same.

Of course, it's easier to pass along trade secrets these days. Working in the electronic realm, DV filmmakers can immediately disseminate production notes, storyboards, location stills, audio clips, and raw footage around the world with relative simplicity. But why would 21st century storytellers feel more compelled to expose their methods than the filmmakers of the last 100 years? It may be that these computer-literate enthusiasts wish to repay a debt to the Internet, using it to warn their brethren of dangers past while using it to troubleshoot the current crop of problems. They have become a breed of artists who lead as they follow, who curry the flock as they blaze the trail. Many of these online forums—the websites, the e-zines, the chat rooms—produce truly invaluable tips. Yet, it's a different voice of authority; it lacks the anecdotal color of an old studio hand or the cynical disdain that Tinseltown legends seem to have for newcomers.

By this measure, *The IFILM Digital Video Filmmaker's Handbook* speaks to the new crop of filmmakers in more ways than one. Carrying the feeling and flavor of those net-based discussions to the printed form, it bridges the gap between those who get their education from books and those who like their information hot off the computer screen. It's more of an apprentice's notebook than a master's memoir, and more comprehensive because it doesn't assume the audience is either celluloid throwbacks or new-age digerati. The aim is to give both groups a tour through DV production.

Where its insights may seem to cover old territory, they are shared with an enthusiasm that is fresh and infectious. When it tackles cutting edge concepts, it leads the blurry-eyed reader into fundamentally clear explanations that are best characterized as unintimidating. Sprocketheads, those well-heeled filmmakers who prefer to skip its wealth of pre-production advice on lighting, audio recording, lens filtering and tracking equipment, will invariably rely on this volume when the gray areas of digital post-work get a little too fuzzy. Everyone else will simply appreciate the breezy, linear progression of the book, a step-by-step explanation of the entire filmmaking process, not just the zeros and ones of the digital world.

•   •   •

SCOTT SMITH is the Senior Editor of *RES:The Magazine of Digital Filmmaking* and a featured columnist on the Adobe.com website, where he writes extensively about the emerging technologies and techniques used by today's digital filmmakers. He is the co-founder of Silver Planet Studio, a DV production company whose digital effects work on feature projects includes director Frank Grow's groundbreaking DV debut, *Love God*, and Todd Solondz's latest film, *Happiness*. He is also the author of two books—*The Film 100* (Citadel Press), a ranking of the most influential people in the history of cinema; and *Making iMovies* (Peachpit Press), a primer on video for the web.

■ ■ ■ ■ ■ ■ Introduction to the Revised Edition

Greetings, and welcome to the world of digital filmmaking!

When I first launched The DV Filmmaker's Website (www.dvfilm-maker.com) and self-published the first edition of *The DV Filmmaker's Handbook* in 1998, it was primarily a result of my frustration at the limited digital filmmaking information readily available. Although many of us shared our DV experiences at filmmaking workshops and via the Internet, there were no books covering the diverse range of topics that encompassed this rapidly developing new art form. Seeing a need, I spent an intense three-month period researching, writing and publishing *The DV Filmmaker's Handbook.*

Since then, the book and website have helped and inspired thousands of filmmakers around the world. Now, with Lone Eagle Publishing making this new revised edition available to bookstores, schools and libraries, even more filmmakers like yourself will have access to this information.

The text has been completely updated (with the generous assistance of *Res* magazine Senior Editor Scott Smith), to reflect current DV hardware and software. We have also added a case study that details the evolution of my documentary film, *Paper Chasers*, from initial idea through post-production. As an added bonus, the book is also packaged with a DVD featuring a trailer for *Paper Chasers* and behind-the-scenes looks at several other digital productions.

So grab your highlighter—unless of course you're a cash-strapped filmmaker reading the entire book in the café of your local bookstore, in which case grab a note pad and a pen—and get ready to go into your creative zone. The information in this book, combined with your own initiative and resourcefulness, can help you make your films a reality. Good luck!

■ ■ ■ ■ ■ ■ Introduction

Me, DV, and Personal Films

I'm ready to make another film. No . . . I *have* to make another film, and soon! My hunger for creative expression battles with my need for a professional career boost.

Never mind the fact that my directorial debut, *Hacks*, languishes in post-production limbo or "in hock," as so aptly phrased by indie film guru, John Pierson. After two years of toiling and pushing my resources to the limit, *Hacks*, though still a work-in-progress, has opened many doors for me.

Yet, my videotape masters sit inaccessible at a fantastic, supportive post house in Baltimore. My film negative remains on lockdown at a lab in Virginia, likewise waiting for me to raise a pretty hefty bail. My mind, however, is haunted by the thought of how much I could do today with the $30,000+ I begged and borrowed from family and friends to film and edit *Hacks* thus far.

With $30,000 I could purchase all the equipment required to shoot and edit a feature, completely finance the production costs, transfer the video to film, and have money left for marketing and festivals!

Wait! Before you trash this book with the notion that I'm insane, I promise that I'll prove to you just what $30,000 can do as we dig deeper into specific issues that will help us create high-quality DV films. But first, let me introduce myself . . .

A Lil' Something About Me

I have worked professionally in film and television for close to eleven years. My interest in filmmaking was sparked after coming in contact with many film producers and directors while working at Black Entertainment Television (BET) in the early '90s.

I left BET to further pursue my interest in filmmaking, and worked on a variety of low-budget and studio-budget films. I also produced several music videos and short films, including a half-hour supernatural thriller entitled *Mind Games.*

In June 1996, I co-produced fellow Baltimore filmmaker Darryl Wharton's debut feature film, *Detention*, "an urban *Breakfast Club*" story about five very different students forced by a dedicated teacher to spend an afternoon together.

A few months later, I made my writing and directing debut with my feature, *Hacks*, the story of a day in the life of a group of illegal cab drivers and the characters they meet while working the streets of Baltimore.

Detention was filmed in twelve days on color Super 16mm film. We got the film in the can for a little over $12,000 plus some debt and deferrals. However, Darryl had to raise far more to get the film to print. In fact, because of the high cost of Super 16mm blow-up to 35mm, he ultimately ended up getting a $14,000 16mm print made from his video cut of the film!

This print has been screened at many festivals nationwide—The Urban World Film Festival, Pan-African Film Festival in Los Angeles and The Atlanta International Film Festival, just to name a few.

Hacks was also filmed in color Super 16mm. Principal photography was completed over a tight fourteen-day period. The film broke several rules of low budget production by featuring over fity speaking roles with the majority of the production taking place in cars traveling all over town. We got *Hacks* in the can for about $24,000 plus a lot of debt and deferrals. Additional money was invested to edit a rough cut of the film.

I spent about a year working on the rough cut and trying to raise the $40,000 required to finish *Hacks*. The work-in-progress received excellent feedback when it screened at the September '97 Independent Feature Film Market (IFFM), but I had no luck raising completion funds. However, I did establish fantastic relationships with several filmmaking professionals and companies. Encouraged by these contacts, I finally relocated to the Los Angeles area.

Since then, I have shared my production experiences as a panelist at filmmaking workshops at The Showbiz Expo West and the IFP West's Film Financing Conference. I've also taught for the prestigious UCLA Extension Program, in addition to helping launch their digital filmmaking curriculum.

I had been researching the viability of video as a medium for independent film production to film for many years. But, after being disappointed with other video formats such as Hi-8, I shifted my attention back to film while keeping an eye on the emerging digital technology.

Then in late '97, I had an opportunity to work with a DV camera and was immediately impressed with the quality. Inspired by the initial impression, I extensively researched and experimented with digital video production and post-production. I have seen many video-originated films projected from 35mm film and I am now convinced that DV represents the future of low-budget filmmaking.

Making the Most of This Handbook

If you have already flipped through this book, you probably noticed that I make extensive reference to various websites and Internet resources. With DV technology evolving so rapidly, the Internet provides a near instantaneous method of keeping abreast of new developments.

The IFILM Digital Video Filmmaker's Handbook is designed to provide, in print, detailed, practical information on DV filmmaking that you can repeatedly reference. This information is built around key technical and filmmaking concepts that often remain applicable even as the technology changes.

However, these concepts are supplemented by specific examples. The DV Filmmaker's website (www.dvfilmmaker.com), my newsletter, the *DV Filmmaker's Report*, and the additional Internet resources listed in the appendices will help you keep up with the latest DV filmmaking news, products, services, and information.

If you are not yet online, you can still benefit from the book, but you will certainly not be getting the most out of it. Internet access is now available at most U.S. public libraries and at colleges and universities.

This book is geared towards first-time filmmakers and film professionals. Experienced filmmakers can skip through and pluck out all of the relevant DV production details, recommendations, and references, while novice filmmakers will receive an introduction to the entire filmmaking process. Along the way we will delve into the mechanics and craft of creating personal films.

The Era of Personal Films

Encouraged by the fairytale-like successes of indie filmmakers such as Richard Linklater (*Slacker*), Spike Lee (*She's Gotta Have It*), Kevin Smith (*Clerks*), Ed Burns (*The Brothers McMullen*), and numerous others, people of all walks of life have now taken on filmmaking as a hobby and profession. The result is . . .

A glut of Indie films!

Great films, mediocre films, and films far worse than you can ever imagine are now being produced. And the boom shows no signs of slowing down, particularly with the advent of DV technology. So, what should this mean to you?

It means that if you enter into this arena with the realistic understanding that the odds are very slim of your film ever being picked up and released by a major distributor, then you will be okay.

But if your passion is driven by the belief that your film will instantly make you the next Robert Rodriguez (*El Mariachi*), you're probably setting yourself up for disappointment. And if you have blown your credit cards along the way, you are setting yourself up for serious financial troubles.

Sure, you may be a great writer or director, but this does not always mean your film will be able to compete in a crowded marketplace.

Herein lies the beauty of DV films . . .

It's a whole different ball game when you are spending $5,000 to $30,000 to create a film. This is a much smaller amount of money to raise *and* recoup. With this awareness, you do not have to be as concerned about chasing a distribution deal to earn back a whole lot of money. Ultimately, the low budgets of DV films create a whole new genre of films. Let's call them . . .

Personal Films

With a personal film, suddenly you don't have to be as concerned about marketplace trends, audience tastes, or other abstract realities. Instead, you can focus on your personal agenda.

Maybe you want to create a work that showcases your ability to write and/or direct a feature-length story. Or, as an actor, you might want to produce a film that showcases your talent. Even musicians and singers can produce showcase works. In these instances, personal films can be an excellent opportunity to work on your craft until you can step up to the next level.

Or maybe you don't want a film career, but you have a passionate desire to communicate a story or message to an audience. Whatever the case may be, personal filmmaking makes it a possibility.

So, what do you do with the films once you have labored to create them? Personal films are distributed by whatever grassroots means possible: the Internet, private home screenings, videotapes passed from person to person, public screenings in theaters with video projection systems, public access TV, leased access TV, community group sponsored screenings, etc.

Am I saying that personal films cannot be commercially viable in today's theatrical market? Not at all. However, it boils down to mathematics. There are a whole lot of films and far fewer movie screens.

But in the near future, the Internet and DVD will become the distribution medium of choice for these projects, furthering the paradigm shift that is occurring in film production and distribution, and creating a viable way of recouping your investment with greater control over your own marketing and distribution.

Don't get me wrong—for years to come, 35mm film will continue to be the premier acquisition and distribution method. And it will be the brass ring for which many of us continue to reach. But for now, between video and film, there is another option, a rapidly evolving hybrid that is not video or film, but rather, digital film. We represent the first generation of digital filmmakers. Are you ready to tell your story?

The 10 Rules of DV Filmmaking

circa Summer 2000

1. No matter how "artistic" or "commercial," the story is more important than the medium.

2. DV in . . . DV out . . . digital all the way.

3. Record the best audio possible.

4. Be professional regardless of the camera size.

5. You really don't need the newest technology.

6. Don't believe the hype . . . judge for yourself.

7. Feed people good food frequently.

8. You never know too many people . . . network, network, network.

9. Technology and artistry can coexist.

10. What you learn today may not apply tomorrow . . . but keep learning anyway.

1

■■■■■■ Television and Film—
Trying to Work Together

Before we begin exploring this merger of video and film technology, we need to have an understanding of some essential basics. Although both television and film communicate pictures and sounds, the mechanics by which they operate are very different. These differences create some challenges when combining the mediums.

Motion Pictures

In the late 1800s, photographers and early filmmakers discovered that the illusion of motion could be created by displaying still pictures in rapid succession. Each individual picture was called a *frame* and the rate at which they were shown was expressed as *frames per second* (fps).

Experimentation led to the discovery that the human eye and brain perceived smooth motion when pictures were shown at 20 fps or more. Specifically, the range of 24 to 30 fps captured and projected movement that looked natural to people.

Even more importantly, it was discovered that this range "felt" natural to viewers. The brain recognizes even slight variations from this range that may not be visibly obvious. So, while 22 fps or 32 fps may look like normal movement, they register differently in the viewer's mind. This factor becomes important later in our discussion of the challenges of making video look like film.

Television and Video Fundamentals

Video captures images by using lenses to project a picture on a light-sensitive device that quickly scans the picture. This device scans diagonally, from left to right and from top to bottom, converting dark portions of a picture into a strong signal (high voltage) and lighter portions of a picture into a weaker signal (lower voltage).

For color video, a lens element splits the image into the three primary colors (red, green, blue, a.k.a. RGB). Each of these colors is then scanned separately.

Prior to the early '80s, the instrument most often used to scan the images was a glass *camera picture tube*. Today, most cameras use a *charged coupled device* or CCD, a silicone chip that is far more efficient and much smaller than camera tubes.

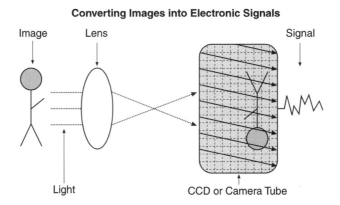

Converting Images into Electronic Signals

The NTSC television system adopted by the U.S. and several other countries, scans images at 30 fps using 525 lines. The PAL system used in England and other countries scans 25 fps using 625 lines, as does the slightly different SECAM system used in countries such as France and Russia. PAL is becoming an increasingly popular choice for DV filmmakers who are enticed by the extra lines of resolution and the ease at which the format can be transferred to 24 fps film.

Video Fields and Frames

In the early days of television, a whole picture could not be scanned line by line because during playback the glowing, phosphorous element of a TV picture tube could not glow long enough to show the whole 525 lines. By the time the last lines of the image were recreated, the top lines had disappeared.

To compensate for this, a system was developed that rapidly scans a picture twice, each time grabbing every other line of the image to capture half a frame. This half of a frame, called a *field*, contains half of the picture information. Each NTSC field equals 262.5 lines.

To recreate a whole image back on the television, the two fields are quickly combined, or *interlaced*, back together to create the illusion of a whole picture on the screen. The scanning and interlacing process causes the scan lines that are so noticeable on old projection TVs. Scan lines are also a major issue when transferring video to film.

Once an image has been scanned by a CCD or picture tube, the information can be transmitted or recorded on a recordable media such as videotape.

The audio portions of television signals are created using microphones that respond to various sound levels and frequencies while converting them into electronic signals. The audio and video signals are combined to create a television signal.

Television signals use a system of *synchronization (sync) pulses* to keep the timing of all of this critical interlace, picture, and sound information coordinated throughout the process.

Analog vs. Digital

Until the advent of digital technology, audio and video signals were captured, transmitted, and recorded as *analog signals*. Analog information is created by monitoring variations in the voltage levels and frequencies of electronic signals.

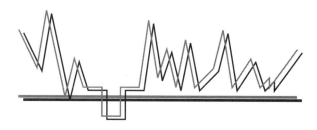

Voltage is the strength of the signal as measured from the top of a peak to the bottom. The time or distance between peaks is called a *cycle* and is represented by a unit of measurement called *hertz* (Hz).

Frequency is the number of cycles a signal makes in one second and is also represented by Hz or kilohertz which equals 1000 cycles (kHz).

As the video and audio information undergoes these conversions, various forms of interference can be introduced throughout the process. This interference, or *noise*, appears as "snow" in video pictures or as undesirable sounds in the audio playback. Noise is present in all signals in varying degrees.

The *signal-to-noise ratio* is a number that expresses the strength of a signal compared to the noise inherent in the signal. This ratio is expressed in *decibels* (dB). The higher the ratio, the better the video will look and the better the audio will sound. For example, the audio from a standard VCR is around 40dB while audio from a CD is roughly 90dB.

However, even if you start with a high signal-to-noise ratio for your video and audio, the disadvantage of analog signals is that anything that affects the levels of the signal being transmitted or recorded on tape introduces noise, thereby also affecting the image and sound quality.

This interference can come in many different forms. It can originate from something as simple as lightning during transmission or the noise added with every copy made from a copy of a tape. (Think about how bad the third copy of a VHS tape looks compared to the original.)

In the digital world, analog signals are *digitized*, converted into digital information, by a process that quickly samples the high and lows of an analog signal, and then translates it into a chunk of computer data. The more times a signal is sampled per second, the more faithful the digital information is to the original signal.

Digital sampling rates are also expressed in kHz. The higher the kHz, the more times a signal is sampled per second. In addition to the frequency of a sample, another variable is the size of the sample. Larger samples mean that for any given portion of your signal, you are digitizing with greater detail.

The size of a sample is expressed as *bits* which are the smallest unit of measurement in computer data. An 8-bit sample means that each time a segment of a signal is sampled, it is broken up into eight little pieces. Sampled at 12-bits, that same segment will be broken up and recorded with 4-bits more detail than the 8-bit.

As a point of reference, the CD audio recording standard has a sample rate of 44.1 kHz at 16-bits per sample (often written as 44.1/16). Many DV cameras offer better than CD quality at 48 kHz of 16-bit samples (48/16).

Once the signals have been digitized and converted into computer data, the information can be stored, reproduced, transmitted and converted back to analog without the introduction of noise. The result is that the material is nearly always reproduced with the same quality, i.e. the same signal-to-noise ratio, as the original—the video and audio are accurate reproductions of the original.

Film Basics

Unlike the electronic process used in television and video, film is a very physical process. Film cameras operate by taking a rapid succession of pictures. Lenses project an image onto a frame of film that is quickly *exposed* (the chemical process that takes the picture), before advancing to the next frame. At 24 fps, 24 pictures are taken per second when filming events at normal speed.

This high-speed process requires some precise mechanics to ensure that everything runs smoothly. Interestingly, although motion pictures appear to be moving, each frame must be a high quality still picture that is properly focused and exposed to the right amount of light.

Poor focus results in blurry images. *Underexposure*, too little light, and the image is filmed dark. *Overexposure*, too much light, and the images lose detail because they are too bright. The key elements in this process are:

- The film stock;
- The film transport mechanism;
- The shutter; and
- The lens.

Film Stock

Film stock is an acetate-based photographic strip with one side covered in a photo-sensitive silver-halide, crystal-based emulsion. It is these crystals that give film an often discernible "grainy" look. Even the high-quality microscopic grain patterns found in the best film stocks available today are registered by the mind. This grain is an important part of the "look" of film.

Film images are captured by the exposure and development of the light sensitive silver-halide crystals. Black and white film features a single layer of emulsion that responds to the entire range of visible light. Color film is made up of three layers that respond to the red, green, and blue primary colors. When later combined, these three colors can recreate the entire spectrum of colors.

Film stock features perforations, called sprocket holes, on the side that allow the film to move through the camera a frame at a time by the transport mechanism. This mechanism is either a spring driven or electric motor that uses a claw that slips into a perforation then moves a frame in place, holds it still until the frame is exposed, then moves the exposed frame out while moving the next unexposed frame in place.

The Shutter

The camera *shutter* is a mirrored device that controls exactly how much light reaches the film frame. It also works in sync with the transport to regulate how long the film frame is exposed to light.

The light reaching the shutter comes from lenses featuring high quality glass optics designed to collect and focus the light reflected off the images being filmed.

Much like the rolls of film used in everyday still cameras, film negative must be developed, then printed before it can be projected. There are some less frequently used film stocks, known as *reversal stocks*, which can be developed and then immediately projected without having prints made.

Motion Picture Sound

Unlike video, motion picture sound is recorded using a separate sound recording device. Traditionally, this recording device was a 1/4" tape based reel-to-reel machine, the industry standard is called a *Nagra*. However, in recent years, *digital audio tape* (DAT) recorders have rapidly become the primary sound recording instrument.

Since picture and sound are recorded separately, a method must be used to synchronize them. The classic way to accomplish this was the use of a *clapboard*. Held in front of the camera at the start of every scene, the open clapboard would be clapped shut generating a distinct sound that was recorded by the sound recording device.

The picture and sound could later be matched up by finding the exact picture frame where the clapper was shut and matching it to the exact point where the clap was heard on the audiotape. That *sync point* allows the picture and sound for the rest of the scene to stay synchronized.

Editing Film

For decades, film editing was just as much a physical process as filming. The film picture and sound elements were literally cut and taped or glued together to eventually create a negative master of the finished picture. Today, most people edit their films digitally, then make a final *negative cut* based upon their digital version.

And, in some instances, especially when *computer generated images* (CGI) are involved, computers are also used to scan film and manipulate the images, or create original images that are then recorded onto film.

Once all of the pictures and sounds have been edited, the final negative is "married" with the final audio track to create a *composite negative* from which a final print can be made. This print will most commonly feature an *optical audio track*, where the sound is represented by impressions burned into the side of the film, or one of an assortment of *digital audio soundtrack* systems, that are frequently used for big-budget films.

The film projectors play back the rolls of film at 24 fps, projecting the images onto the screen using a strong light and lens system, while playing back the audio from the optical or digital tracks.

Aspect Ratios and Film Formats

Most of us have seen films shown on television in a *letterbox* format where there is a black band at the top and bottom of the screen that makes the picture look longer. Well the fact is the picture *is* longer. The width-to-length *aspect ratio* of standard television is more square compared to the rectangular shaped frame size of the 35mm film most commonly used in feature films.

Usually when 35mm films are transferred to video, portions of the picture frame are lost in a process called *pan and scan* that cuts off portions of the picture to fit on a TV screen. When 35mm film is transferred letterboxed, none of the image is lost.

Aspect ratios are typically expressed as number calculated by dividing the width of a picture by its height. For example, standard television has a ratio of 4 units wide by 3 units tall. This ratio is usually expressed as 1.33:1 (4/3= 1.33) reading 1.33 to 1. On the other hand, the standard 35mm film has a ratio of 1.85:1.

There are a couple of other common film formats and a new video format that all have different aspect ratios.

Format	Aspect Ratio
Normal TV, 16mm film, Super 35mm	1.33:1
Super 16mm film	1.66:1
New 16:9 Wide Screen and High Definition TV format	1.78:1
35mm film	1.85:1

16mm film is frequently used for television programs since the aspect ratios are very close. Many low-budget films have been photographed on 16mm and Super 16mm film. In the case of 16mm, these films can be projected from a 16mm print or blown up to 35mm film.

Super16 film is 16mm film perforated on only one side, extending the image area into the space normally used by the soundtrack and perforations. This results in a larger image area and more rectangular aspect ratio. While super 16mm films cannot be shown theatrically, it is a popular format because the aspect ratio is closer to 35mm and offers excellent quality when blown up to 35mm.

The 16:9 wide screen TV format was introduced to prepare for the new generation of digital televisions and high definition broadcast. Several high-end cameras and a few lower priced camcorders can record in 16:9. The rectangular shape of 16:9 also blows up to 35mm very well.

Like Super 16mm, Super 35mm uses single perforations and extends the image area. The additional space provides a better quality image. Super 35mm is mostly used for television programs.

Video and Film Resolution

Resolution is a measurement of the number of individual elements that make up a single picture. As I mentioned earlier, NTSC television features 525 lines, although only 486 are used to create a picture, the rest are used for other signal information.

When capturing video on a computer, NTSC resolution is considered to be 640 pixel elements by 480 pixels, and DV has a resolution of 720 x 480 pixels.

The microscopic crystals that comprise a frame of film cannot be measured in such a manner. In fact, different formulations of film can have very different crystal sizes and resolutions.

The quality of a film image is also related to the size of the picture frame. A frame of 16mm film is about 21 percent the size of a frame of 35mm film. So an image photographed on 35mm film is going to have a much better resolution than the same image filmed on 16mm film.

While the resolution of video cannot be directly compared to film, consider the following example. When film is scanned into computers to create computer-generated effects that are going to be re-recorded on film, the scanning is done 2000 pixels by 2000 pixels! This constitutes far more detail than the 525 lines, 640 pixels by 480 pixels of standard NTSC television.

As a result, most current video formats transferred to film will always have varying degrees of blocky pixelation that are more noticeable under some situations than others. Even the best high-definition television system featuring 1152 lines, still much less resolution than film.

Transferring Film to Video

The different frame rates of film and video create some timing conflicts when transferring film to video. Remember one second of film footage equals 24 frames (24 fps) while one second of video equals 30 frames (30 fps). So, how do you stretch one second of film out to 30 frames? If you just speed up the film, it will play back on video 20 percent faster than the way it was recorded. That won't work.

Obviously, you must have a way to add six frames of film. You could repeat some of the film frames, but then the film played back on video will have a disconcerting jerkiness.

To transfer film to video, a system was devised called the 3:2 pulldown. With this process, those extra six frames of film are added by taking one film frame and recording it on two fields (1 frame) of video. However, the next film frame is recorded on three fields of video (1.5 frames).

This blending method is called *interpolation*. It continues for the entire transfer, allowing those 24 frames of film to be evenly spread across 30 frames. This effectively keeps one second of film equal to one second of video and maintains smooth motion.

The 3:2 pulldown is done as the film is transferred to video using a *telecine machine*. Rolls of film are strung up on the machine, then electronically converted into video.

These complicated and delicate machines can perform incredible image manipulations while transferring to video. The most common is *color correction* that offers unbelievable control over the way your film images appear on video.

Transferring Video to Film

Achieving a quality video-to-film transfer is much more challenging than film-to-video. In addition to incompatible frame rates, you also have to deal with the issue of interlace scan lines and video's lower resolution.

There are three basic processes used for video-to-film transfers: *kinescopes, film recorders* and *electronic beam recorders* (EBRs). In addition, several companies have developed their own unique and often proprietary variations. These methods vary greatly in quality and cost.

Note that in the price examples listed below, companies have different policies on what they deliver. Some companies only do the transfer and provide you with a negative which you have to take elsewhere to have a final print made. Some others provide you with a print, but require that you come back to them for more prints or purchase the negative from them (usually at a very high rate). So evaluate all the pricing for yourself.

Kinescopes

Kinescope is the oldest system for transferring video to film. A kinescope is a small, very high quality video monitor that is synchronized to a special film camera that literally films the video off of the monitor. The camera's shutter and motor are timed to match the video frame rate while dropping selected fields of video as it films. In addition to reducing the video's 30 fps to 24 fps, this helps reduce the scan lines.

Trinescope is a derivative of the kinescope that uses three separate monitors, one for each primary color (RGB again). The images from the three monitors are focused and combined using lens that direct the image on to the film. Trinescopes offer sharper color reproduction than regular kinescope.

Kinescope and trinescope are the most affordable video-to-film transfer process. Below is a sampling of rates from several established companies. Contact information is listed in the appendices.

- **The National Film Board of Canada**
  Trinescope   16mm   CA$70/min.
  Approximately US$47 at time of print.

- **Film Craft Labs**
  Trinescope   16mm   US$75/min.
                         35mm   US$230/min
- **Duart Film Lab**
  Kinescope   16mm $75/min.

Film Recorders

These extremely high quality machines were originally designed for combining short segments of film with computer generated effects. The equipment is expensive and the processes are basically not very cost effective for most filmmakers. However, this technology is starting to be applied to long form projects.

Film recorders use two methods of reproducing video and/or computer images. Both methods use computers to scan each frame of video. The means by which they output the image to film are different. The first method, a CRT-based system, is similar to trinescope except that the three color monitors utilized have a far higher resolution and the color reproduction is superior. The video frames are photographed at a rate of 15-40 seconds per frame, a very slow process.

The second method is a laser-based system that uses three colored lasers to precisely recreate the video frame image on a frame of film. This produces the best quality film images. At six seconds per frame it is faster than CRT-based systems. However, it is still generally unpractical for long projects. Laser film recorders are also the most expensive of all video/digital imaging processes.

Electronic Beam Recorders (EBR)

Between the quality of kinescope and film recorders are electronic beam recorders that offer excellent video-to-film transfers at relatively reasonable rates for long projects.

EBRs cannot record in color so the process converts the video information into three separate electronic beams, again one for each primary color. These beams basically "draw" the video image on to three separate rolls of black and white film. Each roll represents a separate color element for each frame. This process is very precise and much faster than film recorders.

After the film has been exposed to the EBR, the resulting rolls of film representing red, green, and blue are then printed frame by frame onto color negative. Each frame is printed three times, once for each color.

This *optical printing* process is not real-time but is fairly automated and proceeds much faster than you would expect.

Once complete, you will have a color negative that is ready to be printed like any other film. Some companies can only use an EBR to create a 16mm negative. They must then blow the 16mm up to 35mm for a 35mm print.

There are several different systems used in EBR to deal with the frame rate incompatibility. The most common method is a reverse of the 3:2 pulldown, where every fifth field of video is simply thrown out, effectively reducing the 30 fps down to 24 fps. However, this process can sometimes result in jerky motion if there is a lot of movement in the picture frame.

Other proprietary systems use various methods to combine and delete fields. This averaging process allows for smooth motion from video frames with a lot of movement.

There are also techniques for dealing with the scan lines that result from interlaced video. Some EBR processes, such as that used by the Sony High Definition Center, *up-convert* the 525 line NTSC video signal to make it a 1125 line high definition format. While this does not add resolution, the 525 lines are spread across the 1125 lines by using an interpolation that adds lines. The addition of these lines eliminates interlacing artifacts and results in a less video-looking image.

Other methods use computers to change video from interlaced fields to frames of *progressive scan* video that contain two fields of video information in a single frame. Some video cameras, such as the Canon XL1, offer progressive scan modes that perform this very beneficial function.

Although a top of the line EBR transfer can cost $50,000+, you can end up with a top quality product. Below is a sampling of EBR transfer rates. Again, contact information is in the appendices.

- **4MC (Four Media Corp.)**
  16mm $180/min.
  35mm $425/min.
- **Cineric**
  35mm $400/min.
- **Sony Hi-Definition Center**
  35mm $648/min.

Is it worth it? That's been the big debate for the past couple of years. In my opinion, even at these expensive rates, given the relatively low upfront acquisition and editing costs for video, it is still far less expensive than shooting and finishing in film.

Video-to-film transfers are a fast growing, rapidly evolving industry. Companies such as Swiss Effects (www.swisseffects.ch) and Film Team (www.filmteam.com) have invested heavily in researching and developing proprietary processes, offering new developments with lasers, film scanners, computer graphics and film printing devices. All of this has greatly improved the quality of the video-to-film transfers. And now, as the volume of work goes up and the field becomes more competitive, the cost of transfers will start to go down.

Making Video Look Like Film

In the U.S., video is still often looked down upon when used for dramatic works, with the exception of soap operas. Viewers and industry people typically associate video with television news shows, sitcoms, and pornography. On the other hand, the expenses of shooting on film are so much higher than video, that it just isn't economically practical in many cases to shoot film.

In the late '80s, several companies began to experiment with video treatment processes that manipulate video images to make them appear more like film. For many years, the leader among these companies was Filmlook™ Inc. (formerly Woodholly). Many people erroneously use the term Filmlook to describe the wide range of video treatment processes now offered as a service by many different post-production companies and specialized *service bureaus.*

Video treatment processes use customized computer programs to manipulate color, add simulated film grain patterns, and modify the motion of video to simulate the characteristics of film. Some of the services even allow you to match specific filmstocks. When used on quality, well lit video footage, these processes can be quite impressive.

On the other hand, at $45 to $95 per minute, video processes can be pretty costly. There are many companies now offering the service, and several are listed on the resources page. Shop around and review demo tapes carefully. Be sure to ask about their experience with DV.

And now, using two high powered computer programs, Adobe After Effects and Digieffects' Cinelook plug-in, it is possible for you to effectively do very good quality video treatment processes on your home computer. These programs go through your project frame by frame and modify each image according to a variety of adjustable characteristics.

Cinelook also includes settings that allow you to match your video to a range of film stocks.

Unfortunately, because of all the computer processing power required by these programs to modify, render and redraw each frame, you must have a very fast computer with a lot of memory. Even then, you often have to leave the computer on for *days* to complete long projects. In addition to the computer, the powerful software is a hefty investment as well. Still, despite the inconvenience, Cinelook is another step toward self-sufficient production, and the results are on par with the services offered by service bureaus.

Some filmmakers have video treatments done to their videos prior to distributing tapes to festivals or potential investors or distributors. Others use the process as a final step before distributing their film on home video.

Video treatment processes should not be used to create your master tape if you plan on transferring that tape to film. The modifications done by these processes do not translate to film well and result in poor image quality. However, since DV can be dubbed with no quality loss, it is simple to create one copy for your film transfer and another that has been processed.

The progressive scan modes found on some camcorders create video images that look much more film-like than typical interlaced video images. This mode on the Canon XL1 camcorder is called the *frame movie mode*. When properly lit, the frame movie mode offers a very unique look.

Other techniques used to make video look more like film include the careful use of filters to soften the video image, experimentation with shutter speeds, and in camera features like *posterization* and *strobing*. However, with most of these features available when editing, it is best to try to record your video images without effects to keep it as clean as possible.

2
■ ■ ■ ■ ■ ■ So What's DV
All About Anyway?

Digital video (DV) is a high-resolution video format that treats video and audio as digital data. In this format, the data can be stored, manipulated, and relayed just like any other computer data without degradation to the picture or sound quality.

Since its introduction to American consumers in 1994, DV has rapidly grown in popularity. About two years later, desktop DV editing systems became available. Together, the DV cameras and editing systems provide consumers with unprecedented quality.

DV offers users several important benefits including:

- Portable and relatively inexpensive cameras;
- Excellent images with over 500 lines of resolution and component recording that provides fantastic color reproduction by treating the video information as three separate signals (very important for your transfer to film);
- CD quality stereo sound recording;
- The ability to use a high speed connection and cable called a IEEE-1394 interface (also called FireWire or I.link) to transmit video and audio in and out of a computer or other DV device. This is a digital transfer with the quality of the copy identical to the original; and
- Affordable, high performance DV editing recorders and computer-based DV editing systems.

Five Flavors of Digital Video

As is often the case with new video technology, digital video comes in a few different formats. (Remember beta vs. VHS?) In some cases there is significant difference between the cost, features, and quality of the formats. In other instances, the difference is less about quality and more about a company's efforts to develop their own proprietary hardware that requires that all cameras, tapes, and editing equipment be purchased from them.

Although there are new DV systems being introduced and proposed, presently there are five readily available formats: DVC/Mini-DV, DVCAM, DVCPro, Digital Betacam, and the undisputed champ of them all, *High Definition Video* (HD Video).

DVC/Mini-DV

Digital video consumer format is most commonly referred to as DVC. The format was developed and adopted by a coalition of video manufacturers including JVC, Sony, Panasonic, Canon and others.

Initially offered as an alternative to the finicky Hi-8 format, DVC was quickly embraced by video professionals attracted by the low cost and excellent quality.

One problem with DVC is that since the cameras and editing equipment are consumer oriented, they often lack certain precision controls and features found on professional equipment.

However, for the most popular cameras, many companies and individuals now offer add-on products and modifications to compensate for some of the shortcomings.

DVCAM

This is Sony's exclusive, higher priced "professional" version of DV. Technically, the video format is no different than DVC. However, the audio formats and the size of the data track recorded on tape are different.

DVCAM records in a *locked audio* format. This is a system where audio is recorded using a timing method that exactly "locks" it with the accompanying video. The less precise *unlocked audio* format used in DVC effectively keeps audio and video synchronized but theoretically is allowed to drift +/-1/3 of a frame. There have not been many reports of this being a problem.

DVCAM equipment offers more professional controls and features. Additionally, the format is designed to provide the durability required in high volume production environments such as *electronic news gathering* (ENG) broadcasting.

The width of the data track recorded on DVCAM tapes is nearly 50 percent wider than DVC and consumes nearly twice as much tape. But according to Sony, this design makes the format more reliable and better for editing than DVC.

DVC tapes can be played back on DVCAM machines. They can also be used for recording on a DVCAM machine, however their record time will be cut in half.

DVCPRO

DVCPRO was designed by Panasonic as another professional DV format, however, DVCPRO equipment is also manufactured by other companies. As with DVCAM, the video information recorded by DVCPRO equipment is of no higher quality than DVC. However, the equipment does feature professional features.

Like DVCAM, DVCPRO uses locked audio as well as the ability to record an analog audio track. This track is useful to editors because it allows them to hear audio when *shuttling* and *jogging* tapes back and forth to look for material.

The tape format is also more durable than DVC, although DVCPRO can playback DVC and DVCAM tapes. However, DVCPRO tapes can not be played back on DVC or DVCAM machines. Panasonic has also introduced a higher-end format, DVCPRO-50, which features higher resolution and better color processing. This format has not been widely adopted yet.

Digital Betacam (also called Digi-Beta)

Also designed by Sony, Digital Betacam is an excellent, high resolution, component digital format offering top notch audio and video quality. The popular Sony DVW-700 camera offered some of the first glimpses into the possibilities of digital cinematography. The camera has many professional features that make it ideal for shooting projects for video-to-film transfer, including a 16:9 wide-screen option.

Unfortunately, digital Betacam cameras and editing equipment are very expensive. However, because of its popularity, it is very accessible. The format's quality and durability, have made digital Betacam a top choice for creating the master tapes.

High Definition Video (HD Video)

In this hierarchy of video formats, HD video is indisputably the king. Once again led by Sony, HD video offers more than twice the resolution of current broadcast and video systems. The newest version of HD video, HD24p, records video at 24 fps in a progressive scan mode that captures entire frames of video rather than interlaced fields. When transferred to 35mm film, HD24p video is nearly indistinguishable from film originated images. George Lucas is using HD24p cameras for the second installment of the *Star Wars* prequels.

Of course, this quality comes at a high price. And while HD video equipment is now readily available, it comes at a price of $100K plus, and is still in the hands of only a few people. However, this will change in the next couple of years, particularly as American broadcasters convert to digital TV.

Other DV Formats

There are some other DV formats entering the market. Sony's Digital8 camcorders were introduced to give 8mm Handycam owners a way to upgrade to a digital format without losing years of analog footage. Unlike the popular MiniDV format, Digital8 cameras record sound and images on standard 8mm or Hi-8 tapes. Plus, they are capable of playing back 8mm or Hi-8 cassettes—so it's a great way to convert 8mm and Hi-8 analog video to a digital signal before transferring video to the computer through a FireWire (IEEE-1394) interface. The Digital8 format offers the same quality as MiniDV, with 500 lines of resolution, but you should use the metal-particle Hi-8 tapes to avoid artifacts during digital recordings.

There are also digital camcorders which record full-motion video directly to a magneto-optical disc instead of linear tape. Some experts believe systems, like the Sony MD Discam (DCM-M1), hold great promise for the future because they access clips instantly, without racing along in fast forward mode to view your scenes. Disc-based video recorders create icons for each sequence in your footage, helping you find a favorite moment quickly by jumping to it instantly. Because of this random access, magneto-optical formats allows you to perform on-the-spot editing through touch-screen features, circumventing the software in your PC altogether. Although the MiniDisc format only captures video at 400 lines of horizontal resolution, and the cartridges can only

A COMPARISON OF DIGITAL VIDEO FORMATS	
FORMAT	*FEATURES*

DVC
Manufactured by
Sony, Panasonic,
JVC, Sharp
	Resolution: 720x480 (NTSC)
	Sampling: 4:1:1
	Audio: Unlocked
	        2 channels of 16 bit 48kHz.
	        4 channels of 12 bit 32kHz.
	Tape Capacity: miniDV=80 min.
	        Standard DV=3 hours

DVCAM
Sony
	Resolution: 720x480 (NTSC)
	Sampling: 4:1:1
	Audio: Locked
	        2 channels of 16 bit 48kHz.
	        4 channels of 12 bit 32kHz.
	Tape Capacity: miniDV=40 min.
	        Standard DVCAM=3 hours
	Can play back DVC tapes.

DVCPRO
Panasonic, Hitachi,
Philips, Ikegami
	Resolution: 720x480 (NTSC)
	Sampling: 4:1:1 (DVCPRO-50 4:2:2)
	Audio: Locked
	        2 channels of 16 bit 48kHz.
	        4 channels of 12 bit 32kHz.
	Tape Capacity: miniDVCPRO=63min.
	        Standard DVCPRO=2 hours
	Can play back DVC and DVCAM tapes.

Digital Betacam
Sony
	Resolution: 720x480 (NTSC)
	Sampling: 4:2:2
	Audio: Locked
	        4 channels of 16 bit 48kHz.
	Tape Capacity:
	        mini-Digital Beta Tape=40min.
	        Standard=3 hours

High Definition Video
Sony, Ikegami
	Resolution: 1080 Lines
	Sampling: 4:2:2
	Audio: Locked
	        4 channels of 16 bit 48kHz.
	Tape Capacity: mini-HDCAM Tape=40min.
	        Standard HDCAM=3 hours

store up to twenty minutes of footage, it does have the advantage of playing back extremely clear images in slow motion.

Some DV cameras don't record to a tape or disc format at all—they transfer video images directly to your hard drive. Many live events are recorded this way to be streamed immediately over the Internet. Other web-based digital video systems include the immersive 360° cameras, which captures moving images in a complete circle so that audiences can navigate the video as they view it in a browser window. These innovations are merely a glimpse at the future of video; as these digital formats advance, they are incorporating many of the editing functions traditionally performed on a computer on the camcorder devices instead, expanding the possibilities for filmmakers.

DV vs. Film

The DV vs. film debate has raged for a couple of years on several Internet message boards, in filmmaking publications, as well as film production conferences. If you care to catch up on some of the discussion, visit www.dejanews. com and search for "DV vs. film."

In summary, DV offers the following advantages over film.

The Advantages of DV over Film

- The ability to economically have a high shooting ratio, i.e. shooting a lot of footage. This is especially beneficial for documentaries;
- The option of affordably using multiple cameras to shoot faster;
- Being able to immediately review material without having to wait or pay for expensive film to video dailies;
- Small cameras that are less intrusive and more discreet than film cameras (try to sneak a shot at a train station with a film camera); and
- Affordable, professional level camera supports, such as jib arms and the Steadicam Jr., that add to production value.

Of course, DV has its limitations that must be carefully accessed before you begin your production and considered throughout shooting and editing of your feature.

The Shortcomings of DV

- Video's limited resolution, especially when blown up to film, does not handle detailed wide shots very well. That beautiful panoramic shot of cascading mountains will lose a lot of detail;
- Fast motion often proves to be a challenge for NTSC video transfer to film.
- DV image quality can rapidly deteriorate under low light and high contrast situations as well;
- The video-to-film transfer processes, particularly the low-cost processes, do not respond well to shots with a lot of fast motion in the frame or a lot of camera movement; and
- Despite the fantastic variety of impressive computer-generated special effects offered with desktop editing systems, lower priced transfer processes often have difficulty retaining the quality of effect when converting to film.

With these considerations in mind, let's take a look at the process of using DV to produce your feature film.

The DV Filmmaking Process

When creating a DV film, you'll go through all of the steps of traditional filmmaking, with a few variations to accommodate for the strengths and weaknesses of DV.

DV Filmmaking

Develop Your Story
↓
Budget and Schedule Your Shoot
↓
Raise Funds
↓
Plan Your Shoot: Pre-Production
↓
The Shoot: Principal Photography
↓
Editing: Post-Production
↓
Prepare Your Project For Exhibition

In the following pages we will review each of these steps. Preparing your project for exhibition is actually an aspect of post-production, but I choose to list it as a separate step for several reasons.

First, your feature or documentary will be technically presentable after you finish the video and audio editing.

Second, for many of us, the project will be in this form when it is publicly screened, submitted to festivals, or submitted to companies or investors to seek funds to transfer it to film or have the video treated to look more like film.

Finally, the fact is that for many projects, you should not spend the thousands of dollars necessary to take the project further. One of the greatest benefits of DV filmmaking is that it provides an opportunity for people to cultivate and nurture their craft.

After finishing your DV feature, you may decide it's best left in a locked closet in an area permanently inaccessible to family, friends, or general reviews. But what did you lose? Some time? Maybe a couple of thousand dollars? Unlike filmmakers who spend tens and hundreds of thousands (or in the case of Hollywood, millions) of dollars, only to realize they have created a piece of—let's just say that as with any art, not every creation is a masterpiece.

On the other hand, look what you gained from the experience—an opportunity to organize a production, work with actors, work with a crew, hear your dialogue, see characters brought to life, and an overall excellent chance to tell a story.

When I first became involved with filmmaking, I was very intimidated by the technical aspects of production. As a result, I immersed myself in every book, class, and seminar I could afford about filmmaking. But after a few projects, I became aware that while the films I produced were technically excellent, my storytelling skills were coming up short. So after five years of producing, I finally realized . . .

3
■■■■■■ It All Begins with a
Strong Story

You must have more than just a good idea. Ideas without solid execution aren't worth the energy required to make them. You have to put that idea in a form where it can be easily communicated to others.

Believe me, I know the anxious drive to get to "the good part" and be on set with your cast and crew making your film coming to life. But without a solid story as the foundation, you are starting on shaky ground.

If you are producing a narrative, then you have to write a script or have a script written for you. Ideally, it's a great script featuring well-developed characters, a tight plot and a strong, compelling theme. I don't want to hide this crucial fact away in a bunch of text, so let me reiterate . . .

Start With A Great Script!

Even if your project is going to use a lot of improvisation, it is best to rehearse with your cast and build a script out of these rehearsals. This is the technique used by British director Mike Leigh (*Secrets & Lies*). Your script is not just an outline for telling your story but also the key to planning and managing a well-organized production.

This section is simply a primer on some important script and story issues, as well as comments on my personal process. There are many excellent books, classes, and seminars that can help you learn how to write good scripts. I encourage you to investigate these resources and invest the time required to fully develop your idea.

With that in mind, here are a few of my highly opinionated thoughts on scripts and story.

Be Original—or At Least Be a Good Copy

Since people are already going to be biased when they discover your project was shot on video, the best way to win them over is with material that captures and holds their attention. Films like *Clerks* and *She's Gotta Have It* certainly weren't visual masterpieces, but the characters won the love and disdain of many viewers.

Speaking of these successful films, don't spend your time and effort simply rehashing other films. Anyone who has attended the Independent Feature Project's annual Independent Feature Film Market can tell you about the dozens of films that try to recreate the tones, characters, and themes of films by Kevin Smith, Quentin Tarantino, and other popular independent filmmakers.

But, if you *are* going to do a film that is a knock-off of another film, add your own twist or individual mark. This is especially true in the tempting low budget world of genre films, most commonly called B-movies.

Far too often, B stands for Bad—bad script, bad acting, bad directing, bad lighting, and bad sound. However, B-movies have an important role in the economics of home video, cable, and the international film market (though greatly diminished compared to the '80s). In most cases, it is much easier to sell a video originated action, horror, or erotic thriller, than a drama or comedy.

So, if you have your eye on a small bite of the B-movie economic pie, but you also want your film to boost your filmmaking career, then you need to make your story work within the confines of its genre, while adding your special flare.

There were other low budget zombie movies before *Night of the Living Dead*, but its gritty cinema verite style and distinct edginess took horror films in another direction. Take a chance with your script and see what conventions you can shake up.

Use What You Got to Get What You Want

The challenge is to create an original, refreshing script that you can produce with your available resources, your unique talent, and with the
financial, scheduling and technical limitations of low budget DV films.

To accomplish this, you often have to build your script around elements that are readily available including locations, props, wardrobes,
vehicles, and talent. A realistic assessment of your available resources
makes your life far easier when you begin production.

Available resources do not just mean what you personally have, but
rather, what you can access. This is an advantage of working with a collective of people. Everyone brings more to the table.

Do You Have Stunts?

As a writer, I understand that it can be very tempting to throw in just
one quick little highway chase scene, while rationalizing to yourself
that you can find bold actors and a small gung-ho crew daring enough
to pull it off. But what about when you accept the reality that it can't
happen? Does that leave a gaping hole in your story?

If it does and you can't get the shot, then you will have to rewrite
the scene. And if it doesn't, then you don't need the scene anyway (if
it's not advancing your story or character development, toss it).

Of course, if you have access to a Grand Prix race car, a driver, a race-
track *and* you can genuinely integrate it into your story, then go for it.

Do You Have Special Effects?

The very same low-cost computers you will be using for editing can
produce special effects on par with many early '90s Hollywood productions. However, most of these do not translate well to film when using
the consumer DV formats and the mid-range video-to-film transfers. If
your sincere intention is to stay on video, then certainly add them to
your writer's tool box.

But again, keep in mind the importance of substance over hi-tech
wizardry. As we have seen with many Hollywood features, crash-bang-
zap-stomp may make for lively trailers, but it doesn't keep people sat-
isfied for 90+ minutes.

Writing your script based on available resources should ultimately
make you focus more on story and character.

Research, or How I Became a Cabby

I'm one of those people who finds it difficult to create without having a deep well of information and research to draw upon. In fact, when I begin a script, I have to research relevant topics from multiple angles until I feel completely familiar with the subject matter. Most frequently, I end up with notebooks filled with pages of notes.

This habit has been dramatically aided by the seemingly infinite information sources provided by the Internet. I can spend hours behind my computer to keep up on topics, communicate with experts, and survey people.

During the planning of my film *Hacks*, however, I learned that there comes a time when you must hit the streets. Literally. For many months, I researched cab history, gypsy cabs and hacks—the illegal cab drivers in Baltimore.

I held interviews with people working as hacks, and talked to passengers. But when I put the research behind me and took my car out and actually started hacking, suddenly I found myself no longer an observer, but a participant as well. This new perspective radically changed the direction of my story from a comedy to a drama.

Are you allowing yourself to step from the world of academic research into the atmosphere and circumstances of your characters? I'm not saying you should use drugs just because a character does, or otherwise put yourself in jeopardy, but to the degree possible, seek the depths of human experience that cannot be easily conveyed from afar.

I'm not one of those people who believes that a person is unable to effectively tell the story of characters outside of their own race, ethnicity, social class, religion or personal experience. However, I do believe that you must take your research to a level that reflects a near metaphysical comprehension of your subject matter.

Organize Yourself

As you conduct your research, you can begin developing a well-organized, detailed outline. Even if you don't plan on writing the script yourself, this process helps develop your idea and structure it in a format that can be easily communicated.

Much has been written about the use of 3x5 index cards as a tool for organizing the many tidbits of information that will ultimately evolve into your script. I have found this to be a very effective technique that allows me to keep track of random script elements as they come to my mind.

I use a set of cards labeled as: *Scene cards, Character cards, Plot cards, Theme cards* and *Music cards.*

Scene cards are for individual scenes. They include a couple of words as a distinct header and a few lines of summary about key action and characters in the scene.

Character cards feature specific, concise information about characters including their background, relationship to other characters, motives, and unique attributes.

Plot cards have summaries of significant turning points in the story, including the timing between them or the place where they are to occur in the story. These points are the cornerstone of the overall story structure.

Theme cards note various themes that I am attempting to integrate into the story. These themes may be related to the overall story or individual aspects such as imagery.

Music cards note the types of music I'd like to include in a certain scene. Music influences my writing tremendously. These personal notes help me when writing scene descriptions and during character development.

As you complete a large number of scene cards, you can begin to create an outline in your word processor based upon these many informational sources.

Or, you can first use the popular technique of using push pins to arrange your cards on a wall or corkboard, adding and deleting scenes, or adjusting the arrangement as required.

Finally, after a certain point, you've done enough research and enough planning, and the hour has arrived to put up or shut up, because now it's time to . . .

Write the Damn Thing!

I know . . . I know . . . it's easier said than done. In many cases, it is not an issue of not being prepared, or not having the talent to execute the story, but simply a matter of sitting down and facing the blank screen.

Here are a few of my most common excuses for not writing:

- I need to make some phone calls.
- I'm hungry.
- I need to check my e-mail.
- I need to research online real quick. (Ha!)

- I'm burnt out from writing all day yesterday (trying to play catch up).
- I'm feeling disconnected from my characters (after not having written for a week).
- I don't like the direction of this draft but I don't feel like starting over so I'll let it simmer for awhile.
- And a half dozen more . . . .

Of course, ultimately there is no progress, as the days and weeks go by, until I sit down and commit to making progress. In recent years, I have learned that even more than talent, training, and experience, it is this discipline and commitment that separates want-to-be filmmakers from soon-to-be filmmakers.

I have had the pleasure of conversing with many professional film and television writers since I moved to Los Angeles. At one particularly festive reception, a very inebriated, frequently employed writer of direct-to-video movies bragged that the extent of his formal training consisted of overdue library books. And yet, he was earning far more money than friends who spent fortunes at the major film schools.

But in the midst of his gleeful boasting, this self-proclaimed hack said something that continues to be significant to me. "At 8 a.m. six days a week, whether I've got a gig or not, I sit at my computer and I don't get up until I have written something. A lot of it is mostly crap that no one will see, but it's like a famous boxing champ getting up to make that early morning run, even when no fans are around. He knows that if he doesn't, he's not going to stay on top for long. Well that's me, I'm writing my way to the top and can't nobody make me to do it but me."

I think about that almost every time I'm ready for another game of solitaire.

Script Readings

Script readings are one of the greatest script development tools I have experienced. Basically, you put your script in the hands of a group of actors and have them perform a straight read with little or no direction from you. A narrator usually reads the scene descriptions.

The readings can be private events in your home with just a few friends and family. Or, you can organize a semi-public event held at a theater, community center, or coffee house.

I enjoy public readings because they give me an opportunity to receive blunt critical feedback that is often difficult to obtain from people close to you. I usually create a detailed questionnaire to seek opinions on specific areas of the script.

Readings such as this can raise some completely unexpected issues. As you sit anxiously in a corner of the room listening to the actors, you might suddenly be aware that something you considered skillfully subtle is in fact quite ambiguous.

Or in a question and answer session afterwards, a question may be asked that really makes you ponder a character's motives, or at least the way you communicated it on the page.

Certainly, the reading ability and presence of the actors reading can affect the audience's perception. Yet, if you are attentive and honest with yourself, you can differentiate bad reads from script problems. Videotaping and/or audiotaping can also help tremendously.

Working with Writers

If you are committed to finding a writer to help you develop a script, I commend you. There are plenty of people who have a story to tell, but lack writing experience and/or the desire to learn to write a script. This is another area where acceptance of your personal strengths and weaknesses should supersede your ego in an effort to create the best film you can.

However, even if you're going to be working with a writer, in most cases you still need to refine your ideas as much as possible. You should be able to succinctly communicate the distinctive elements of the story and the characters.

Most commonly, when you mention to someone that you are producing and/or directing a film, their response will be, "Oh yeah, what's it about?" You should be able to provide an answer without a lot of deliberation.

If you have some basic writing abilities, you can compile your ideas and notes into a two to five page *treatment* of the film that at the least:

- Summarizes the story;
- Introduces the key characters;
- Broadly covers the beginning, middle, and ending of the film;
- Makes note of the important conflicts; and
- Highlights important themes.

The treatment does not have to be written like an eloquent literary work. It can be a straightforward presentation of the elements that are most important to you.

In addition to being a tool to help you communicate with your writer, a treatment can also be registered with the Writers Guilds of America (in Los Angeles and New York) to help provide some protection for your creative work.

If the thought of writing anything at all just does not appeal to you, consider using a small portable tape machine to dictate story notes.

Collaboration vs. Work-For-Hire

It is certainly possible for you to begin with just a simple idea and work with someone to develop it into a full story, but this relationship requires you to rely heavily on someone else's vision. When a producer and/or director is very much in sync with the writer, this type of collaboration can be very productive.

At the same time, you must realize that the idea that originated with you is no longer solely yours, creatively or, perhaps most importantly, legally. Unless a contract is established that dictates otherwise, the work created by you and the writer will be considered a collaborative work with ownership belonging to both of you.

Alternately, you can contract with a writer to produce a script on a work-for-hire basis. In this arrangement, you present the writer with your idea and pay a predetermined amount to have it written. The contract may allow for small changes after the first draft, but there are additional fees for subsequent re-writes. However, depending on the terms, you have complete ownership over the finished work.

Many writers, understandably, will not do work-for-hire scripts on a deferred payment basis. The work is far too demanding to hand over a script and walk away with neither ownership nor financial compensation.

However, it is not uncommon to find an ambitious, talented writer willing to collaborate on a project on a deferred payment basis, with the confidence that they have a vested interest in the project.

As you can imagine, the line between collaboration and work-for-hire can at times become blurred. Fortunately, the Writer's Guild of America has standard guidelines and contracts to help in this distinction. This information in the hands of a good lawyer can help you and your collaborator or contractor develop legal documents that will protect everyone involved.

Finding a Writer

With so many people secretly craving success as a screenwriter, finding a writer is not difficult at all. Finding a good writer is far more challenging. Finding a good writer willing to work for little or no money is just pure luck! It is this reality that ultimately leads many people to write their own projects, even if their primary creative interest is elsewhere.

Your search for a writer can begin in the dramatic arts departments at local colleges, as well as local theater companies. Although playwriting is a different art than screenwriting, many writers are now crossing genres.

Some colleges also have non-degree oriented professional development programs that include scriptwriting or creative writing classes. You can contact professors in these programs to seek referrals to past or present students.

There are also writer support groups in many cities that have newsletters, telephone hotlines, and websites to post messages for writers.

Advertisements in national film and television trade publications and scriptwriting magazines will yield an avalanche of submissions that can require a substantial amount of time to evaluate.

Regardless of the approach you use to solicit writers, it is important for you to be forthright about your previous experience, budget level, and expectations. Additionally, be certain to communicate that your film will be professionally shot on DV. There are still many people who will object to video, so you should establish that fact from the top.

4
■ ■ ■ ■ ■ ■ It Takes Time
And Money

Too little time or money and you're out of luck. On the other hand, the availability of too much money during principal photography can allow you to become comfortable with unchecked spending. If you're not careful, you'll be pinching pennies months later during the important and expensive steps of post-production.

Film scheduling and budgeting is an art that benefits tremendously from hands-on production experience. By spending time in production offices, on other film sets, and sitting in on editing sessions, you will learn some of the ways people effectively or ineffectively make use of their time and money.

In this chapter, we'll examine some of the general scheduling and financial issues that should be taken into consideration in the early stages of your project.

Script Considerations

Scheduling and budgeting begins once you have completed a *shooting script* that accurately represents the major elements of the story as they are to appear in the finished film. Scenes in this script are numbered to allow the production team to quickly and easily be able to refer to a given scene.

Although there are certain to be changes and additions, substantial changes in the shooting script could radically alter the entire *shooting schedule* and budget for principal photography.

The shooting script elements that most significantly affect a production's schedule and budget are the:

- Size of the Cast. The larger the cast, the more difficulty coordinating schedules (especially with volunteers), the more paperwork to deal with, the more personalities to temper and the more mouths to feed.
- Number and Proximity of Locations. The more time spent moving from location to location, the more hours and days you will require. More days equal more money.
- Number of Night Exteriors and Large Interiors. Lights are expensive to rent and purchase and require time to set-up. On the other hand, you cannot shortchange yourself by not getting enough lights. More on this later.
- Set Decorations, Props, and Wardrobe Needs. A production set in the past or future will most likely require more time and money to prepare.
- Stunts and Special Effects. If you must have them, be prepared to spend the time and money required to do them properly and safely.
- Special Equipment Requirements. Any equipment critical for the execution of a scene adds to the cost.

Scheduling

A *script breakdown* is performed on the shooting script by meticulously scrutinizing each scene and making note of all of these details. Everything from a small, but crucial, piece of art to the fifty extras you insisted on including in a scene must be accounted for in the budget.

The shooting schedule is created by assessing the breakdown and arranging scenes in the most logical and most efficient order. This is why most films are often shot out of sequence; it saves time and money to shoot every scene that occurs at a particular location while you are there, as opposed to bringing cast, crew, and equipment back and forth.

For many years professionals performed script breakdowns using *production boards* composed of color-coded strips of paper representing different elements. Today this job is done using specialized computer software that works with script and budgeting programs.

However, even without these programs you can breakdown your script using a word processor or spread sheet program to create tables with the vital information for each scene listed in rows in a format similar to this:

SAMPLE DAILY SCHEDULE IN TABLE FORMAT						
Scene#	Description	Pgs.	Location	Cast	Props	Extra
33	Rue & Tate Driving	1/4	Ext. Street— Day	Rue Tate	Coffee cup.	Rue's Car, Tow Truck
82	Tate Chases JD.	1/8	Ext. Alley— Day	Tate, JD	Belt	Tate's Car
	Total	3/8				

Each day in your shooting schedule will have a table with scenes arranged by priority for that day. You can cut and paste between tables to adjust the schedule.

For most small casts with limited location shooting, aim for ten to fourteen days for principal photography and one or two days later for pick-up shots. This schedule is long enough for you to get a lot of shooting done when paced properly, but short enough to not burn-out an unpaid cast and crew.

Shooting on weekends and evenings is another way to accommodate your cast and crew schedules, although this can create many continuity challenges and extend the length of the principal photography over a much longer period.

Budgeting

Your budget is highly contingent on the specific elements of your script, and the deals you are able to negotiate. The trick is to be realistic in your projections, while trying to stretch every dollar without compromising the safety and efficiency of the production or the quality of the finished film.

If you are fortunate enough to have a cast and crew working for deferred payments, your main expenditures will be:

- Equipment
- Food
- Tape Stock
- Misc. Expendables

- Post-Production Services
- Video-to-Film Transfer or
  Video Processing

Attention to detail when budgeting is just as important as it is elsewhere in the production. The consistent failure to anticipate minor expenses can quickly lead you to exceed the budget.

If your prior budgeting experience is limited, seek feedback from experienced production people on your budget line items. While many of them may be accustomed to working at far higher budget levels, they can draw attention to items that you may have overlooked.

The following is a sample DV budget. We'll go over each of these items in detail in the following chapter. The first column is based upon having free access to equipment, while the second column has comparable rental rates. Note that this budget does not include video transfer or video processing.

Keep in mind that there are many enthusiastic camera and editing system owners out there who are seeking to work on feature projects. If you have a good story and are well organized, chances are you will be able to find people willing to work for deferred payments. Later, I'll tell you how I've connected with some great folks and how you can as well.

HOLLER IF YOU HEAR ME! DETAILS		
13 Day Shoot 4 Week(s) Rough Cut 2 Week(s) Fine Cut 4 Week(s) Audio Editing	90 minute project 8:1 shooting ratio 12 total hrs of footage	
Category	*W/Deferrals*	*W/Paid Rentals*
Cast	$ 0.00	$ 0.00
Crew	0.00	0.00
Equipment	270.00	4384.00
Tape Stock	361.00	361.00
Food	650.00	650.00
Post-Production	1500.00	8250.00
Miscellaneous	222.50	222.50
Sub-total	$ 3003.50	$ 13867.50
10% Contingency	300.35	1386.75
TOTAL	**$ 3303.85**	**$ 15254.25**

Fundraising

Perhaps the greatest reality I have had about "independent" filmmaking over the last couple of years is the fact that you really are VERY dependent on many people—your cast, your crew, labs, distributors, and more than anyone else—your investors.

But raising funds for highly speculative ventures like indie filmmaking is far from simple. However, most of us have a much better chance of coming up with $2,000 to $10,000 to do a DV film than the $20,000, $50,000, or $100,000 required to complete a 16mm feature. (The key word here is "complete.")

There are many books that provide details about researching and writing the business plans required by most investors. I'll briefly discuss some of my fundraising experiences.

Investors

Frustrating. That's the first thought that comes to mind when I think about my experiences trying to find investors. The Washington D.C. area (not far from my hometown) has the fourth highest concentration of millionaires in the country. With a lot of networking I would consistently meet potential investors who were very attracted to the entertainment industry from afar.

But by the time my very thorough business plan would get through their accountants and attorneys, they would be advised that the risk was too high. Several people would make small investments, but I was never successful in raising more than $1,500 from an individual investor.

Still, for a DV film, that $1,500 could be nearly the whole budget. If you are seeking investors, it's much easier finding ten people to invest $300 than ten people to invest $10,000.

Renewable Promissory Notes

The low budgets attached to a DV filmmaker's projects can also help you avoid some of the expensive legal paperwork required when seeking large investments. This is especially helpful in instances where people are basically making donations to support your project.

In the past, for these small amounts, I have used renewable promissory notes purchased from an office supply store (like Staples or Office Depot). The term of the loan was three years with a low interest and an option to extend the loan if necessary.

These notes help family, friends, and other supporters "investing" realize that I recognized the value of their contribution. Of course, every situation is unique, so you should consult an attorney.

Self-Financing

Likewise, with the budgets we are dealing with, many people can self finance their DV film, either from their income, savings, an extra job or via credit cards. If necessary, you can spread the production over a period of time.

Self-finance is true independence—to not have to turn to anyone else to finance your production. It also frees you creatively from having to account to anyone else.

Sponsors

You might also be able to find companies or organizations willing to support the project if your theme or story is in line with their agenda. I know several filmmakers who have been able to raise money and resources to produce their projects when they aligned themselves with such organizations. One director did an anti-gang short using members of a youth organization and suddenly had all of his equipment and food donated.

Sponsors for projects I have worked on have contributed complete meals for the cast and crew members, clothing, locations, props, and numerous goods and services that I otherwise would have had to spend cash to acquire.

Grants

Finally, apply for every grant you can. I was never a fan of the long, drawn-out grant application processes. I always felt that by the time recipients were announced six months down the line, I would have already raised money and been far into my production. But in reality, that was rarely the case.

Then in late 1995, at the encouragement of another filmmaker, I applied for a grant from the Maryland State Arts Council. I literally dropped my sample tape and application off within hours of the deadline. Imagine my surprise in March of '96 when I found out I had won a $6,000 grant! That money became the seed money for *Hacks,* which was shot later in the year.

5
∎∎∎∎∎ Pre-Production: Think First, Shoot Later

There is no greater investment you will make in your film than taking time to properly plan and prepare for principal photography.

Pre-production is the period where you have the greatest control over the various elements that will comprise your film. Sometimes in our anxiety to get to production, we trick ourselves into believing that the film is made when the cameras start rolling.

That's like thinking that a cake is made when it goes in the stove, when 75 percent of the work was blending the right combination of ingredients.

Pre-production is an art in itself. But unlike the expensive and demanding period of principal photography, during pre-production, your primary investment is your time. Most of these tasks can be completed with minimal cash outlays; meaning, you cannot use the lack of funds as an excuse to not begin working on your film.

And one of the best, low-cost things you can do in the early stages of pre-production is to organize yourself and . . .

Learn to Work the Paper or It'll Work You

By the time you complete your film you will have files full of all types of paperwork, everything from hand scribbled receipts to legal contracts that can make or break your film's chance of ever getting sold to a distributor.

It is to your advantage to start an organizational system early. Every time I begin a new production, I purchase:

- A very large three-ring binder.
- A package of durable multi-colored dividers.
- A small plastic milk crate.
- A box of tab folders.

The notebook is divided to contain any relevant paperwork to which I require immediate access. The milk crate(s) will eventually contain all of the other important records. From that point on, every piece of paper I disburse or collect is categorized in the notebook or filed in the milk crate(s).

Two years after filming *Hacks*, I was still able to easily go back and pull sample paperwork out of my files to include in this book.

This part of pre-production may not be as exciting as casting or scouting locations, but what you are essentially doing is laying the cornerstone of your production. Plus, being organized impresses people, and sets a precedent for what you expect from them. Remember, low budget does not have to mean unprofessional.

Once you have organized yourself, there are many steps in pre-production that contribute to the overall quality of your film. Here are some of the most critical tasks:

Pre-Production Checklist

- Cast your actors.
- Hire your crew.
- Find locations.
- Find props and wardrobe.
- Rehearse.
- Make arrangements for equipment.
- Make catering and craft services arrangements.
- Decide on the intended final format.
- Shoot video test.

Casting

With a great script in hand you will want to find excellent talent to help bring the story to life. Your casting decisions are the first and perhaps most important decisions you will make as a director.

Take your time casting and always choose the best possible talent available. Good acting contributes substantially to the quality of your finished piece, just as bad acting distracts from even the best script.

Finding Talent

If you live in or near a major city, you can place free ads in *Back Stage* and *Back Stage West,* as well as low-cost ads in local alternative weekly newspapers. And if you submit a production notice to *Variety* and *The Hollywood Reporter*, you can receive a free listing that will generate a mailbox full of headshots.

Many cities and states have film commissions with telephone hotlines and newsletters that will allow you to post audition notices. You can also post notices at local theater groups and colleges. Another advantage of networking with filmmakers is that you can refer each other to good talent.

The Internet has some fantastic resources for casting. You can view head shots and resumes online as well as post your own casting messages. It still amazes me how quickly you can begin to receive replies once you put your notices out there. The resource guide includes a list of sites to get you started.

A well publicized *open call* for actors can often generate a long turn out. However, the ability and experience levels of the actors will vary tremendously.

The Screen Actors Guild

Recently, recognizing the growing significance of independent and low budget films, the Screen Actors Guild (SAG) has developed low budget contracts that make it possible to tap into the large SAG talent pool. These contracts should make SAG one of your first stops when looking for talent.

The SAG Experimental Agreement and Limited Exhibition Agreement allow you to use SAG actors at deferred and substantially discounted rates. With these contracts, you could theoretically hire anyone from Tom Cruise to Jennifer Lopez to be in your low-budget film.

Auditions

Auditions are always exciting to me, especially heavily promoted open calls where you have no idea who may come through the door.

Since these auditions are the first contact you will have with your talent, it is important to establish and maintain a sense of professionalism. This means that you must have a support team and a well-organized system of handling the potentially high volume of people attending the auditions.

Also, be certain to hold auditions in an accessible public place. And, unless you are auditioning people you already know, do not hold auditions in a private residence. Most experienced professional actors rightfully know to shy away from going to a stranger's home for an audition, especially women. Additionally, the pervasive view is that anyone unwilling to pay for a space to hold auditions probably does not have the means to make a film.

There are free and low-cost options for holding auditions. Many colleges and community theater groups make their facilities available for little or no money, particularly, if someone in their organization likes your project. And, depending on the nature of your project, nightclubs, comedy clubs and rehearsal halls are other options.

Also, as a first-time director, while holding auditions you may want to seek the services of a *casting director* or veteran actor to aid you in your evaluation of an actor's skills. This person does not necessarily have to be working as a casting director, but should be very familiar with actors and the acting process. I have found that this type of insight helps me learn more about communicating with actors.

Casting Against Type

Casting is a very subjective process that draws heavily on the director's interpretation and vision of the characters in the story. Additional input may be solicited from a casting director and the producer(s), but in most cases the director makes the ultimate decision.

One of the primary casting taboos to avoid is the common practice of *typecasting* actors. This involves casting someone based on physical attributes or personality traits stereotypically associated with a character. While this problem often has its roots in the script, it can be corrected or perpetuated by the casting choices.

As you cast your film, be aware of those subconscious images of what we typically accept as being beautiful, ugly, nerdy, bored, sexy, weak, strong, and any number of common character types. Attempt to avoid casting actors that look or act like these types in these roles.

For example, in *Hacks* I had originally written a role of a shoplifter to be played by a young man in his early twenties. The actor I found to play this role was great, but during rehearsal it became obvious to me that the character as written and performed was somewhat cliché.

As an experiment, I swapped another actor, a man in his late 60s, into the role and had him mix his generation's slang with the current young adult slang. This change added an entirely new dimension to the character in everything from dialogue to musical references.

It often takes a very conscious effort to cast against types. And many times it can be a risky undertaking since audiences must be re-oriented when their preconceived perceptions of a character are challenged. But, that's also why it is so refreshing to cast against type when it can be effectively executed.

Don't Forget the Business of the Show

Always be certain to have a contract with your talent that spells out payment, rehearsal attendance, shooting dates, and re-recording terms, as well as a *talent release form* giving you the right to use their likeness and voice in your film. Distributors will require these releases from you should you get a distribution deal.

One of the benefits of using SAG contracts is that the terms are very standardized. Although the terms can be modified for each actor, by using these contracts most actors know the extent to which their rights are protected should the film become a blockbuster. If you are not using SAG contracts, your attorney can create contracts modeled after the SAG terms.

Create a Cast Information Form

As you hire people for various roles (even if they are not paid, you are still hiring them), it is a good idea to have them fill out a form that helps you keep track of information about them. In addition to basic contact information, some of the additional information I like to know includes;

- Special eating habits or diets.
- Allergies.
- Medications or medical issues.
- Emergency contact person.
- Transportation plans (car, bus, carpool).
- Hours and days of availability.

This quick reference sheet can be invaluable when planning your shoot.

Hiring a Crew

Just as you want to work with the best acting talent available, you also want to try to assemble the most professional crew possible.

There are many professionals currently working in the industry, as well as talented students who are willing to work for deferred payment on projects that will provide them an opportunity to earn a production credit and work on their craft. Be direct about the terms of employment and be sure to use a contract, especially if payment is to be deferred.

Finding a Crew

As with actors, you can find crew people by advertising in the trades and local papers, as well as at the local colleges. But one of the best ways to find experienced people is to volunteer on other productions and network with crew people.

Online Resources

Internet websites, newsgroups, message boards and chat rooms can also connect you with production people with all levels of experience. I have used the Internet to find camera operators, production assistants, editors and musicians for my projects.

Today, many of these websites offer comprehensive services to film and video professionals. Designed as business-to-business portals, many of these websites (such as CreativePlanet.com or iFilmPro.com) create a directory of like-minded professionals, and give you access to a searchable database of thousands of writers, directors, cast, and crew. Some sites offer online ways to manage your projects throughout development, allowing you to create custom phone lists, scout locations, download document templates, and track script changes from anywhere in the world. The message boards and open forums can be great ways to exchange information or announce available positions for your production. Of course, you can also get the latest insider gossip and industry news.

The advantage of using these Internet resources is that you have an opportunity to develop relationships with people and establish credibility (or the lack of credibility). This is why it is appropriate to spend some time online becoming familiar with the proper protocol for the various forums.

When seeking people online to work on your projects, especially for deferred payment, always be honest about your background, the project's specification, the timeline, and the payment terms. Remember, you will be establishing your professionalism from your initial contact.

My favorite Internet networking sites are listed in the resources page.

Crew Requirements

Your production crew requirements will vary depending upon the complexity of your production but the key crew people are:

- Production Manager—Keeps track of all facets of the production including scheduling, budgeting, hiring crew, negotiating deals for equipment and service, etc.
- Director of Photography (DP)—Your camera operator and lighting director.
- Production Sound Mixer—Monitors audio, selects microphones, and directs boom operator (if there is one) on microphone placement.
- Gaffer—Works with DP to set lights.
- PA/Runner—Runs errands, helps on set and helps with food.

This is a small team, but with small projects it can be done. Actually, in certain circumstances such as a documentary, it can be done with one person doing the shooting and sound (the DV documentary *The Cruise* was completed in this way).

I would not try a narrative feature alone. Ideally, you would recruit these people on your team as well:

- Assistant Director (AD)—Helps schedule the production and stay on schedule.
- Location Manager—Secures the locations.
- Script Supervisor—Keeps track of continuity during scenes.
- Production Designer—Helps create the look of the film.
- Grip(s)—Helps the gaffer and manages dollies and other support.
- Boom Operator—Holds the boom mike and maintains audio notes.
- Set PA(s)—Helps the AD on set.
- Craft Services/Catering Person—Helps keep people fed.
- Production PA(s)—Helps the production manager juggle things.
- Make-up/Hair—Keeps talent looking good.

Screen Potential Crew People

When evaluating prospective crew people, you want to carefully review demo tapes, resumes and references. This is particularly true in regards to your DP and your production sound mixer. Bad visuals or sound can quickly kill the quality of your film.

Personally, for key positions, I prefer to work with people I have worked with before or who have been referred to me by people I know and trust. It's not because I favor the nepotistic systems that are common in this business, but the reality is that it is important to have a sense of their skills and work ethics. Principal photography is a high stress environment. Not everyone is able to perform under this pressure.

Forming Partnerships

In your search for a production crew and equipment, you might be fortunate enough to find people who are excited about being involved with your project, are anxious to work with you for the duration of the project and bring some unique talents or resources to the table. When personalities are compatible and the terms of the arrangement are clearly outlined, this situation can offer many benefits beyond just the availability of equipment.

At times, filmmaking can be a very isolated activity. Even with all of the people who become involved with a film during the course of its various stages, there are many moments where the filmmaker is the primary, if not sole effort driving the project towards completion. The demands of this effort can at times be very tough to bear.

Successful partnerships spread the weight of the many tasks and responsibilities among two or more dedicated individuals committed to a common goal. In the best partnerships, people are synchronized to the degree that they complement each other's resources, strengths, and weaknesses.

Look at the growing trend in Hollywood of actors partnering with writers and directors. Many people are realizing that partnerships help you leverage your talent by allowing you to focus on what you do well, while your partners focus on what they do well.

In your case, you might be a writer/director seeking to complete a showcase film and your partner might be a TV news camera operator looking to do a feature length project. Both of you can benefit from a quality project.

Of course, partners must be able to do one key thing more than any other—get along. This means that you must be able to respectfully work through any ego clashes, frustrations, moodiness, and disappointments while fulfilling your respective duties.

So, with carefully placed messages on the Internet, or some networking, you might be able to find a few people in your vicinity interested in working with you. Just make sure to take your time to get to know the people with whom you will be going into battle.

And most importantly, once you develop the terms of your partnership, create a contract. This has nothing to do with trust as much as serving as an explicit, unquestionable reference aid should the relationship get off track or be terminated. Some of the issues to address include:

- Specific task and duties.
- Content ownership if the partnership ends.
- Income distribution.
- Strategies for conflict resolution.

Your attorney can create a partnership agreement to incorporate these and other legal matters. The last thing you want is a disgruntled former partner owning half of your work.

Create a Crew Information Form

As with the cast information forms, crew information forms provide you with a way to maintain useful facts about your crew. In addition to the information listed on the cast information form, there are a couple of other items it is good to know about your crew, including:

- Professional aspirations.
- Locations, equipment and resources available to the production.

While in pre-production for *Hacks*, I was contacted by a man who wanted to work on the film, but then he became unavailable. However, because I asked the above questions, I found out that his stepfather was a mechanic with a tow truck and a junk yard. This resource was a major breakthrough for us. His stepfather and the stepfather's business partner worked diligently during the entire shoot.

Locations

Hopefully you will have developed your script with the confidence that certain locations will be available to you during principal photography. If not, you will be required to track down and secure the locations for your shoot.

By "track down," I mean going through your network of friends, family members, extended family members, and associates to find people who are willing to let you have access to their properties for the long hours and days you will be shooting. Once you have some places in mind, scout the locations paying attention to things such as:

- Security.
- The electrical systems, i.e. condition, number of outlets, access to circuit breakers, etc.
- Proximity to streets and highways.
- Potential noise sources.
- Staging (working) areas for crew and cast.
- Storage facilities.
- Lighting conditions at various times of the day.

Get a Signed Location Release

When you find a suitable location, you should be honest with the owner/resident about the duration and hours you will require access. Also, be blunt about the terms pertaining to issues such as payment, damages and overtime. All of these issues and more should be incorporated into a location release drawn by a qualified attorney.

Securing the location means that you have a signed locations release with the owner/resident and you have made entry arrangements to gain access to the property.

Don't slack on your locations. Great locations can contribute to a film both explicitly and subtly.

Props/Wardrobe

Again, careful planning while writing your script can help diminish the often challenging task of finding just the right prop or wardrobe for a scene. However, skillful usage of props and wardrobe can greatly enhance the look and production value of a film.

Thrift stores, yard sales, flea markets, and swap meets can be good sources of odd and ends, depending on the time period for your film.

I have also had luck finding local vendors willing to contribute products in exchange for a credit in the film. I know filmmakers who have gone to manufacturers directly and received seconds or off-season items for little or nothing.

Rehearsals and Pre-Visualization

The importance of rehearsals can not be understated. Every hour spent preparing yourself and your cast will increase your odds of creating a film that will meet your expectations.

Far too often, rehearsals are viewed as a time-consuming task that is a low priority when compared to all of the other pre-production items. This is especially true when the director is also producing and/or acting in the film.

But believe me, it is a terrible feeling to make it through the weeks and months of pre-production and principal photography, only to sit in front of a monitor and suddenly realize that your key talent is giving you a terrible performance.

I like to videotape rehearsals because it is quite different watching expressions and body movement in the confines of a picture frame. Plus, the tapes provide an opportunity for me to see how the actors are developing in their roles.

I do know a couple of directors who feel strongly that rehearsals reduce spontaneity, but they are working on large budget shoots where they have the luxury of taking their time to experiment and allow actors to flub their lines. While video allows you to have a higher shooting ratio to accommodate experimentation and mistakes, time is always an issue on low budget shoots.

Rehearsals also help you pre-visualize scenes so that you can create your *shot sheets* and/or *story boards*. Shot sheets list shot by shot how you plan to shoot a scene. Storyboards use rough sketches to communicate the same information. By using these tools you can walk on your set and easily relay to key people the way you plan on handling a scene.

It is also advisable to try to have your DP and production sound mixer attend some rehearsals before you shoot. This provides the DP an opportunity to see the range of skin tones he/she will be lighting. It offers the sound mixer a chance to consider some of the microphone situations that will be encountered.

Although this preplanning may seem excessive, it is better to be too organized than unorganized, particularly when you have a couple of dozen people volunteering their time and effort to your production.

Instead of limiting your creativity, rehearsals, shot sheets and story boards free you to capture spontaneous moments with the confidence that crucial material has been already been videotaped the way you wanted it to be.

Securing Equipment

Gaining access to DV equipment is becoming easier everyday as more people purchase their own equipment. Most professional video equipment rental houses now also rent complete DV packages.

In the next chapter we will review in detail the exact equipment you will require for production, but in this section, I want to focus on how you can go about securing equipment for your shoot.

Purchasing Your Own Equipment

Purchasing your own equipment is another step towards true independence. However, before you rush out and spend a big chunk of money you should carefully consider the investment.

Consumer video equipment depreciates very fast. The $3,000 camera you buy today will almost certainly cost $2,500 a year from now. Of course if you have consistently utilized that camera, then the purchase was worth it. But if you just used the camera a few months out of the year, then you might have been better off renting the camera and putting the extra money into your production. The same is true for video editing equipment.

For example, as I write this, you can purchase the popular Canon XL1 camera by mail order for about $3,400 and you will need to add another $500 for a tripod, extra battery, and camera case.

In the Los Angeles area, you can rent this camera, complete with the accessories for $125 per day or $500 per week, which gives you seven days for the price of four. For a two-week shoot, $1,000 is a substantial savings over purchasing the camera. To be fair, as we'll see later, many people will be using the camera for a few weeks of editing as well.

Just to give you an idea on what you might spend, here are sample purchase prices for the three equipment packages specified in the next section. Of course, these prices are subject to change (they have probably gone down already). The prices are based on averages from several mail order and retail consumer electronic stores.

SAMPLE COSTS FOR PURCHASING EQUIPMENT			
Production Equipment Total	*Basic*	*Mid-Range*	*High-End*
Camera, Support, Accessories	$1,875	$4,040	$6,072
Audio Package + Accessories	592	1,287	3,102
Light Package	0	880	1,760
TOTAL	$2,467	$6,207	$10,934

Purchasing by Mail Order

Mail order prices are significantly less expensive than retail stores, especially including savings on sales tax. However, if you have problems with your equipment during production, you will be forced to ship it back to the dealer as opposed to swapping it at a local dealer.

If you decide to purchase by mail order, you can refer to the resource listing for some companies to get you started. When dealing with mail order companies, be certain to check the return policy. Some places only allow store credit for returns.

Also, when comparing prices, be aware that some less-than-legitimate mail order houses charge you an additional amount for accessories that are ordinarily standard parts of the equipment. So, be certain to ask questions and if possible, have quotes faxed to you with details on what items are included in the price.

You can often find good deals on used equipment as people upgrade to newer models. But again you need to be careful—electronics are very delicate instruments that have components that can wear out or become improperly calibrated.

For video cameras, common problems arise with the *viewfinder* or CCD getting burned out. The heads used to read DV tapes can also get worn out after regular usage, especially if not cleaned properly.

When purchasing used gear, try to deal with companies that have warranties. Or, if purchasing from individuals, have the equipment evaluated by an authorized repair agent.

Renting Equipment

As pointed out in the section above, renting your production equipment is often an economical option. Here are the Los Angeles area weekly rental rates for the same equipment packages:

SAMPLE COSTS FOR RENTING EQUIPMENT (per week)			
Production Equipment Total	*Basic*	*Mid-Range*	*High-End*
Camera, Support, Accessories	$360	$500	$1,000
Audio Package + Accessories	168	188	658
Light Package	0	180	260
TOTAL	$528	$868	$1,918

You can begin your search for a rental house by looking in the yellow pages under video cameras, video production, or audio-visual rentals. In most mid-size towns, you should find a company with no problem.

If you live in a smaller town, you might need to contact a local video production company and see if they rent out their gear (most small shops don't), or if they can refer you to a rental company. Provide some details about your project and you may find an equipment owner who may not want to rent their gear, but may be interested in working with you on another aspect of the production.

Dealing with Rental Arrangements

Typically, to make rental arrangements with a rental house, you will have to have a credit card with a certain limit as a deposit against rental fees and damages. Some rental houses have their own insurance and will allow you to pay large cash deposits. Other companies require that you provide a certificate of insurance or pay an extra fee of 5 percent to 10 percent of the rental rate for insurance.

Before you approach a rental house, you might want to investigate production insurance policies. If you can find an affordable policy that will cover equipment, I suggest you get it. On one of my shoots, a single professional walkie-talkie was lost. The replacement cost was close to $1,100, but fortunately my $600 insurance policy covered it.

Many rental companies rent equipment on a four-day week, meaning that you pay for four days, but get to keep the equipment for seven. For longer term rentals, you can often negotiate better deals.

Craft Services and Catering

There is one low budget filmmaking rule you should never break when trying to maintain the energy level and morale of your unpaid or under-paid cast and crew, that rule is to . . .

Feed People Good Food Frequently!

Eliminate the concept of fast food from your mind while in principal photography. Bags of greasy burgers convey the message that the needs of your cast and crew are an afterthought.

Conversely, good craft services and a well-planned catered meal that accommodates individual eating habits serves the purpose of satisfying appetites and reaffirming your gratitude for their contribution to your project.

Craft services and catering should be adequately budgeted, even when you have cut everything else to a minimum.

The Craft Services Table

Craft services are assorted snacks and drinks that keep people going between meals, such as:
- Assorted fruit
- Bagels
- Muffins, doughnuts, cookies
- Coffee and tea
- Juice and spring water
- Hard candies and chocolates (M&Ms are a favorite)

The craft services table can definitely put some calories on you and your cast. Yet allowing people to grab a snack while still working is essential to their ability to sustain the energy required for the production.

Catering

After long, demanding hours, good catering provides the substantial meals that truly replenish people. The information listed on your cast and crew information forms can help you plan menus that accommodate different diets.

I'm not implying that every person should have their own special entree. Indeed, to customize meals in this way would be time consuming and expensive. Instead, seek to provide alternative menus whenever possible.

Catered meals do not have to be extraordinarily expensive as long as you pre-plan.

Call in the Troops

The most economical method is when you are fortunate enough to have family members who can cook. Just be certain that they can handle cooking and transporting large volumes of food.

Additionally, have them pay special attention to their use of spices and seasonings. Not everyone has the same tolerance for these ingredients.

Be certain that they understand the importance of delivering and setting up food in a timely manner. My mother likes to jokingly tell people that I fired her as my caterer after one of my early short films. And I have to admit . . . I did.

The food she cooked was always delicious and prepared within budget, but she was consistently late. And not just a few minutes; once, she was two and a half hours late! We ended up having to order some other food as a snack that cost more than the food budget for the whole day.

Eventually, I learned how to schedule her to arrive early and I would send a production assistant over in advance to keep us up to date.

Friends and Sponsors

There was a little doughnut shop near my home that I would visit every few days to get out of my house while writing a script. I'd order a muffin and juice and sit there reading over my pages.

After awhile, I became friends with the shop owners and when I started my shoot, they insisted on offering me free fresh baked doughnuts and muffins for the first week! I truly appreciated this gesture, as did my cast and crew.

I also found good deals on catering from restaurants I frequented. Everyone—from the local Boston Market to a fantastic Indian restaurant—was willing to offer free or discounted food as long as I provided them with a credit in the film. Most of them were very excited about being involved in the production.

Some of these deals were based upon relationships with the owners, but in most cases, it was simply being genuinely cordial anytime I'd visit a place.

Bite the Bullet

If you are unable to have good cooks at your disposal and you cannot get deals from local restaurants, then you will have to contract with a catering company.

When comparing companies, be blunt in expressing the limitation of your budget and seek suggestions for meals. Also, be certain to let them know the schedule and conditions under which you will be working. A company that is used to catering weddings may not always be able to handle a low budget set.

And, as with every other important relationship you develop for your production, check references and get contracts. This is especially important, since you will be required to pay cash advances.

Planning Your Final Format

One important decision you will need to make during pre-production is the final format you intend for your finished film. Will you simply keep it as regular video and distribute on VHS or maybe even DVD? Will you treat the video with a process to make it look less like video? Will you transfer your video to 16mm? Or, are you aiming for 35mm film?

This decision is important because you have to decide what aspect ratio you will use to compose your shots. For example, if you are staying on home video, you do not have to do anything different, and you have a greater flexibility as far as using computer generated effects and animation.

But if you are planning on going to 16mm or 35mm, you will want to be sure to compose your shots within the 1.33:1 or 1.85:1 aspect ratio respectively. Otherwise, your image will be cut off at the top and bottom when transferred to film. Or, you will be forced to have the entire square shaped image shrunk down to fit into the rectangular shaped frame.

Some people frame their shots for 35mm then letterbox the video for videotape. Others compose for 35mm but make certain that the image in the entire video frame is usable.

Shooting Video Tests

Before you commit yourself to a final format for your project, or even before committing to a specific camera, it is critical that you and your DP (if you are not shooting it yourself) shoot video tests. These tests will help you better understand the strengths and weaknesses of DV as a format, as well as the strengths and weaknesses of your specific camera.

Ideally, when shooting video, test what you will shoot under a variety of conditions that accurately represent the range of circumstances that exist in your story and your particular directing style. For example, if you decide you want to do a lot of hand-held shooting with jump cuts, close-up shots and bright colors, shoot some test footage under these conditions.

Conversely, if you are planning on taking the color out and creating moody black and white images, try different lighting and camera settings to determine what works for you. Be sure to make notes to yourself about the settings you are using.

If you are on a very limited budget, you might want to shoot a couple of small scenes with the understanding that you might need to reshoot them later depending on the success of your test.

If you are planning on using a video treatment process or video-to-film transfer, most companies will charge a nominal amount to do a two- to five-minute test on your footage. While these expenses can add up, these tests are invaluable in helping you and your DP make decisions about how to create the best images possible for your project.

Other Important Items

There are a few pre-production issues that I'm hesitantly including in this broad category.
- Legal services
- Accounting services
- Insurance
- Permits

Each of these items is very important and using them ultimately offers you greater protection from the many hazards of film production and distribution. However, I recognize that many cash-strapped filmmakers will not be able to have these services at their disposal. Still, if you are successful with your film, then, at some point down the line, you will require them.

And in many instances, if you use the same tenacity you used for negotiating your other arrangements, you can make some deals for these services as well.

Legal Services

If I were only allowed to work with three people for my entire film-making careers, I would choose a great actor, a great director of photography and a great lawyer.

There are innumerable legal matters that arise during film production and even more in the predatory world of film distribution. Having a good attorney can add significantly to your battlefield armor.

But you must have the right lawyer. Entertainment law is a very specialized field that requires attorneys to be familiar with and current on many different subjects. In fact, there is an amazing amount of specialization even within the entertainment industry. Unfortunately, this fact is often overlooked by filmmakers and overly ambitious lawyers.

If you read the trades, you have probably read articles discussing a particular deal where they mention the names of half a dozen attorneys. Have you ever wondered why? Consider just a few of the legal issues that arise in the life of a typical feature:

- Securities Exchange Commission (SEC) Laws pertaining to offering shares in your production and terms for soliciting investors.
- International Copyright/Ownership Laws to protect your creative work from those who will steal it outright or create derivative works.
- Copyright Clearances to ensure that you have permission to use other people's artistic works including music, photographs, and text.
- Talent Contracts to secure a commitment from that celebrity whose involvement becomes the key to investors agreeing to finance the film.
- Merchandising Rights to provide manufacturers with the rights to create products and services based on elements of your film.
- Distribution Contracts, a critical document dealing with the terms of the relationship between you or your production, and the distribution company.

Your local personal injury lawyer may be excellent in that field of law, but does he/she have experience with the complex distribution contracts that determine whether you stand a chance of getting paid anything from your hit film? The entertainment business is notorious for contracts where the difference between a few words, *net profits* and *gross profits*, can make a world of difference in your future financial participation in what was once your film.

You can find qualified attorneys by once again, turning to your network of fellow filmmakers as well as other artists such as recording artists. Or, you can call the local law firms and seek referrals to entertainment lawyers.

In many major cities, there are also non-profit organizations that offer free and low-cost basic legal services for artists. Contact local arts organizations such as theaters and companies to receive a reference.

If you have a decent project, the odds are you can find a qualified attorney willing to work with you in exchange for a small profit participation in your film. If you are fortunate enough to make such an arrangement, just remember to have another lawyer review the contract presented by the first.

Accounting Services

Accounting services go hand in hand with legal services when you consider all of the exchanges of money that occur during the life of a film, even in a film that never earns back a dime.

While you may not initially need professional accounting services, you should be certain to keep track of records and receipts for every dollar you spend at all stages of pre-production, principal photography and post-production. This is important if you have investors since you will have to account for how you spent their money.

But, even if you are self-financing your film, small amounts accumulate quickly, and the total represents your *equity* in your film. Should you later have to bring in investors to help you cover the substantial expense of transferring the video to film, your equity becomes your leverage when negotiating the terms of investment.

You can maintain your financial records using simple computer spreadsheets such as Microsoft Excel or specialized programs such as Quicken or Quickbooks. By making record-keeping a habit early, you will be better prepared when you finally need the services of a professional accountant.

Insurance

Insurance is another service that often gets nixed in efforts to cut the production budget, often without the realization that all it takes is one incident to bring the production to a halt.

The running and gunning pace of filmmaking creates a hazardous work environment for cast, crew, locations and sometimes the public at large. Accidents occur on even the most professional shoot.

These risks are increased on low budget guerrilla film shoots because the crew is often comprised of people with various levels of professional experience. Inexperience combined with an assortment of heavy, high voltage lighting and grip equipment can make for a dangerous situation. Without insurance, an accident on your shoot can open you up to serious lawsuits.

And if these threats are not bad enough, there is also the fact that you are frequently carting around equipment that is *very* expensive to replace should it be lost, stolen or damaged. As I pointed out previously, even the replacement cost of a couple of professional walkie-talkies can be in the thousands.

There are a variety of production insurance policies available to provide you liability protection from accidents. General liability policies offer broad coverage for damages and accidents that may occur to individuals and locations while filming, while workman's compensation insurance protects you and your crew in case a crew person is hurt on set. Some locations will not allow you to film without general liability insurance.

There are also policies that protect your equipment and pay to replace lost, damaged, or stolen equipment. In fact, many rental houses will not rent to you without certificates of insurance.

The exact terms of production insurance coverage varies greatly. Some policies only provide coverage for the duration of your shoot, while others provide annual coverage. Similarly, there are many different arrangements for the amount and payment terms of premiums.

I have had insurance on all of my shoots and every time it proved to be valuable, either by replacing damaged or lost equipment, or by making locations available because people had the security knowing that they could be compensated for any damages. Anytime I needed to rent something or secure a location it was simply a matter of getting the insurer's relevant information and faxing it to the insurance agent to have it added to the policy.

On one of my shoots, I actually did not have an insurance policy myself; but my production manager and close friend had purchased an annual policy for one of her projects. She allowed me to produce my project under her company's policy.

Shop around for insurance policies, especially outside of the major markets. You can sometimes find insurance agencies that offer general liability policies that may not be geared specifically towards film and TV production, but can provide coverage for you. This is the type of policy I had for my productions.

It was offered by Hagan Insurance, a company in Maryland that provided insurance for most of the independent film and video producers in the area. At the time, the policy was very affordable (compared to insurance agencies in New York and Los Angeles) at only $600 per year.

One way to find a company is to call a local rental house, and ask for referrals to companies from which they frequently receive insurance certificates.

Permits

Permits are documents provided by city and/or state agencies authorizing you to shoot at a particular location. This includes public places as well as private locations where the presence of your shoot may be disruptive to other people. Some cities require a fee and have other stipulations such as insurance coverage and security requirements (including paying an hourly rate for city police officers).

A permit provides you legitimate access to certain locations, while frequently offering amenities such as reserved parking places or being allowed to cordon off a street. With permits, I have filmed in public train stations, malls, busy streets, and parks and had the complete cooperation of the local authorities. And, my experience has been that most city agencies that require permits will go out of their way to make it easy for you to obtain them.

The disadvantage of permits is that in some jurisdictions, they can be expensive. Thus, permits add to the expense of meeting the required insurance and other stipulations. And if your schedule rapidly changes, it can be inconvenient to keep on top of the required permits.

While filming *Hacks*, we often did not know what street we would be filming on the next day until we finished the current day's shoot. But even more constraining was the fact that we would have had to pay for police escorts while towing our picture cars up and down the street.

Fortunately for us, the television show *Homicide: Life on the Street* has been shot in Baltimore for the past several years, and now nearly everyone in town is used to seeing production crews and equipment. As we were filming, police officers would drive by and ask knowingly, "*Homicide* second unit?" What do you think our response was . . . ?

6
■■■■■ DV Production Tools

DV cameras and editing equipment are rapidly evolving. We are already seeing second generation cameras and third generation editing systems. In this chapter we will cover the equipment you will need to shoot your project. We will discuss editing options later.

The equipment recommended here will remain viable for the next couple of years. However, be certain to ask potential vendors or better yet, ask online for suggestions about the latest or comparable versions.

Your basic equipment requirements will fall in one of these categories:

- DV Camera, Accessories, and Support
- Audio Packages and Accessories
- Lighting and Grip Packages and Accessories
- Tape Stock and Miscellaneous Expendables

DV Cameras and Accessories

With new models of DV cameras being introduced every few months, it can be hard to keep up with the bells and whistles offered by the latest models. Still, there are common features you should evaluate when deciding which camera to use for your production. These include:

- Lens Specifications
- CCD Specifications
- Audio Recording Specifications
- Camera Control Features
- Special Camera Modes
- Ergonomic Design

Most of this information can be found on the camera specification sheets available in catalogs or online, or by asking qualified technicians. Salespeople might have some difficulty answering questions about the more technical specs.

The first two items listed, the lens quality and the CCD specifications, directly affect the video quality your camera will produce.

Lens Specifications

Video cameras rely on a precise assembly of optical lenses to accurately capture light reflected from a scene and focus it on the CCD(s). The quality of the optics of a lens is the first critical factor in the camera's overall image quality. As a result, lenses are the single most expensive component of a camera. In fact, many high-end video cameras use *detachable lenses* that can cost as much or more than the camera body alone.

Interchangeable Lenses

In efforts to keep production costs low, most consumer DV cameras feature undetachable *zoom lenses* that are fixed to the camera's body. These lenses are not as high quality as the far more expensive, high precision lenses used in photography, film production and professional video equipment. And, since they are built into the camera, you have few options relative to the expansion of their functionality.

However, the introduction of the Canon XL1 in December 1997 made detachable lenses an option for consumer cameras. Using a special EOS lens adapter, the XL1 can use a variety of 35mm photography lens. Other low-cost cameras, such as the JVC GV-DV500, now offer this feature as well.

Zoom Range

In addition to optical quality and lens interchangeability, another important lens consideration is the *zoom range*. A zoom lens allows you to vary the *focal length* of the lens and make a focused image smaller or larger in the frame without moving the camera. This focal length is measured in millimeters (mm).

The zoom range is the distance between the widest shot a lens can get (i.e. 10mm) and the furthest shot (i.e. 100mm). This range can also be expressed as a whole number that represents the *magnification factor* of the lens.

For example, the Sony VX1000 zoom lens has a 10x magnification factor that allows the lens to go from a 5.9mm wide shot to a 59mm telephoto shot (5.9mm x10=59mm).

A higher magnification factor offers a longer zoom range, and ultimately provides more flexibility when shooting, especially if the lens is not detachable.

Many cameras also include a *digital zoom* feature that uses special computer processing to greatly expand a camera's zoom range. However, this digital trick comes at the expense of degraded picture quality. When comparing cameras, be certain to compare their optical zoom range.

Image Stabilization

A camera's *image stabilization system* is another specification that often relates to the camera lens. *Optical stabilization* uses a system of motion detectors and lenses to reduce the effects of shaky camera movement and vibration on an image. This feature is especially helpful when shooting hand-held shots with small camcorders.

There are also *electronic image stabilization systems* that perform the same function. However, these systems operate by electronically manipulating the video image. And, as with digital zooms, this digital manipulation degrades the images. Although this degradation may not be noticeable or may be very slight, remember that the main objective is to record the best images possible.

CCD Specifications

As we learned earlier, CCDs are the essential component for converting images (reflected light) into electronic signals. The effectiveness of a CCD is determined by its size and the number of *active pixel elements* it contains.

Number of CCDs

The size of a CCD is measured as a fraction of an inch. Larger CCDs typically result in better images because they contain more pixels. For example, Sony's popular DV camera, the VX1000, uses 1/3" CCDs with 410k (k stands for thousand) pixels. The lower-priced TVR900 uses 1/4" CCDs with 380k pixels each.

However, there are some Panasonic and Canon cameras, that use a technology called pixel shifting to achieve higher resolution from fewer pixels. Canon's XL1 camera uses 1/3" CCDs with 270k pixels, but has an effective resolution slightly higher than that of the Sony VX1000.

One Chip or Three Chip

In addition to the size of the CCDs, another issue is the number of CCDs utilized. Some cameras use a single CCD to scan pictures, and then derive color information using a filtering system. This single CCD (also called single or 1 chip) design is very economical and commonly used in lower priced cameras.

However, these savings come at the expense of the single CCD's ability to reproduce and manipulate the individual primary colors. So while single CCD cameras can reproduce excellent images, they often fall short in the amount of color detail they can capture.

Higher-end DV cameras like the VX1000 and XL1 use three separate CCDs, one for each primary color. This means that you are recording basically three times as much color information as with a single chip camera. The result is that *three CCD cameras* (also known as *3 chip cameras*) reproduce colors much better and more accurately than single CCD cameras.

Three CCD cameras are certainly the first choice for DV filmmakers. However, single chip cameras can be used, especially if you plan on reducing or eliminating the color to create a black and white or otherwise *monochromatic image.*

Low Light Operations

The final consideration is the CCD's responsiveness under low light situations and the signal-to-noise ratio.

Camera manufacturers often note the minimum light under which their cameras can reproduce an image. This measurement of light intensity is called *lux,* with 0 lux representing complete darkness. The higher the lux, the more light required by the camera to produce an image. Sony's TRV-9 camera has infrared circuitry that allows it to record an image repeatedly, up to one hundred feet away, in complete darkness.

But, just because a camera can produce an image under low light, does not mean that it is a good image. In low light situations, some cameras generate a lot of noise relative to the usable video signal (remember signal-to-noise ratio?). This noise causes the images to appear "grainy" and smeared. Higher quality cameras maintain a higher signal-to-noise ratio that produces better images in low light.

Audio Recording Specifications

In the late '80s, *compact discs* (CDs) first introduced consumers to the excellent sound quality and benefits of digital audio, while digital audio tapes became commonplace in professional recording environments. Naturally, DV incorporates digital audio as well.

The DV audio uses a recording process called *pulse code modulation* (PCM) that offers two different audio recording modes. However, not all cameras support both modes.

Sample Rates

Early DV cameras and lower priced DV cameras use a 32kHz, 12-bit sampling rate that is lower than the 44.1 kHz, 16-bits used in compact discs. However, even this lower rate provides outstanding sound recording quality with a range than is more than adequate for human voices and most music recording situations.

The DV specifications allow for up to four channels of 32 kHz, 12-bit audio. This can be four individual mono tracks or two stereo tracks (with one left channel and one right channel). Most DV cameras only allow you to record two 12-bit channels of audio at a time, requiring you to *dub* (add) the additional tracks later. Typically, the cameras allow you to playback all four tracks at the same time.

The second mode offered by the DV format uses 48kHz, 16-bit samples that allow you to record your audio at a quality that is better than that used for CDs. The mode supports a single stereo track or two mono tracks. The higher range provided by 48kHz, 16-bit sampling is particularly beneficial in complex music recording situations. The Canon XL1 and Sony TVR900 both offer this mode.

For DV filmmaking, the 48kHz, 16-bit mode is preferential because of our goal of starting with the best audio and video possible. However, your camera decision should not just be based solely on this factor.

Audio Connectors

Another audio issue that you should be aware of is the type of microphone input connector provided by the camera. Currently, all consumer cameras accept microphones that use a small 1/8" wide *mini-plug* to plug into a *mini-jack* that is on the camera. This fragile connector is like the ones you use for the headphones of your portable radio or CD player.

The mini-plug is an *unbalanced line* input that allows for one stereo microphone or two mono mikes. This means that the microphone cable uses wires that are not *shielded* from outside line noise that may come from other electronic signals. As a result, unbalanced audio lines over ten feet become very unreliable and prone to interference.

Professional cameras use *balanced line* inputs that feature a type of three pronged connector called an XLR. Balanced lines are shielded to protect the audio signal from outside interference and line noise and can be used over much longer distances than unbalanced-lines. Most professional mikes use balanced XLR plugs.

The XLR connector is a much more durable jack and plug than the mini-jack and mini-plug. The mini-jack on some consumer cameras are known to develop electrical shorts after excessive usage. These shorts make the audio input useless.

Many people feel that the camera manufacturers intentionally did not add XLR inputs to the higher end consumer DV cameras to deter professionals from using them. However, it did not take long for other companies to begin manufacturing professional quality *mini-to-XLR adapters* to allow for the use of professional mikes. Additionally, a new generation of low-cost cameras—such as the Sony PD100, PD150 and JVC GV-DV500—offer built-in XLR adapters.

Camera Control Features

Along with the lens quality and the CCD specifications, there are many variables that can affect the flexibility you have when you shoot your scenes and the quality of the images and audio you record. These include the *zoom lens control, focus control, audio gain control, white balance, exposure* and *shutter speed.*

Many consumer cameras have auto modes that adjust these variables for you. But for the greatest control, your camera should allow you to override the auto mode so you can manually set them.

Zoom Lens Control

Most cameras have variable speed zoom controls that allow you to adjust how fast or slow the lens zooms in or out when you push your zoom button. Many professional camera operators express dissatisfaction at the sensitivity of the controls, noting that it is often difficult with consumer cameras to start and stop zooms smoothly or change speed during a zoom.

Manual zoom control allows you to bypass the push button zoom control and zoom in or out by directly turning the *zoom ring* that is a part of the camera's lens. This offers the greatest zoom control.

However, many cameras use an electronic sensor to read manual zoom settings. This sensor does not provide an accurate relationship between the position of a zoom ring and the zoom current setting.

Focus Control

Manual focus is another essential requirement. There are many excellent *auto-focus* systems that can accurately focus on a stationary object in the frame. But, when you are in the middle of an important scene, the last thing you want is for the camera to begin shifting focus on its own.

As with manual zoom, manual focus allows you to turn a focus ring on the lens to set and adjust the focus. Unfortunately, most cameras also suffer from the same shortcoming as manual zoom rings whereby the electronic sensors do not give precise control over the manual focus.

This is not a problem when all of the action in a scene takes place in the same part of the frame (the same *depth of field*). But it is a problem when characters are moving close or further to the camera, and you must *rack focus* to shift focus to another part of the frame.

Understanding this limitation, many DV filmmakers simply plan their scenes accordingly. Recently, a lens was developed for the Canon XL1 to work around this problem. For more details, see the VX1000/Canon XL1 comparison on page 73.

Audio Record Level Control

Automatic *audio record level,* also known as *automatic gain control,* adjusts the strength of your incoming audio signals in an effort to record the audio at a consistent level by reducing loud noises and enhancing softer sounds. This is especially important for digital audio because extremely loud audio that falls out of a recording range is simply recorded as completely unusable distortion.

Manual control over your audio levels ensures that you can find just the right settings for your particular scene. In most instances, your sound mixer will be monitoring and adjusting audio using a separate audio mixer that plugs into your camera's audio jack.

White Balance

Video cameras are especially sensitive to the color differences that exist in various forms of lighting. Although our eyes notice that a sunset is more red than a fluorescent light, the difference in the *color temperature* of these light sources registers as a substantial difference to a CCD.

Color temperature is expressed in degrees Kelvin—the higher the temperature, the cooler (bluer) the light, and the lower the temperature, the warmer (redder) the light. For example, a typical sunset has a color temperature of about 2,000° K, while a fluorescent bulb is around 4,800° K.

White balance is a function that allows the camera to adjust the way it filters colors to compensate for the current lighting conditions.

Automatic white balance means that as you shoot, the camera attempts to make these adjustments based on lighting conditions read by its light sensors. This can result in the color of your picture changing drastically from one set-up to another.

Manual white balance allows you to set a white balance for your current lighting conditions, then have the setting remain constant.

To perform a white balance, typically you aim the camera at a white object such as a piece of paper or a white T-shirt, then simply push a button. The camera adjusts for the correct color temperature based upon the reading it takes.

Exposure

While the camera lens focuses reflected light towards the CCDs, the amount of light actually allowed to pass through the lenses, the *expo-*

sure, is controlled by an adjustable circular opening called the *iris* or *aperture*.

When the iris is closed, no light is allowed to enter the camera. The iris can be opened up incrementally to allow more light to enter. These increments are expressed as a number called *F-stops*.

Common f-stops used for video cameras, from the largest iris opening to the smallest opening, are f-1.4, 2, 2.8, 4, 5.6, 8, 11, 16 and 22. One of the tricky things to remember about f-stops is that the larger the number, the less light that reaches (is exposed to) the CCD.

As with automatic white balance, when using automatic exposure, the camera attempts to adjust the iris based on its own light readings. Depending upon the available light, it will open up the iris or close it down a little to try to keep an image from being underexposed or overexposed.

Automatic exposure proves to be a handicap when you must have complete control over the exposure. Say, for example, that you are moving briefly between light and dark environments, or you want to create a dark, moody atmosphere, manual exposure control offers that flexibility.

Many cameras also feature adjustable automatic exposure that has several preset settings based upon a variety of light situations.

Shutter Speed

Shutter speed is the duration for which the CCD is exposed to an image. The rate is stated as a fraction of a second. For example, 1/60th of a second is the standard shutter speed for NTSC cameras. This corresponds with 60 fields of video recorded each second.

Faster shutter speeds allow you to record better shots of fast action, because the camera is capturing more images per second. However, since the CCD has less time to scan the image, recording video at high speeds requires more light than normal shutter speeds.

Slower than normal shutter speeds, for example at 1/30th to 1/4th, can help improve low light sensitivity by providing the CCD more time to respond to the light falling on it. Unfortunately, this additional exposure time can cause images to appear blurry, and the motion to be stuttered in a stroboscopic effect. Some people find this useful as a dreamy effect, but it is undesirable for video that is to be inter-cut with video recorded at a normal shutter speed.

Special Camera Modes

In addition to the usual assortment of automatic and manual control features available on DV cameras, new recording and playback modes are being introduced to add still more functions to the cameras. The usefulness of these features depends on the degree to which they affect the image quality of your video or truly improve the performance of the camera.

Long Play Mode (LP Mode)

The concept of long play mode is well established in consumer video recorders. The basic idea is that by slowing down the recording device and reducing the amount of picture information recorded, users can stretch the record time of the tape. While this results in a deterioration in picture quality, tape record time can be doubled or tripled.

Many DV cameras are now beginning to offer LP modes that allow you to record up to 90 minutes on a 60 minute DV tape. And guess what? There is *no* difference in the video quality between SP and LP modes. This is because the DV format always requires that data be sent at the same rate.

But, before you get excited about turning that into a 50 percent tape stock saving, you need to know that LP mode is accomplished by crowding more data into an already crowded tape. This can make the tape much more susceptible to errors and playback problems.

Additionally, there are reports that some LP mode tapes have difficulty playing back on machines other than the one that it was recorded on.

Because of these potential risks, LP mode is best left for casual use.

16:9 Mode (also known as 16x9 or 16 by 9)

Considering the recent launch of digital television and the migration towards 16:9 as a standard video format, it's no surprise that 16:9 mode is becoming a common function on DV cameras.

To view 16:9 video, it must be played back on a device capable of properly displaying it. Because of the difference in ratios, 16:9 video appears stretched when viewed on regular televisions or monitors. It must be viewed on a digital television, or through a DV tape player where 16:9 can play the video letterboxed on a regular TV.

Unfortunately, for most consumer cameras, the process used to create 16:9 video from the standard 4x3 CCD also reduces the camera's video resolution. In some cameras, the 16:9 images are noticeably less sharp looking than normal recordings. Some video to film transfer companies have already optimized their processes for 16:9 modes on these cameras. As 16:9 devices become more common, the DV cameras will begin to offer true 16:9 modes at full video resolution.

Photo Mode

Photo mode allows you to use your camera to capture high quality still pictures. Once taken, they can be stored on video tape, often with short audio comments. Some cameras also allow you to store sets of photos on small memory storage cards or floppy disc. The photos can later be viewed on a television, or loaded into a computer from the disc or via FireWire.

If the camera features a progressive scanning mode, then the photos will already be free of the interlace video lines common when combining video fields to create a single frame image. If not, an interpolation is performed to do this on the photo. This eliminates the digital, pixilated look.

Most DV editing programs also allow you to take single frame photos as well.

Frame Movie Mode

Frame movie mode is an extension of the progressive scan still photo mode that performs this function on full motion video. The video recorded in this format has a distinctly different look than normal interlaced video. Some have compared it to the look of film, although in my opinion, it's far from that. However, it is an interesting look that can definitely add a unique feel to projects.

However, when planning for a DV to film transfer, you must be certain to consult with the company that will be providing the transfer for you. Some companies say frame mode produces better images using their process, while other say it creates serious problems for them.

PAL Playback

PAL playback allows you to play PAL tapes in your camera, and view them on your NTSC television. This is a welcome feature for filmmakers opting to shoot PAL.

Ergonomic Design

For many people, the basic physical design and weight of a camera is an important issue. If you are going to be shooting hand-held for long periods of time, you will want to use a camera that is comfortable for you. This is certainly one reason why, before you purchase a camera, if at all possible, you should spend some time shooting with it.

Physical Design

When news organizations began to use high quality Hi-8 camcorders in the early '90s, one of the primary complaints from professional shooters was that the cameras were just too small!

For a person used to hauling around a 20+ lb. Betacam SP camera, the little cameras had a physical and psychological effect on their shooting style. Although they were much bulkier, it was easier to shoot stable hand-held shots from a big camera because it was designed to be used on the shoulder. However, camcorders had to be supported by the arms.

With DV camcorders, this continues to be an issue. In fact, the cameras have gotten even smaller. Although many of them now benefit from various forms of optical stabilization, your shooting style will be very much dictated by the camera's physical size and bulkiness.

Weight

Likewise, the camera's weight will also determine how well you can shoot with the camera for long stretches at a time. This is especially true for cameras that have interchangeable lenses or other attachments that may shift the balance of their weight towards the front. The camera's weight will also be a factor when considering various accessories and camera support systems.

Controls Accessibility

The ability to easily access camera controls, particularly manual controls, zoom, and focus are important. You don't want to have to take your eye away from the eye piece to look for a button while shooting. This is really an issue on some cameras that rely on extensive computer menu systems to modify certain control settings.

Comparing Cameras

While there are many different DV cameras being used in DV filmmaking, there are currently two specific models that have won the respect of filmmakers—the Sony DCRVX-1000 (a.k.a. VX1000) and the Canon XL1. While there are newer models introduced almost monthly, I'll use these two popular cameras to illustrate the comparative strengths and weaknesses you might consider when deciding on a DV camcorder.

Sony DCRVX-1000

The VX1000 was one of the first consumer DV cameras introduced. It immediately became a hit because of its small size, durability, and excellent video quality.

One of the greatest advantages of the VX1000 is that it looks so much like a regular camcorder. This allows you to inconspicuously take the camera places that "professional" cameras are not allowed to go. As a result, many documentary filmmakers use the VX1000.

Also, because of its lightweight, the VX1000 can be used with the low-cost Steadicam Jr. which provides users with stable, professional looking shots as the camera appears to move freely through the air.

The camera also has the benefit of being a mature product that has the support of many third party vendors offering a variety of customized accessories.

The VX1000 has a few shortcomings. One of the biggest complaints from users was the marginal quality of the camera's lenses and the inability to use other lenses.

Professional videographers often complain about the lack of professional controls, especially in relationship to the ability to manually focus the camera. While the VX1000 can be focused manually, it uses an electronic sensor system that makes it difficult to set and return to predetermined focus spots.

This inability to "follow focus" requires careful planning when setting up shots which require the talent to move a lot or an action to happen at various depths of field. The same issue also plagues the XL1 lens. However, a new lens option can now work around this problem.

The final shortcoming of the VX1000 is that it can only record 32kHz, 12-bit audio two channels at a time. Furthermore, it does not offer 48kHz, 16-bit audio at all.

Canon XL1

Canon introduced the XL1 to eager videographers and filmmakers in late 1997. Considered a second-generation camera, the XL1 sought to address the VX1000's lens complaints by allowing for interchangeable lenses.

The XL1's 16x zoom lens has a longer range than VX1000s and users can easily switch between a variety of other high quality lens. Canon lens are renowned for their quality. Under certain situations, the lenses offered for the XL1 provide a better image than the VX1000.

The zoom lens provided with the XL1 suffers from the same focus control shortcomings of the VX1000. However, a California filmmaker named Michael Pappas recently developed a system that combines Canon's lens adapter with a set of 35mm photography lens resulting in a lens that provides excellent manual focus control.

The Pappas Lens System allows *directors of photography* to operate the XL1 much like they operate and set focus on a film camera. The lens arrangement is sold by ProMax Technologies, listed in the appendices.

Filmmakers have also been excited by a special shooting mode offered by the XL1 called *frame movie mode.* When shooting in this *progressive scan* mode, the camera captures images as an entire frame as opposed to the process used traditionally, where video images are captured by two separate fields of information that are then interlaced (combined) to create a frame. The video recorded in frame movie mode has a softer, less video look to it.

On the audio side, the XL1 also features some improvements by providing the ability to record two channels of 48kHz, 16-bit audio or four simultaneous channels of 32kHz, 12-bit audio.

It's fair to say that the XL1 is a well-supported camera. Many companies make special lenses, teleprompter extensions, and sound packages that conform to this unique Canon model. Other accessories for the XL1, such as a *monochrome viewfinder, 14X manual zoom lens, floppy disk still image recorder* and *remote controller* add even greater expand-ability to an already versatile camcorder.

The XL1 has received some criticism from users. People have com-plained about its front-end heavy design that makes it awkward and uncomfortable for long periods of hand-held shooting.

Canon offers a shoulder mount that offsets this problem. The shoul-der mount also includes XLR adapters to allow professional micro-phones to be plugged into the camera.

Another complaint stemmed from people hoping to use the Steadicam Jr. with the XL1, but found that at nearly twice the weight of the VX1000, the XL1 was far too heavy. Steadi Systems, the manu-facture of Steadicams, responded with the Steadi DV system capable of supporting the XL1 and heavier DV cameras. However, the Steadi DV rig costs $2,000 compared to the $725 Steadicam Jr.

Which One?

This debate question has been asked and debated since the introduction of the XL1. And, unfortunately, the answer depends primarily on the conditions under which you will be recording and your personal pref-erences. The potential for slight differences in image quality is not enough to be the sole determining factor. And in many cases, it would be ideal to have an XL1 (primary camera) *and* a VX1000 (Steadicam and secondary camera) on a shoot.

Sony VX-2000 and PD150

Sony released an update of the VX1000 in two newly reshaped varia-tions; a consumer version dubbed the VX2000 with improved audio and three amazingly crisp 1/3" CCDs, and a professional version called the DSR-PD150; essentially, it's the same camera but with substantial upgrades. Namely, the PD150 has two XLR audio inputs for connecting professional microphones, complete with channel independent level controls. Sony also lets you switch recording formats between DV to DVCAM on the professional PD150.

Canon GL1

Less ergonomic than its predecessor, the new Canon GL1 camcorder holds a 3-chip imager in a body style that's both rugged and portable. For those who are shooting DV for green-screen effects, the GL1 has picture technology that reduces color shifting, noisy shadows, and edge details. It has a frame movie mode which shoots de-interlaced images that Canon XL1 users will be familiar with, but it is only a psuedo-cinematic gimmick. The overall image is similar to the XL1, but the price is just $2,800.

Others

There are other cameras that are increasing in popularity among DV filmmakers. The Sony TR-9 is a 1-chip camera popular because of its low-cost. The 3-chip Sony TVR900 includes 48kHz, 16-bit audio and other improvements over the VX1000 at a lower cost. However, it has smaller CCDs and less pixels.

The Sony DCR-PC1 and DCR-PC100 are the compact camcorders seen in many feature films as the hand-held choice of documentarians. These $2,000 miniatures carry all of the bells and whistles found on Sony DVcams with a single 1/4" chip and sharp Zeiss optics. The PC100 has an advanced HAD CCD imager to reduce noise levels and double the clarity of dark scenes. Sony's DCR-PC5 is their smallest Mini DV camcorder yet, it features a 2.5" touchscreen LCD Monitor, 120x digital zoom, and a respectable 680,000 pixel CCD chip. The camera offers both 16-bit stereo sound, or a 12-bit *audio dub* mode records digital audio in two stereo tracks.

The JVC GY-DV500 is blurring the line between pro and consumer DV camcorders. A 3-CCD 1/2" color model with interchangeable lenses, XLR mic inputs, and two channels of 16-bit digital audio outputs, it incorporates the inexpensive Mini-DV format and FireWire in its 11 lbs. body. It features a special *super scene finder* to help you flag up to 134 scenes with a "Take" or "No Good" marker as you shoot. The only professional thing that the consumer-level filmmaker might not like is the $6,000 price.

Panasonic's AG-EZ30 is billed as the world's smallest and lightest three CCD camera. Weighing only 1.52 lbs., it packs a lot of quality into a $4,000 package. The AG-EZ30U includes manual controls over focus, shutter speed, and white balance. Like many broadcast-quality camcorders, it includes a zebra-level indicator to control exposure. And because it has a highly-sensitive signal-to-noise ratio, it gives you a more dynamic range of light and color. Of course, it's got a FireWire connection, full audio/mic inputs, and a remote control. And like many of today's camcorders, it has a photo-frame function so you can take high-resolution stills with the same equipment.

There are other DV models by Sony, Panasonic, JVC and Sharp that all produce great images as long as you become familiar with their limitations and light each scene properly. The next generation of DV cameras should improve the quality even more.

On the high-end of $10,000+ DVCAM and DVCPRO cameras are the Sony DSR-500, the Panasonic AJ-D200, and the Panasonic AJ-D810 which all feature high quality lens, professional features, and true 16:9 wide screen recording.

And of course there is also the venerable Sony 700 digital Betacam camera. And the HDW700 high definition camera if you can afford the $1,500 per day rental.

But in the worse case, it is about using whatever DV camera you can afford or have access to, then pushing it to its limits. I'm not trying to diminish the camera selection process. But if it comes down to waiting until you can afford the 3-chip camera with all the bells and whistles, or taping with a borrowed 1-chip, remember: use what you got to get what you want.

Camera Accessories

You will require a few important accessories to make the most from your camera. Batteries, power supplies, and camera cases are essential. Lens converters and filters allow you to tailor your video image, and field monitors provide you with the benefit of seeing scenes as they are being prepared and recorded.

Batteries and Power Supplies

DV cameras can be powered using battery sources or AC power supplies. Small lithium batteries can be plugged into the camera to provide thirty to eighty minutes of recording time depending on the batteries charge capacity and the conditions in which it is used. These batteries can be recharged in approximately forty to 150 minutes (2.5 hours), depending on the batteries *recharge rate.*

As an alternative to the camera's on-board batteries, there are also high capacity *battery packs* available. These battery packs can usually be slung over the shoulder by a strap or worn around the waist as *battery belts.* Several DV camera manufacturers offer their own high capacity batteries, while battery packs manufactured by companies such as Bescor and NRG can provide as much as eight hours of recording time.

Priced less than $300, these battery packs are crucial for recording in the field or remote locations, as well as when using devices such as a Steadicam Jr., where mobility is a must. However, the recharge time for these batteries is so long that they usually must be recharged overnight.

AC power is a practical option when it is available and does not interfere with the camera's movement. The power adapters plug into the battery connection on the camera. These adapters often serve the dual purpose of being a battery charger for the on-camera batteries. Many cameras allow you to recharge the batteries while also powering the camera. Additionally, some batteries also have DC power adapters that allow you to plug into a car cigarette lighter for a recharge.

Plan your power requirements carefully, and monitor your battery usage without relying on the battery recording times provided by manufacturers. You don't want to be stuck at a remote location without power. I know it sounds basic, but I have seen it happen.

Cases

A good case is important to protect your camera from the obvious rigors of production, as well as the less obvious threats of dirt, dust, static electricity, and other things that can damage the fragile optics and electronics.

Hard shell cases provide the best protection by isolating the camera in a rigid exterior, padded interior structure. In this case, the camera can be stacked and packed with other equipment. Plus, they frequently have interior designs to accommodate camera accessories such as cables, filters, and small lights. However, their design makes them very conspicuous and often awkward to transport. Additionally, they can easily cost several hundred dollars.

Soft cases provide a basic means of transporting the camera when it is kept close to you. They can be used to carry most camcorders on an airplane. And, while you do not have the benefit of the hard shells protection from rough handling, the camera is still protected from the elements.

Miscellaneous Accessories

You will also want to pick up a few other odds and ends. Head cleaner tapes remove residue and dust from the heads of your DV camera and/or deck. If you notice odd patterns when you play back tapes, then you might need to clean the heads. Similarly, you should purchase a small can of compressed air to blow dust out of the camera. You will also want lens tissue to properly clean your lens. You can find these items at any photography shop.

Len Converters

Lens converters attach to your camera's zoom lens, and allow you to create a wider or a more telephotographic lens. The degree by which it widens or narrows is expressed as a number that can be multiplied by the zoom range to provide the new zoom range. For example, the Sony VX1000 ordinarily has a zoom range of 5.9mm to 59mm. With the optional .7 wide angle lens, the widest angle becomes 4.13mm (5.9mm x.7=4.13mm), and the narrowest 41.3mm. The same type of math applies with telephotographic lenses.

The lens converters are attached to the zoom lens by a threaded adapter ring that allows them to be screwed onto the end of the zoom. To be compatible with your camera, the lens adapter ring must be the same diameter as the your zoom lens. This diameter is expressed in millimeters. Consumer camcorders commonly use 37mm, 52mm, and 72mm diameter adapter rings.

Be aware that some lens converters, particularly wide angle lenses, have been known to slightly distort your images at extreme settings. Sometimes this distortion is a slight shift in focus, at other times, it is an odd optical *vignetting* that may not be visible in the viewfinder. However, it can usually be noted on a monitor.

Lens converters are offered by camera manufacturers as well as camera accessory manufacturers. Century Optics is one of the leading companies. Be careful of low-cost converters that use cheap plastic or poor quality glass lenses.

Filters

Lens filters allow you to modify characteristics of the light entering the camera which determines the way it is perceived by the CCD. When used properly, filters allow great control and enhancement of your images.

Like lens converters, filters attach to the end of the zoom lens. However, unlike converters, filters can substantially decrease the amount of light entering the camera, requiring you to increase the exposure. Filters are rated by the *filter factor*, which indicates how much of an f-stop of light is lost when using a particular filter.

Filters cost $25 to $75 each and are often sold in sets that feature varying degrees of a particular effect. Some of the most common and useful filters include:

- Ultra Violet (UV)–Cuts down on the amount of UV light which helps reduce haze. Since UV filters do not affect the image and have minimal filter factors, people often keep them in place to protect the lens from getting scratched and damaged.
- Neutral Density (ND)–Allow you to cut down on light and decrease contrast in a scene. ND filters will be one of your most commonly used filters.
- Polarization–Changes the angles at which light is entering the camera to reduce reflections and glares.
- Fluorescent–Helps decrease the odd color and flicker created by fluorescent lights.
- Diffusion–Used to create a softer, "dreamier" look. Another frequently used filter. Tiffen Pro-Mist filters are among the most popular.

Field Monitors

Monitors are used by the DP when preparing scenes and by the director and crew while scenes are being shot. One of the amenities of video is the ability to view a monitor and see an image that is an accurate representation of what the camera will be recording. This proves to be invaluable while lighting scenes and composing shots. There are many types of small portable televisions and monitors that are suitable for use as a field monitor.

Many people also use the small LCD color televisions, such as the Sony Watchman. There are special mounts available that allow you to attach them to the top of your camera. While they are useful up close, larger televisions and monitors typically provide more details.

The least expensive option is simply a 5"–13" portable television with the ability to be powered by batteries, a DC car battery adapter, and AC power. If it does not have that feature, you can rent or purchase a 12V DC to 120V AC power converter from an electronics supply store that will allow it to operate off of a battery.

Also, be certain that the television has RCA connectors for audio and video input. And, view color bars generated by a camera or videotape to be sure that the picture tube can accurately reproduce colors.

To reduce glare from the sun and lights, and to view the screen better, a protective hood can be created from small pieces of cardboard extended from the top and sides of the TV and held in place by tape.

While portable televisions can get the job done, true field monitors offer professional features such as detachable hood screens, S-VHS input for better picture quality, higher resolution images which aids greatly for checking the cameras focus, and *overscan/underscan* modes which allows you to view the video image area not seen on regular televisions. Additionally, these monitors can often be powered for hours by large battery power packs. The JVC TM-550U ($900) is a good model to purchase or rent.

Camera Support

When combined with optical or electronic stabilization, camcorders and palmcorders are great for hand-held shooting. And even without it, once you become familiar with your camera you can accomplish some very effective shots, especially if you are going for the hand-held look popularized by TV shows, such as NBC's *Homicide: Life on the Street.*

However, other times you may require a more traditional cinematic look and feel for your project. That's when its time to turn to a variety of camera support options such as shoulder rests, tripods, camera stabilization systems, dollies, and jib arms.

Shoulder Rest

With a shoulder rest, your camera is attached to a device that allows you to support the camera using your shoulder and a single hand. The rest is designed to help stabilize the camera by distributing its weight between the lens and the contoured pad at the rear. For lightweight cameras, shoulder rests can add much needed weight.

Instead of having to balance the camera near the front by holding it in your hand, some shoulder rests include *pistol grips* which extend from the bottom of the front of the rest. This arm position is more comfortable when shooting for extended periods of time. Some pistol grips connect to the camera and allow you to control camera functions such as recording, zooming, and focus.

Tripods

Since cinema's early years, tripods have provided a stable camera support by balancing the weight of the camera on three adjustable legs. The camera's height can be raised and lowered by adjusting the tripod. The camera's movement and position is controlled by a *tripod head* attached to the tripod that uses a set of rotating joints to allow the camera to *pan* left and right or *tilt* up and down. Handles can be affixed to the tripod head for precise control.

The camera is attached to the tripod using a *plate* that screws onto the camera and tripod. These days, most plates are *quick release plates* that can lock into the tripod without screws.

The quality of tripods can vary tremendously. Inexpensive plastic tripods may not have the weight necessary to ground the camera enough to make it very stable, especially with lightweight cameras. Plus, these tripods frequently use inexpensive *friction heads* that make it difficult to perform smooth camera movements.

Professional tripods are usually made out of a much more durable, heavyweight aluminum. Even lightweight professional tripods are designed to provide the most stable support possible. And the *fluid heads* used on professional tripods allow for much smoother camera movement.

Professional tripods, heads, and plates are usually sold as separate units. However, most manufacturers recommend certain combinations or market whole units as a particular model. This is to allow for the option of using the tripod with a variety of cameras and accessories such as a jib arm.

While camera manufacturers usually offer their own tripods and accessories, the industry leader is Bogen. For years they sold products under their own name, however they now market them under the Manfrotto brand name.

The 3140 model is a favorite with DV cameras. It costs just under $300 and includes the 3046 model tripod and the 3063 model mini-fluid head.

Dollies

Although tripods are excellent for *lockdown shots* where camera movements are limited to pans and tilts, there are other occasions where you might desire to have the camera smoothly follow the action in the scene.

Dolly shots allow you to accomplish this by mounting the camera on a wheeled device called a *dolly*. The dolly, camera, and camera operator are pushed and pulled about the set, sometimes rolling on tracks, expanding the range of camera movement. Dollies can add a substantial feeling of depth to a scene when used properly.

Some high-end dollies mount the camera on a *boom arm* attached to the dolly. This arm can move up and down to create yet another axis of movement.

Despite the seemingly simple operation, correctly handling a dolly during a scene takes some experience. This job is typically performed by a *dolly grip* who communicates closely with the director and DP to determine the timing and pace of movements.

Professional dollies are very expensive to purchase and rent. They are also very cumbersome to move and set-up and are best used under the supervision of an experienced dolly grip.

There are low-cost dollies available. The most basic dollies are sets of wheels which attach to the tripod to allow it to roll across the floor. However, because the camera and tripod are so lightweight, this arrangement only works on very smooth surfaces.

Other inexpensive dollies are variations of *doorway dollies* or *skateboard dollies*. Doorway dollies are like a child's wagon; they are essentially a board with a set of large wheels on the side. The tripod and operator stand on the board and the dolly grip moves the unit with a large handle.

As the name implies, skateboard dollies are basically a large board with skateboard wheels mounted at an angle on the underside, The board is laid on top of a "track" made from the inexpensive PVC tubing used for plumbing and drain pipes. Again, the tripod and operator stand on the board and are moved using a handle. This simple dolly can be built for less than a $100 and works quite effectively. Plans to build a skateboard dolly are available for free online. The website URL is included in the resources list in the appendix.

Wheelchairs are a long-time favorite for many filmmakers seeking a quick and convenient dolly solution. They are very inexpensive to purchase and can often be found at thrift stores such as Amvets and Goodwill.

Jib Arms and Cranes

There are many times where directors seek even more camera angles and movement than can be provided with dollies. Jib arms and cranes offer that option.

A *jib arm* (also known as a boom arm) is a long attachment that fits on a tripod head and extends out several feet with the camera mounted on the end. It can make use of the tripod heads panning and tilting ability and a system of pulleys to move the camera to a variety of horizontal and vertical angles, from low close to the ground to high in the air. The longer the arm, the higher the jib arm can be raised.

Basic jib arms allow for this range of movement, but provide little or no control over the camera's functions. More sophisticated jib arms offer camera control as well as a camera head on the end of the jib arm that can be tilted and panned to further vary the shot.

There are now several companies offering jib arms for under $500. One such unit offered by ProMax Technologies is called the Cobra Crane (it's actually a jib arm). There are also plans on the Internet for building a low-cost jib arm. The URL is in the appendices.

Like jib arms, *cranes* are also used to move the camera on a vertical plane; however, they are large, stand-alone units that move the camera and the camera operator. This offers greater control than a jib arm by allowing the operator to compose and alter the shots at will.

Cranes are expensive to rent and very difficult to transport. Additionally, larger units must be operated by trained *crane operators*.

Camera Stabilization Systems

Offering the mobility of hand-held shooting and the fluidity of dolly and crane movement, the introduction of the Steadicam™ camera stabilization device in the mid-'70s offered a new tool for cinematic expression. The device uses a system of springs and weights to isolate the camera from the operator's movements while keeping it balanced, even as the operator moves it about. This makes it possible to smoothly perform extremely complicated moving and *tracking shots* that follow action in a scene.

Because of their precise design and popularity, Steadicam units are very expensive. However, there are now many companies that offer professional stabilization systems similar to the Steadicam.

A few years ago, the manufacturer of Steadicams, Cinema Products, introduced a Steadicam Jr. system to be used with small lightweight camcorders. Although it costs less than $600, with a fair amount of practice, its performance is very impressive. It allows you to mimic many of the shots performed with the professional version.

A new version called the Steadicam DV accommodates heavier weight camcorders such as the Canon XL1. However, it costs twice as much as the Steadicam Jr.

Several lower priced alternatives to the Steadicam DV system are now available. While they have the same basic intention, they all use a variety of stabilization methods.

Two notable products for DV cameras are the Glidecam V-8 from Glidecam Industries and the Steadytracker sold by ProMax Technology. Both units cost less than $600.

When purchasing or renting a camera stabilization system, be certain to allow yourself sufficient time to learn to use the device. They are very finicky instruments that must be carefully calibrated. Learning to get professional results requires an investment of time and effort.

Audio Package and Accessories

Just as you want to strive for the highest quality visuals for your production, you must also make sound a priority. This can be accomplished by using the best audio equipment you can afford, and knowing how to use it effectively. The basic components of your location sound package are:

- Microphones and mic accessories
- A shock mount and boom pole
- Headphones
- Cables and adapters
- Field mixers

Microphones and Accessories

There are dozens of assorted microphones available for many different recording purposes. You will probably do the bulk of your production with shotgun, lavaliere and hand-held microphones.

Shotgun Microphones

A *shotgun mic* is a highly directional mic featuring a *unidirectional pickup pattern* that is most responsive to the sounds that it is aimed towards. In the hands of a good operator, they provide the ability to separate dialogue from background noises.

Physically, the mics are tubular shaped and can vary in length with a *short shotgun mic* measuring several inches long to varieties of *long shotgun mics* that are several feet long. The length of the mic is one of the factors that determines its attributes.

Short shotguns offer the flexibility of being used for interior and exterior recording. Long shotgun mics are excellent for exterior recording but, when used indoors, are often more sensitive to a room's echoes.

A mic's cost and sensitivity is also determined by the type of mic element and powering method it uses. The less expensive *electret condenser* shotgun mics are internally powered by low voltage AA or button batteries, while the more sensitive and more expensive *condenser* shotgun mics are powered by external 12 volt battery power supplies or 48 volt *phantom power* provided from a source such as an audio mixer.

There are several models of short shotgun mics that are popular for high quality dialogue recording. They vary in price and quality, although quality is not always determined by the price. Highly recommended mics include:

Audio-Technica AT835b ($280)

Despite its low cost, the AT835b is one of the best short shotgun mics for interior and exterior dialogue recording. However, it has a short range and must be used from overhead within 1.5 to 2.5 feet of the subject.

Sennheiser K6/ME66 ($430)

Sennheiser is the industry leader in professional mics for film and video. With a range comparable to the AT835b, the ME66 is also an electret condenser short shotgun mic module that attaches to the K6 power module.

Audio Technica AT4073a ($680)

This is a condenser short shotgun mic that offers greater sensitivity than the AT835b, the AT4073 can record dialogue from up to six feet away.

Sennheiser 416 ($1,230, Rental: $45/day)

This is by far, the leading short shotgun mic for film and video sound recording. This mic has a range about a foot shorter than the AT4073a, but is a very durable and reliable mic.

Windscreens

Because of the mic's sensitivity, it should be covered by a foam *windscreen* that helps reduce rustling noise from wind blowing across it, as well as odd breaths and noises made by people when pronouncing certain sounds.

For very windy exterior shooting situations, you may require a more expensive *furry windscreen* (approx. $120) which provides better protection or even a high-priced, hard-meshed *blimp windscreen* (approx. $300) that cuts wind noise substantially in even the worse conditions. A low-cost but effective alternative is the use of several layers of cheesecloth wrapped around the mic and covered with a tube sock.

Boom Poles and Shock Mounts

Shotgun mics are mounted on the end of long adjustable length *boom poles* which allow the mic to be suspended above the performers. The mics are attached to the boom poles with a *shock mount* that helps reduce the noise generated by the boom operator.

A six-foot boom pole, such as the model 557 offered by Gitzo, is available for around $110. However, you will probably want the flexibility and range of a longer nine- or twelve-foot model.

The Audio Technica's AT8415 shock mount for short shotgun mics is another industry standard. The mount is available for around $50.

Boom poles and shock mounts can also be rented for a few dollars per day. Some rental houses include them as part of a complete audio package that includes a mic, boom pole, shock mount, and cables.

If the purchase or rental price is still too high, some creative folks have effectively used paint roller poles for boom poles and rubber bands and Styrofoam to create shock mounts.

Lavalieres

You might occasionally turn to small, battery powered lavalieres mics to record audio in certain situations. They can be discreetly clipped on clothing or planted on set. Their *omnidirectional pickup pattern* makes them sensitive to sound coming from a wide range of directions.

Hard-wired lavalieres use cables to connect to the camera or audio mixer. They are useful for interviews and other situations where an inconspicuous mic is desired. *Wireless lavalieres* rely on radio transmitters to send audio signals to the record device. They are practical for very wide shots where the mic can not be boomed without being seen.

Quality hard-wire lavalieres, such as the Sony ECM-77 and Sennheiser MKE-2, can be purchased for a less than $300 and rented for about $10 per day. Be cautious of low-cost lavs that can cause audio to sound thin and hollow.

Handheld Mics

Handheld mics are most often omnidirectional and are most useful in situations where several people must share a mic, such as an interview, or where it is desirable to pickup background sounds, like when recording sound effects and *natural sounds.*

Most handheld mics have a *dynamic mic* design that uses a sensitive electromagnetic capsule which generates electric signals in response to sounds. The advantage of this capsule design is that it is very rugged and able to tolerate the demands of field audio recording conditions. The disadvantage is the mic's limited range and sensitivity.

Handheld mics can be hardwired or wireless. Good quality hardwired handheld mics are very affordable.

Wireless Mics

Wireless mics rely on *radio frequencies* (RF) to send the audio signals from the *transmitter* attached to the mic to the *receiver* at the camera, or audio mixer. Wireless mics can be sold with the transmitter and mic as one unit or in modular systems that can be used with most lavaliere or handheld mics.

Wireless units transmit either using VHF (Very High Frequency) or UHF (Ultra High Frequency) transmitters. VHF is a very crowded bandwidth used for everything from pagers to remote control toys to broadcast television. Wireless mics used in these frequencies can be very susceptible to RF interference from these other sources. This is especially true as the distance between the transmitter and receiver grows or if they are separated by obstructions such as trees or buildings. Despite these problems, many low-priced wireless units transmit using VHF.

On the other hand, UHF has a much broader bandwidth than VHF. Although it is becoming increasingly popular for wireless applications, it is still much more reliable for top quality wireless transmission. However, UHF wireless systems are far more expensive than VHF.

When evaluating wireless systems, you will frequently encounter mics being billed as *diversity mics*. Diversity systems use a variety of techniques in attempts to reduce problems with interference. The basic concept is to use two or more signal paths to transmit and receive, then at any given time, use whichever signal is strongest or has the least interference.

Low-end professional wireless mics are available from manufacturers like Telex (the ENG1, $300), Samson (UM1, $600) and Azden (400UDR-Receiver and 41BT-Transmitter, $600). The top quality professional wireless units from leading companies such as Letrosonic, Sennheiser, Sony, and Shure can run into the thousands and are usually quite expensive to rent.

However, for shoots making extensive use of wireless mics, particularly in RF congested urban areas, these units are certainly worth the rental rates.

Audio Adapters and Cables

Since most consumer camcorders use a mini-plug jack for mic inputs, you will be required to use special adapters to connect professional mics that use XLR connectors. Additionally, you will require long XLR audio cables to connect various elements of your audio package. To avoid introducing undesirable noise and distortion to your audio, it is important that you use quality audio adapters and cables.

Professional audio adapters basically fall into two categories, XLR adapter cables that simply change the connectors and match the electronic levels, and XLR adapter boxes that add additional features.

A straight adapter cable that allows you to physically change an XLR connector to a mini-plug can be purchased from most electronic stores. However, these cables lack the electronic component necessary to properly match the difference in the electronic signal levels used in XLR lines and those used in mini-inputs. When used as is, they typically create a very distinct buzz in your audio.

Fortunately, you can purchase adapter cables that have been modified to compensate for the electrical differences. These low-cost XLR adapter cables are now available from many sources, usually for less than $50. Beachtek manufactures a popular model.

In addition to converting the connectors and line levels, XLR adapter boxes also add features such as:

- Additional inputs that allow you to connect more than one mic;
- The use of 1/8" plug mics to connect other audio equipment such as a CD player;
- Audio level controls for each mic; and
- Mono/stereo switches which designates whether one mic feeds left and right audio channels.

The boxes are designed to be small, durable, and unobtrusive. Most of them can be mounted under the camera.

Quality XLR adapter boxes are manufactured by Beachtek (the DXA-4 for the VX1000–$250, the DXA-4P–$270 for other cameras), Studio1 (XLR-PRO for the XL1–$220), and Elite Video (Diamond 4–$230). Additionally, the Canon MA-100 shoulder rest also adds XLR inputs to the XL1 camera.

Similar care must be used when selecting audio cables. The length and durability of these cables are especially important when using a boom operator. Beware of thin, low-cost cables that may not be properly shielded and, as a result, are subject to line noise. Also, look out for poorly wired XLR connectors. A good quality ten-foot cable can be purchased for less than $50. They can be plugged together to extend the length. However, to avoid signal loss, try to keep cable lengths under twenty feet. Custom length cables can also be made at a local audio and music equipment house.

Headphones

Good headphones are crucial for monitoring audio while recording. To be effective, they must completely eliminate outside noise. The small earphones used with portable radios and CD players are not acceptable for this purpose. Professionals rely on expensive but lightweight *ear wigs*.

When purchasing a pair of headphones, be certain to check that the audio plug used fits your camera headphone jack or the audio mixer jack.

Recommended models include the Sony 7506 Headphones ($90) and the Sennheiser FDFP ($100).

Field Mixers

Field audio mixers are portable multiple input devices for monitoring and adjusting audio levels prior to the signals entering the camera. While XLR adapter boxes also allows record level adjustments, audio mixers provide additional functions such as allowing the production sound mixer to:

- Visually monitor record levels using graphic *VU meters*;
- Pan the balance between left and right channels of stereo tracks;
- Modify sounds by selectively adjusting or *equalizing* (EQ) the various high, low, and mid-range frequencies that comprise sounds;
- Filter out selected frequencies;
- Provide phantom power required by some professional mics.

Field mixers offer the greatest level of audio control for location sound recording. In single mic situations, they allow the production sound mixer to do his/her job without having to be near the camera. In multiple microphone set-ups, a mixer is crucial for combining the various levels and sound characteristics of different mikes.

As with most audio equipment, you have to pay the price to achieve professional results, or run the risk of having inferior components and designs ruin your otherwise pristine audio. Among the best buys are the Shure M267 ($425) and the Rolls MX442 ($800). You'll have to spend several hundred more to purchase the Shure FP33 ($1,230), one of the leading field mixers.

However, the Shure FP33 can usually be rented for less than $40 per day. With most mixers, you will also still require an XLR to mini adapter cable to feed the output from the mixer to the camera.

Lighting, Accessories and Gaffer Tools

Because of the ability of most video cameras to produce acceptable images under low light conditions, many people consider lighting to be a secondary consideration. This may work in certain situations where you desire the effect of natural lighting.

For example, the DV film, *The Celebration*, was recorded almost entirely with *available light*, with the exception of a small light mounted on top of the camera.

Similarly, for a documentary you may have neither the desire nor time for elaborate lighting. Documentaries often require quick set-up time with as little equipment as possible.

But for most feature films, lighting is the key to making your video look more like film. This is especially true if you plan to use a video treatment process or plan on transferring your video to film. Good, artistic lighting design adds production value and becomes another means to further personalize your film.

Lighting design is accomplished by the manipulation of light intensities, colors and shadows. Even with low budgets this can be accomplished by creatively using an assortment of professional lighting instruments, low-cost light fixtures, accessories, and various gaffer tools.

Lighting Instruments

Professional lights come in a range of shapes, sizes, and intensities. There are also common household and work lights that can be used to light your project as well. By understanding the basic characteristics and limitations of these lights, you will be able to use them to create the type of atmosphere you desire for your film.

Professional Lights

Professional lights are available for field recording and studio production. Field lights are lightweight portable units with collapsible stands and additional options to expand their functionality.

Field lights also include handheld lights, frequently known as *sunguns*, as well as a variety of small lights that mount on top of a camera, which can range from generic low power 10w lights to the popular and extremely versatile Frezzolini line.

Studio lights are much heavier, larger, and many times, more powerful than field lights. They are most often designed to hang from poles suspended from a *light grid* of beams high in the ceiling of film and television studios.

On-set, professional lights are referred to by an assortment colorful names like mickey, tweenie, baby, baby-baby, inky and many others. These names are derived from their physical size, wattage and light characteristics. Conversely, most field lights are referred to by their make and model.

Despite the extremely diverse variety of professional lights, they can all be categorized into three types: *floodlights, fixed-focus lights* and *focusing spotlights*. Within each of these categories are variations that have slightly different features and attributes.

Floodlights

Floodlights offer broad, diffuse light that can be can be used to illuminate wide areas. While the light is not very controllable, it does not create hard edges and can be used very effectively to reduce shadows.

Softlights are a particular type of large floodlight designed specifically for the purpose of providing shadowless light. Softlights often have large, half-moon shaped light heads or rectangular panels with white or reflective material on the inside. Larger units commonly use more than one long, tube-shaped bulb. Lightweight aluminum framed softlights can provide a tremendous amount of light in a very portable unit.

Fixed focus and focusing spotlights can be made into softlights by directing the light towards accessories such as the reflective *umbrellas* commonly used in still photography, and the diffusion boxes manufactured by Chimera.

Broadlights provide more intense light and less diffused light than softlights. They are also more controllable than softlights. Adjustable flaps or *barndoors* can help widen or narrow the light spread. Some broadlights are very boxed shaped while the popular *scoop lights* are a very elliptical shaped flood unit.

There are many different softlight and broadlight instruments to select from when renting professional lights. Many times you can simply request a softlight and broadlight by the desired wattage as opposed to a specific model or manufacture.

If you are purchasing a couple of portable floodlights, the Lowel Tota-Lights™ ($135) are a favorite among news and documentary crews. These small rectangular units can easily be held in your hand but, depending on the bulb used, provide up to 750 Watts (w) of lighting. They are hinged on a long side, and snap open to reveal the bulb (i.e. a FLZ-500 watt, $18) and reflective material inside. This design allows you to control the spread of light by adjusting the angle of the opening.

Tota-Lights can be used with accessories such as a lightweight stand like the nine-foot Bogen 3333 ($50) and a *gel frame* (Lowel model TI-20, $30) which allows you to color the light using colored, flame retardant gels.

Tota-Lights are usually available for rent in kits that include three lights, stands, and gel frames for around $50 per day.

Other portable flood units include the Arri Mini-Flood which can use bulbs up to 1000w ($290) and the 600w Colortran Minibroad ($350)

Fixed-Focus Lights

Fixed focus lights use glass lens elements in front of the bulb to direct light into a very precise and controllable beam. The angle of spread of the beam is fixed and is a factor to consider when selecting a light unit. Many units offer very wide coverage but allow for the use of barndoors to control it.

Among the most commonly used professional fixed focused lights is the HMI PAR light, a 3,200° K lamp that is frequently used to accent or simulate sunlight.

Among portable lights, the Lowel Omni-Light ($150) features the advantages of a fixed focus light in a small square-shaped light. When operated by battery it can put out up to 250w. While operating on AC power it can produce up to 650w of light. Lowel also offers the larger DP Light ($165) which goes up to 1000w and is more directional than the Omni-Light.

Tota-Lights, Omni-Lights, and DP Lights are available in various combinations for purchase as kits. For example, a DP Kit includes two Tota-Lights, one Omni, three stands, gel frames, and one umbrella for around $800. The lights can also be rented as part of a three light kit.

Focusing Spotlights

Focusing spotlights perform similarly to fixed spots, except they allow the angle of the light beam to be varied. The most common type of focusing spotlight is called a Fresnel, named after the adjustable Fresnel lens system it uses.

Using knobs on the sides of the unit, the angle of the light beam can be changed from a very focused spotlight to a much broader floodlight. This flexibility is what makes Fresnel lights some of the most important lighting instruments on set.

Many companies produce Fresnel lights but camera and lighting manufacture, Arri Systems, is one of the top producers. They provide a wide range of Fresnel lights for studio and field production. Popular portable units include the Arri 300w Fresnel ($330), the Arri 650w Fresnel ($330), and the Arrilite 1000w ($300). Mole-Richardson is another leading company, especially for studio lighting instruments.

Professional lights can be very expensive to purchase, and in most instances you will be renting a large lighting package for the duration of your shoot. However, you might consider purchasing a small light kit and supplementing it with low-cost consumer lights.

Low Budget Lighting Fixtures

There are inexpensive home and work lights that creative filmmakers have found success using in their productions. Keep in mind that in most cases, these lights do not provide the level of control offered by professional lights. On the other hand, they are very cheap and readily available.

The most popular of these are: halogen household lamps, halogen work lamps, Chinese lanterns, photofloods, and practical lights.

Halogen Household Lamps

These high wattage lights can usually be purchased for less than $30 from office supply and department stores. Most often they are free standing lamps with adjustable dimmers. They work best as background lights used to bring up the overall light level in a room. They have a tendency to be "warm" adding a reddish or orange tint, especially as the bulbs get older.

Halogen Work Lamps

These lights are comparable to the household lamps except that they are available in higher wattage. They also cost less than $30 and come attached to tall stands or with hooks to allow them to be hung. They have protective grills in front of them that can cause the light to appear uneven. But these grills can also be used to attach flame retardant gels to add color.

Since the spread of the light can not be easily controlled, these lights work best as fill lights when bounced off of a reflective material such as a white wall or white foamcore. However, be careful because they get very hot and can ignite flammable materials.

There are also rechargeable, battery operated handheld halogen work lights, often labeled emergency lights, that can effectively be used as a low-cost sungun or backlight. They can be purchased at home supply stores for about $50. Also note that as with the household halogen lamps, these lights are warmer than professional halogen lights.

Chinese Lanterns

Chinese lanterns are inexpensive globular or tube shaped lighting instruments made from wire or wooden frames covered with flame resistant paper or cloth. They use regular household bulbs and provide an even, soft light. Most often they are hung from the ceiling.

Chinese lanterns have long been a favorite with film cinematographers because they are attractive and can be included in a scene without drawing attention to themselves. Renowned director of photography, Phillipe Rousselot (*Interview with a Vampire, Mary Reilly*) is noted for his use of Chinese lanterns. You can find Chinese lanterns in a variety of sizes in furniture stores such as Ikea.

Photofloods

Photofloods are inexpensive, dome-shaped metal light fixtures that accept regular light bulbs and low-cost photoflood bulbs. The reflective inside of the dome helps to focus the light allowing it to be somewhat directable. This allows you to use the light as a key light, although the low wattage of the bulbs requires placement fairly close to the subject.

The lights can be purchased with cheap light stands. Or you can purchase them with spring clips that allow you to clip them on to window sills, doors, low hanging beams, etc.

In his excellent book, *Rebel Without a Crew*, director Robert Rodriguez shares details about lighting his entire film, *El Mariachi*, using only photofloods.

Photofloods can be purchased at camera shops and some home building supply stores.

Practicals

Practicals are light bulbs that can be used in a variety of regular light fixtures. However, the benefit over regular bulbs is that they are available in very high wattages and in various color temperatures.

With practicals, you can replace the bulbs of lights that are a part of the scene, such as lamps and chandeliers, and increase the amount of light they produce and at the same time, create consistency in the color temperature between different lights.

Though it is simple to swap practicals for regular bulbs, their use is best left to gaffers and DPs who are familiar with their usage.

As with most professional bulbs, practicals can be very fragile and are sensitive to the natural oils on our hands. Handling them with bare hands reduces their longevity.

Additionally, since the bulbs are available at very high wattages, it is easy to surpass the maximum load supported by a light fixture, the electrical wiring, and/or a circuit breaker resulting in blown circuits, shorts, or in the worse case, fires.

Practical bulbs are very expensive when purchased individually since most vendors usually sell them by the dozen. But you can buy them in smaller lots from a local grip and electric rental house.

Lighting Accessories

Lighting instruments are aided by accessories that modify the color, intensity, and/or the pattern of the light. In everyday life, the world we see is full of subtleties. These tools help to introduce them into your lighting designs. The most important light accessories are:

- Light Stands—These are important for allowing your lights to be positioned at the proper height. Lights must be frequently aimed at a subject from high above.
- Dimmers—The intensity of lights plugged into these small boxes can be incrementally lowered.
- Gels—Rosco is the leading manufacture of gels. They offer gels in a multitude of colors. A sampler pack is available for $38.
- Diffusion Paper/Frost Paper—Used in front of a light to soften the beam.
- Scrims—Lowers the intensity of a light without diffusing it. Half scrims affect half of the beam.
- Cookies—A paper or metal obstruction cut with a pattern. When placed in front of the light, it breaks up a solid beam to project the pattern and/or add shadows.

Gaffer Tools

In addition to a variety of lighting instruments and accessories, most gaffers and grips rely on other tools to further go about molding complex lighting designs. Among the most commonly used gaffers tools are:

- Gaffers tape—A strong gray or black cloth tape that has the unique property of being very adhesive while doing minimum damage to the surface it is applied to when pulled off. Used for everything from hanging set pieces to binding objects. $15 per roll.
- Spring clamps and wooden clothes pins—Used to hold gels in place and myriad other as needed purposes.
- C-Stands and arms—Foldable three-legged stand that can be used as a light stand. When arms are added, can also support flags, reflectors, a boom mic or anything else that needs to be suspended.

- Flags–Variable sized black cloth in wire frames. Used to block excess light.
- Reflectors–Large gold, white, or silver cards or collapsible circular units used to bounce light towards a subject. Can be created using any reflective material, including white sheets or aluminum foil.
- Foam Core–Large panels of foam, typically, white on one side and black on the other. The white side can be used for a reflective bounce card and the black side as a flag. Other uses almost always arise.
- Black wrap–A very heavy, black aluminum foil. Can be attached to lights to alter the beam. Very useful when using non-professional lights. $35 a roll.
- Organza fabric–A black gauze material that can be used to reduce excess background light coming through windows.

Tape Stock

Unlike a lot of other aspects of production, your selection of DV tape stocks is pretty straightforward. While mini-DV tapes are available from Sony, Panasonic, and JVC, they vary slightly in quality and significantly in price, with the Sony tapes almost always more expensive. One factor that distinguishes Sony tapes from others is that Sony offers a version of its DV tapes with a memory chip built-in. When used with Sony DV cameras, this chip is able to record information about the location of each scene and a still photo from that scene. This data can later be retrieved and used when editing. However, to many people this feature is not worth the extra $10.

DV and DVCAM cassettes are essentially the same products. They both use a *metal evaporated tape* (ME) formulation while the slightly larger, metal cased DVCPRO tapes use a *metal particle tape* (MP) formulation. The quality difference between ME tapes and MP tapes was significant when Hi-8 was a popular format. At that time, MP tapes were less prone to *drop outs*, losses of video information, caused by minute tape imperfections. Fortunately, with digital video, this is not an issue.

The following is a sample listing of your DV, DVCAM, and DVCPRO tape stock options. I have chosen not to include thirty-minute tapes because sixty-minute tapes are much more economical. You can also save by ordering by the box, which usually means five tapes. Be sure to order the correct tape format for your camera.

Sample DV, DVCAM, and DVCPRO Tape Stocks

- Sony DVM60PR
  60 min. mini-DV tape. No memory chip. For camcorders.
- Sony DVM60EX
  60 min. mini-DV tape. Includes chip. For camcorders.
- Panasonic AY DVM-60
  60 min. mini-DV tape.
- Sony DV-120MEM
  120 min. standard DV tape. Not for camcorders.
- Sony DV-180MEM
  180 min. standard DV tape. Not for camcorders.
- Sony PDVM-40ME
  40 min. mini-DVCAM for DVCAM camcorders.
- Sony PDV-64ME
  64 min. standard DVCAM. Not for camcorders.
- Sony PDV-94ME
  94 min. standard DVCAM. Not for camcorders.
- Sony PDV-184ME
  184 min. standard DVCAM. Not for camcorders.
- Panasonic AJ-P33M
  33 min. small DVCPRO. For camcorders.
- Panasonic AJ-P63M
  63 min. small DVCPRO. For camcorders.
- Panasonic AJ-P64L
  64 min. standard DVCPRO. Not for camcorders.
- Panasonic AJ-P94L
  94 min. standard DVCPRO. Not for camcorders.
- Panasonic AJ-P123L
  123 min. standard DVCPRO. Not for camcorders.

Preparing Your Tapes

Prior to beginning principal photography, you should prepare your tapes so that they are ready for use on set. To prepare your tapes you should:

- Clearly number and label tapes and tape cases.
- Fast forward new tapes all the way to the end and then rewind back to the beginning. This simple step helps reduce drop outs by repacking the tape to remove any slack that may have developed, allowing the tape to roll evenly.

- Record at least one minute of color bars. While the color bars generated by most DV cameras do not correspond with true specs of SMPTE color bars, they are still useful for setting up monitors when editing.
- Record black on the entire tape. This lays down a continuous time code track on the tape guaranteeing unbroken time code when recording your shots. Continuous time code is important for certain editing functions. Some cameras have a feature that allows you to record a minute of color bars then automatically begin recording black. Other cameras will require you to put the lens cap on then begin recording black at the end of the color bars.

SAMPLE DV PRODUCTION PACKAGES

	Basic	Mid-Range	High-End
CAMERA AND ACCESSORIES			
Canon XL1			$3900
Sony VX1000		$3300	
Sony TR9	$1400		
Bogen 3140 Tripod	290	290	290
Bogen Quick Release Plate			32
Steadicam DV			1200
Bescor Battery Pack	125	125	175
Tiffen Filter Set(s)		125	200
Camera Case	60	200	275
TOTAL	**$1,875**	**$4,040**	**$6,072**
AUDIO PACKAGE			
Audio-Technica 835b & Windscreen	$290	$290	
Senheiser 416 Mic & Windscreen			$1230
Telex ENG1 Wireless Lav Mic		270	270
mini to XLR Adapter	12	12	12
Shure M267 Audio Mixer		425	
Shure FP33 4 Channel Mixer			1300
Sony 7506 Headphones	90	90	90
Gitzo 557 Boom Pole	110	110	110
Audio Technica Shockmount	60	60	60
10' XLR Cable	30	30	30
TOTAL	**$592**	**$1,287**	**$3,102**
LIGHT KIT			
Lowel DP3 Light Kit	$0	$760	$760
Add. Tota Light+Stand+Access.			
Add. Omni Light+Stand+Access.			
Arri Mini-Flood+Stand+Access.			400
Arrilite 1000+Stand+Access.			400
Rosco Gels and Misc. Gaffer Needs		120	200
TOTAL	**-**	**$880**	**$1,760**
PRODUCTION EQUIPMENT TOTAL			
Camera, Support, Accessories	$1875	$4040	$6072
Audio Package + Accessories	592	1287	3102
Light Package	0	880	1760
TOTAL	**$2,467**	**$6,207**	**$10,934**

7
■ ■ ■ ■ ■ ■ DV Film Production

It's the early morning, a little bit before dawn. You've just spent most of the night anxiously tossing and turning, and yet you are wide awake and extraordinarily alert. After weeks . . . months . . . years of wistful day dreaming, hustling, disappointments, and triumphs, you are about to step on the set of your first feature film.

If you have prepared yourself and planned to the best of your ability and resources, get ready for a wild, adrenaline-driven ride with plenty of unexpected bumps and curves. And hopefully, by the end of principal photography, you can step from the driver's seat confident that you, your cast, and crew accomplished everything you set out to accomplish and more.

On the other hand, if you prematurely rushed into production head first, well . . . good luck to you . . . good luck to you all. Ask your righteous great aunt to say some strong prayers for you.

Pray that your cast stays the whole shoot. Hope that the crew shows up. And don't be surprised if locations aren't available. Or worse, you are beset by the painful tragedy that befalls many indie filmmakers . . . you run out of money half-way through the shoot. Of course, optimistically thinking, maybe the quality of your work won't be affected by all of this stress.

But the reality is that, even without trying to play catch up on all of the issues that should have been handled in pre-production, a successful shoot requires your complete attention on a whole range of time and resource management, personnel, technical, and artistic issues.

Managing Time and Resources

A high-priced lawyer I approached about doing legal work on a low-budget film once game me an analogy that made perfect sense to me. He said that the minutes of his work day are like the premium goods that make up a popular bakery's inventory.

And considering the demand given the limited supply, every minute he gave away instead of selling depleted his inventory just as if the baker was giving away his goods. This analogy applies perfectly to the way you manage your time and resources on your shoot.

Time Waits for No Filmmaker

When you set your shooting schedule, you are essentially determining a specific number of hours that are available for you to complete principal photography and all of the organizational details not covered during pre-production. This amount of time is finite. It only increases or decreases when you allow it to change.

But there are repercussions for such schedule changes. People are planning their time around your time. The changes you make will affect them.

Let's say you thought you could get everything done in ten days of shooting, but now on the eighth day you have completed only 50 percent! Is it a simple solution to just ask everyone to stay on and work for eight more days? Not likely.

Crew and cast costs go up (even with salaries deferred, you still have catering and craft services costs), equipment costs go up, contracts must be redrawn, and quite frequently, the morale of everyone involved goes down, especially if the past eight days have seemed like a month of chaotic, unorganized hell.

It's one thing to ask people for more time after many productive days where it becomes obvious you are behind schedule simply because of poor scheduling or uncontrollable circumstances. But, it's another thing to ask people to continue to invest time and energy when it is obvious that what they have already invested has been squandered by poor management.

Therefore, your number one priority should be to make maximum usage of your time inventory. And, this attitude must trickle down to everyone else in the crew.

Communicate with Each Other

As a producer, you want to maintain control of all facets of the production. As a director, you want to have an atmosphere that is conducive to the acting performance and the visual imagery you will use to tell your story.

To accomplish this, you and your key people—the production manager, AD, DP, gaffer, production sound mixer, production designer and location manager—must all be synchronized about the current production needs, while at the same time, preparing for forthcoming time and resource requirements.

At any given time during principal photography, the production team needs to know:

- How much cash is left?
- How much more cash do we need?
- What other resources are left?
- What other resources do we need? When do we need them by? Where are they coming from?
- How many pages of the script have we completed? How long did it take us?
- How many more pages do we have to complete? How long do we project it will take us to complete, based on our current situation?
- Why are you putting yourself through all of this in the first place?

Once these issues are discussed, action plans should be created that must be communicated and delegated to the rest of the cast and crew. And, most importantly, changes in plans must be quickly and clearly communicated to everyone as well.

This process of Assessing, Planning, Communicating, and Acting Out will occur over, and over, and over again throughout a single production day.

The objective is to have everyone synchronized and operating as a smooth running, harmonious, motivated and highly effective production machine for the duration of your shoot.

Ok, fine, I'm being idealistic; just getting it to be an effective production machine is an accomplishment, at any budget level.

More Paperwork You Can't Ignore

There are several standard production forms that are important tools to help keep the machine running. These forms keep track of the answers to the questions raised above. Some productions treat this paperwork as a mandatory task, rather than realizing that it provides dynamic levels of communication.

Since most scenes will be shot out of order and the shooting schedule frequently changes, it can be very difficult to gauge exactly where you currently stand in the production. Fortunately, these forms can help everyone understand the production's progress:

- Shooting schedules convey the schedule for the entire shoot.
- Call sheets relate the schedule, crew, talent, locations, and resource requirements for individual days.
- Production reports feature information on the prior day's shoot and the total progress to date, relative to the entire project.
- Daily script notes are taken by the script supervisor. They feature information on actor performances as well as comments on camera and sound performance. Very helpful during editing.
- Camera reports feature notes on camera settings and performance.
- Sound reports include notes on audio takes. Especially important when recording a lot of sound effects on location.

Copies of these forms can be ordered from Enterprise Stationery in Los Angeles. You can also find some of the forms online at www.filmmaker.com.

The Director as a Leader

The director establishes the tone and pace of the shoot. And if he/she doesn't, it will be established by someone else—the producer, the ambitious lead actor, the DP, a frustrated gaffer . . . someone will step up. This fact creates a lot of insecurity in some directors.

Most of us have heard stories of the hypersensitive, quick-tempered director ready to fire every person he/she deemed incompetent. As a production assistant on films and TV projects, I could not relate to this mentality.

However, by the time I started producing, I could completely understand the importance of working with talented people who can help you parlay your limited time and resources. Conversely, I could relate to the challenge of remaining patient with people who waste time and resources.

Then when I began directing, suddenly I could completely empathize with the shouting, raving director character. Although my temperament under stress is not like that, at one moment on my first feature set I looked up and realized that the fifty plus non-paid cast and crew people working so diligently, were all there to help me make my vision come to life.

When the assistant director and the director of photography walked up and asked, "What's next?" and all fifty plus people turned around and looked at me questioningly, guess what . . . ?

I was incredibly afraid!

I was unsure that I could communicate the images in my head to my DP. I was afraid I had not gotten my actors where I wanted them to be with their performances. I wasn't sure I had shot enough footage to properly cover the last scene.

And from the producing side, I was scared that I hadn't scheduled enough time for the shoot. And that money was running out faster than I planned. I was even stressed that I had not ordered enough food for everyone that day. But, by far the greatest fear was . . .

I was afraid they could see that I was afraid!

Let me tell you, if you are not prepared, there is no way to lie at a moment like that. This reality is what causes so many directors to lose it.

The pressure . . . the quick decisions . . . the compromises . . . the clock steadily ticking . . . the dollars diminishing and all the while trying to have some artistic integrity.

Fortunately I drew upon something I learned from years of martial arts classes—keep your cool and meet fear head-on. So, instead of racking my brain and spewing out a quick response to prove my preparation and confidence, at that instance I simply said, "Give me a minute to think."

I took a deep breath, and cleared my mind to focus on the current priority, unburdened by the grandiosity of the production as a whole.

That is part of the magical process of directing. When you look through the camera's eyepiece, suddenly all that matters is what you see and hear in the frame, regardless of everything it took to make it happen.

By keeping my cool, I was able to recall my preparation and combine it with a reality of the current moment to confidently answer the question, "What's next?" providing the leadership that is a part of the director's responsibility.

Every director is going to have moments of uncertainty. The question becomes whether you are going to allow those moments to disrupt your entire momentum.

Directing Actors

The relationship between the director and his actors is commonly compared to a parent and child relationship. For some, this may seem a bit condescending, but once you experience working with actors under pressure to perform on cue, it is apparent that the similarities between directing and parenthood are . . .

Trust and Patience.

Without these, you and your actors will consistently be at odds with each other as you both fail to meet each others expectations. And when faced with the stress of principal photography, this problem can quickly turn ugly and dysfunctional.

It is the relationship you establish with your actors during rehearsals that will help you make it through the inevitable challenging moments on set where you or an actor may be out of sync, but the circumstances require you to get the shot and keep moving.

During rehearsals you should become very familiar with your actors, personally and professionally. By understanding an actor's life experiences and background, you are provided with points of reference as you coach them. And by becoming familiar with their acting style, you will also be better prepared to address their individual needs.

The trust that must be developed between actors and the director is multifaceted. First, and most basic, an actor must trust a director's judgment during rehearsals, on set, and while editing.

When actors are truly participants in a scene, it is extremely difficult for them to objectively assess their performances. Given this reality, many have fairly legitimate fears built upon the thought of giving terrible performances and not being alerted of this until viewing the final scenes, possibly projected on a huge screen in front of a room full of people.

But, if actors trust the director, they can have the confidence that the director will be the one to prevent this from happening. During rehearsal the director will work with the actors to develop shared interpretations of characters. While shooting scenes, the actors must trust that the director will catch performances that fail to be true to these interpretations, and have the ability to provide the feedback necessary to improve the performances. And, the actors must confidently know that in post-production the director will select the best takes.

Conversely, the director must trust an actor's ability to deliver the expected performance regardless of personal problems or the high pressure of principal photography. And the director must also trust the actor enough to be willing to allow his/her own perception of the character to grow based upon input from the actor as the actor becomes increasingly familiar with the character.

It is an actor's need for feedback and confirmation that eventually taxes the patience of many directors, especially if extensive time has been spent on rehearsals. A common attitude is that performances are worked out in rehearsals so that the director can spend time composing and blocking shots while on location. However, the reality is that a director never stops having to provide actors feedback, even if it is a simple nod of approval.

A failure to have the patience necessary to address an actor's needs can quickly result in a breakdown in communications that jeopardizes the dynamics of the entire cast and the whole shoot. It is from this terrible reality, that the whole concept of "star treatment" is derived. And while most low budget shoots have neither the time nor money to cater to the whims of an up and coming superstar, that does not reduce the director's basic obligation to his/her actors.

In addition to the issues of trust, patience, and communication, here are a few other items to consider as you develop your own directing style and relationship with your actors:

- Learn when to give directions and when not to. Some actors lose their natural instincts when given too much direction to think about.
- Remember to remind actors of the scene's relationship to the entire story. With the fast-paced, out of sequence nature of principal photography, it is easy for everyone to be solely focused on the scene at hand. The director must remind talent how the current scene relates to previous and forthcoming scenes in the film.

- Allow for spontaneity. Rehearsing scenes in a home or rehearsal hall is much different than being on location with set pieces, props, wardrobe in place and everyone ready to perform. This can create impromptu moments you never imagined.
- Maintain control. Even when discussing the importance of collaborating with and being receptive to input from the cast, the director must also have a strong backbone and the ability to maintain control on set.

The Producer's Role

While the director is the leader, his/her cold-hearted henchman is the producer. The person who determines things based upon minutes and dollars as opposed to the cinematic possibilities.

It almost seems cliché how often a producer must become a firm voice of logical reason among a mob inspired towards overly ambitious artistic heights.

The Person Who Says No

From having walked on both sides of producing and directing, I can appreciate how important it is to have someone you trust shake you by the shoulders and say, "NO!" then offer a completely rational explanation. Regardless of the final compromise agreed upon, the opposing view often makes you really evaluate situations.

If you are directing and producing your feature, try to find a producing partner, line producer, or production manager with whom you can develop this type of relationship. Look for someone to help you keep yourself in check.

But even while being the spoilsport, the producer must also be . . .

The Caretaker

Principal photography is a high stress environment. When you combine that with the challenges of low budgets and less experienced cast and crew people, you can have an extremely high stress situation. I believe producers working under these circumstances have additional responsibilities to their unpaid or underpaid cast and crew.

It is very easy to get caught up in myriad details you are confronted with during production and become desensitized to the needs of your cast and crew. So, let me remind you again of one thing that will always keep them appreciating you, even if they think you're just the bad guy saying "no" all the time. Remember . . .

Feed People Good Food Frequently!

In addition to taking care of people's appetites, here are a few other suggestions that will help you handle the delicate role of low budget film producer.

- Be ready when someone has a breakdown. Inevitably someone will crack. When they do, use whatever restraint required to patiently deal with them by expeditiously working through the situation or removing them from their position.
- Reassign or fire people discreetly. If you must reassign or fire a person, then do it in a manner that allows them to maintain their dignity. It affects your crew to see you disrespect someone who was just working beside them or you.
- Don't lie just for the sake of giving an answer. If you don't know, let it be known and seek out an answer. On the other hand . . .
- At times you'll have to stretch the truth or sugar coat situations. What more can I say? That's the truth.
- Don't worry about looking like the bad guy, as long as your intentions are good.

Shooting Digital Video

Even the least expensive DV camera can create impressive images. But, it is not enough to just pick-up the camera, run around with it, and hope for the best. This is especially true for narrative feature films. Once you have a good script and well-prepared actors, your next goal should be to . . .

Create A Visual Style!

Even if you are doing a documentary or a feature that will be very naturalistic with minimum artificial lights, you can still create images that uniquely accent your story. A visual style is created by:

- Knowing Your Camera
- Using Lights, Gels, and Filters
- Manipulating Depth of Field
- Camera Angles, Shot Composition and Coverage
- Art Direction
- Continuity
- Camera Movement

Proficiency in these areas increases the production value of your film.

Know Your Camera

Each camera model has its own peculiarities under various shooting situations. You or your DP should allow ample time to become familiar with the camera you intend on using.

This familiarity should include a complete understanding of the operation and effect of all of the manual controls. You don't want to have to spend time pulling out manuals on set.

But, it's not just about learning what is in the manuals. In fact, some of the most important information you will need to know is often not included in the manuals, such as any particular nuances that frequently occur with the camera, and how to correct or work around them.

For example, the VX1000 is often criticized for high levels of video noise that result in "muddy" or "grainy" images when shooting in certain low light situations. Experienced VX1000 users know that this is the result of the camera's automatic mode electronically boosting gain in order to make the CCDs more sensitive to light.

This boost can go all the way up to +18dB, resulting in more higher sensitivity to low light, but at the expense of adding much more noise to the picture. In most cases, a gain above +9dB produces unacceptable noise.

However, if you have worked with the VX1000 for some time, you will learn that in manual mode, this automatic gain boost does not occur. And furthermore, you can use a VX1000 option called Custom Presets to adjust the overall preset gain value. By adjusting this value and manually adjusting the shutter speed as necessary, you can effectively attain great images with the VX1000, even in low light.

Most cameras have little tricks like this that you or your DP can learn to improve the camera's functionality. Again, this type of information is another benefit of networking with people, either in person or online.

Art Direction

Art direction is another issue commonly overlooked by first-time filmmakers. Far too many low budget films feature people standing in front of plain white walls.

For many stylized sets, the art direction, as established by the production designer, and the lighting design should complement each other. The tone created by the colors of set decorations and wardrobe can be accented by the lights.

A good production designer knows how to use simple things to enhance a set. A small piece of fabric hung or taped to that white wall can add much more character to an otherwise plain, visually boring close-up.

More importantly, in most cases, art direction is also linked to an interpretation of character or plot elements in the story. As the director, it is your job to work with the production designer to make certain that the sets accurately reflect the subtle or explicit message you are trying to convey about a character or plot.

Use Lights, Gels and Filters

The artistic use of lights, gels, and filters is one of the key ways of crafting a visual style for your film. Used minimally, lights increase a set's illumination to create usable images. But at its best, lighting allows you to establish the time and moods for a scene.

Basic lighting techniques are built around the concept of *three point lighting* where a *key light* is used to illuminate a subject from a high angle near the camera; a slightly lower *fill light* on the opposite side is used to reduce shadows caused by the key light; and a *back light* is used to light the background levels and help separate the subject from the background.

The *lighting ratio* is the relationship between the intensity of the amount of light falling on a subject when the key light and fill light are turned on, compared to the light level when only the fill light is turned on.

Readings of these light levels are taken by using an *incident light meter* held in front of the subject. A typical light ratio is 2:1, meaning twice as much light reaches the subject using the key and fill light compared to the fill alone.

The *contrast range* is the difference between the light level of the darkest item on set that the camera must see and the light level of the brightest item on set for which the camera must discern details. This information is determined by using a *reflected spotlight meter* that samples and measures light reflected from the area you point it towards.

Lighting ratio and contrast range are important to understand because video and film have different light tolerances and ranges. Film accepts a much higher contrast range than video, which is one reason why television programs typically light sets much more evenly.

Additionally, overexposed video will be useless when transferred to film. However, because of film's wider range, useful images can often be created from overexposed film negative.

Although you cannot completely light your DV exactly as you would for film, you will want to emulate the lighting styles used in film. Variations of three point lighting, lighting ratios, and contrast range allow you to create many different looks. The degree to which you use them depends on the lighting style you choose to use: naturalistic, neutral, realistic, or abstract.

Naturalistic lighting is essentially the use of whatever lights are available on location. You adjust your shots and camera settings to compensate as best you can. Filters can be used to reduce excess light or modify color temperatures, but no additional lighting apparatus are used. This style is frequently used with documentaries.

Neutral lighting is where a set is evenly illuminated with a low contrast range. This style is frequently used for news programs, talk shows, and sitcoms.

Realistic lighting is when lighting of colors and the contrast range are of sufficient levels to provide a good image for the camera, while accurately representing the way the set and people look in "real life." The colors and contrast range can be highly stylized and still appear realistic. Colored gels and filters can be used to cheat the look of scenes by slightly accenting or eliminating colors. Frequently used for feature films, TV dramas, and commercials.

Abstract lighting does not stay within the conventions of colors and contrast ranges found in everyday life. The lighting design can reflect personal taste and expression. Gels and filters can be used to radically alter the images and colors while other grip devices can be used to create unusual patterns and designs. Often used for music videos, horror films, and sci-fi films.

Low key lighting is an example of a dark, high contrast abstract lighting style first popularized by the Orson Welles classic, *Citizen Kane,* and later applied to everything from *The Twilight Zone* to *Blade Runner* to most recently, *The X-Files.*

As mentioned in the VX1000 example above, when using low key lighting with DV be certain to pay attention to the gain settings. Also, it helps to keep important details out of the dark areas so that you can expose those areas for the most contrast. This works very well if you plan on your final product being black and white.

However, to produce the best color images that will endure the DV to film transfer, most facilities recommend you maintain a lighting ratio of around 3:1.

Manipulating Depth of Field

By varying the lens *focal length* (the measurement, in millimeters, from the optical center of a camera's lens to the surface of the film or CCD imaging chip inside the camera) and aperture settings (the f-stops), you are able to manipulate the depth of field. A short focal length and narrow aperture will result in a wide depth of field, while a long focal length and wide aperture opening will cause a shallow depth of field. These variations can be used creatively.

Wide depths of field allow background objects to be in focus along with the foreground objects. This can work to your advantage by allowing the actors more range to move about during a shot, which is especially beneficial given the previously noted focusing difficulties of most consumer DV cameras.

Wide depths of field also draws attention to details in the background setting. In film production this is often desirable, allowing you to fully capitalize off the look of the environment you are shooting in.

However, DV tends to lose a lot of this detail when transferred to film. For close-up and medium shots, this may not be too disconcerting, but for wide shots the undesirable results can be very noticeable when projected on the big screen. If you intend on staying on video, it is not much of a problem. If not, you need to plan your shots carefully. The degree to which these wide shots become an issue is based upon your familiarity with your camera's abilities, and the quality of the video-to-film transfer that you will be using.

Another shortcoming of a wide depth of field is that it requires more light than normal circumstances since you are using a smaller aperture setting.

Because of these disadvantages, many DV filmmakers only use wide depths of field when absolutely necessary, choosing instead to use shallow depths of field that "blowout" background details and cause them to be out of focus.

A shallow depth of field is easily achieved by selecting a low f-stop to open the aperture wide, then using a neutral density filter to bring the light level down to the proper exposure.

By experimentation you and your DP can determine the depth of field that works best for your film based on the way you plan on covering the scenes.

Camera Angles, Shot Composition and Coverage

The placement of the camera relative to the action being recorded is the camera angle. While the manner in which the subject fills up the video frame is the shot composition.

Camera angles and shot composition are important tools for visually telling your story. The way you choose to use them is another part of your personal directing style and another reflection of your interpretation of the story.

B-movie king Roger Corman, who has produced and directed hundreds of films, including the original *Little Shop of Horrors*, has been quoted as saying that the effectiveness or ineffectiveness of a scene depends entirely upon selecting the proper camera angles from which to film the scene. The specific compositions of your shots allows you to control what is emphasized or de-emphasized in the picture frame. There is a basic set of shots that are commonly used:

Close-ups (CU) are where the lens is zoomed in tight on a specific area of the subject, such as the face. Useful for relating details. A variation is the extreme close-up (ECU), which is an even closer shot (i.e. the eyes).

Cut-away shots are close-up shots of images that are not visible in the preceding shot but are a part of the scene. Reaction shots of people are a specific type of cut-away. Cut-away shots can tremendously aid editing.

Medium shots provide a wider perspective of the subject relative to the setting with the emphasis still on the subject (i.e. a shot of an actor from head-to-toe.) Useful to show relationship between subject and setting.

Two shots and group shots are based on the shot above but composed in relationship to the total number of key people in frame.

Wide shots prominently highlight the setting with the subject being relatively small, if at all present, in the frame.

Over the shoulder shots (OTS) are subjects framed with a portion of another subject's body in the foreground. These are useful for establishing relationships between people as they talk to each other.

Point of view shots (POV) use the camera to represent an event as seen from the perspective of someone present in the scene.

The way you compose these shots is also very contingent upon the aspect ratio you are aiming for. A close-up framed for the square 1.33 ratio of television is going to look much different than a close-up framed for rectangular 1.85 ratio of 35mm film.

If you are uncertain about the final format of your project, you must be sure to frame your shots by taking into consideration both aspect ratios. Make certain that the shot is completely clear of boom mikes, lights, people or any other items that should not be seen if you have to use the entire frame.

From these basic shots you can derive many shots that can develop into a unique style based upon what you and your DP choose to highlight.

Typically you pick an angle as your *master shot* and record the whole scene from that position before beginning additional *coverage* of the scene from other angles. The various takes from these different angles will later be edited together to produce the complete scene.

Get as much coverage for your scenes as your schedule will allow!

The lack of adequate coverage of a scene is a common problem for inexperienced filmmakers. Unfortunately, the magnitude of the problem does not rear its head until you begin to edit your scenes, only to find that you are lacking shots of important action. Or, you may discover you cannot connect various takes because you do not have transitional shots to connect them. In the worst case, always shoot a lot of cut-away shots.

Coverage should also allow action to overlap between takes.

Pick-up shots are segments of a scene continued from a line of dialogue or action covered in another take. When using pick-up shots, it is important to allow the starting and ending action to overlap similar action from takes that will be edited together.

Let's say, for example, you just recorded a medium shot of an actor walking to a door. Rather than picking up a close-up shot of the actor already at the door, have the actor walk into the close-up shot then continue the action. And before stopping the actors, allow a few seconds of coverage of the ending action.

Overlapping action in this manner, combined with coverage from a variety of angles with a mixture of shots will provide you significant leverage when editing.

Continuity

Continuity is the consistency between shots covering the same action. This includes consistency in the appearance and actions of the actors, direction and movement of objects on screen, lighting, audio and the set elements. Without continuity, shots do not cut together well.

Functionally, continuity is important because discrepancies between shots appear to be mistakes, and most commonly, they are. The script supervisor frequently keeps track of continuity to help prevent problems that can arise later.

However, discontinuity can also be used as a stylistic device. The television show *Homicide: Life on the Street* makes use of the jarring *jump cuts* that are created when inconsistent shots are edited together.

Jump cuts can be used to create a pace of urgency on the screen. But this technique must be used sparingly as people can quickly grow weary of it.

Camera Movement

Subtle camera movement allows you to create feelings of openness by revealing more of the set than was initially perceived. Extreme camera movements draw attention to the camera and can be used to unnerve the viewer as they find it difficult to fix their attention on any particular part of the scene.

You must be very careful with rapid camera movement if you are producing your project using NTSC video, and if you plan on transferring the video to film. As mentioned previously, the transfer process discards some of your video fields which results in rapid movements appearing very jerky on the screen. PAL video transferred to film does not suffer from this problem.

The basic camera movements include:

- Panning the camera. Rotating the camera on a horizontal plane (i.e. turning left to right and vice versa).
- Tilting the camera. Rotating up and down on a vertical plane.
- Dollying the camera. The camera is mounted on a wheeled device that allows it to physically move across a horizontal plane.
- Booming or craning the camera up in the air or down using a jib arm or crane. These shots add production value to your film.

Hand-held shooting can be used to create extreme camera movements, or, in the hands of a skilled operator, provide shots comparable to a tripod.

Hand-held camera work is popular for the feeling it elicits by making the viewer feel like a part of the scene. Another benefit is that it is quicker to set-up hand-held shots than shots where the camera is mounted on a support system such as a tripod or dolly.

For this reason hand-held shooting has become extremely popular in low budget films. Unfortunately, because of its excessive usage, what was once considered a style has nearly become a low budget film cliché.

Stabilization devices can be utilized to move the camera about smoothly while creating well-choreographed scenes such as those featured in *Goodfellas* and *The Player*.

As with every other element of your film, camera movement is a good tool to use when it is properly motivated by the story. In many cases, especially considering the video-to-film motion problem stated above, a well composed shot with the camera locked down on a tripod is more effective than a few slick moves.

Other DV Shooting Tips

A few more general suggestions that apply especially if you plan on transferring your video to film.

- Rely on a field monitor to check focus.
- Lenses perform their best optically at an exposure f-stop of around f/5.6.
- Pay attention to the zebra stripes displayed in most cameras when shooting in manual mode. They will warn you about overexposed areas.
- When shooting in bright light, if possible use the neutral density filter. Decrease the light instead of reducing the exposure.
- Avoid changing your shutter speed from the normal setting of 1/60. Faster and slower speeds affect the way the camera records motions. Be aware that some cameras change this automatically in low light.
- Do not use in-camera effects such as strobe or posterization. Most of these can be done in post-production if you choose. You want to keep your video images as clean as possible.
- Do not shoot in 16:9 mode with consumer cameras. Currently, the 16:9 mode on most of these camera derives the 16:9 image by

stretching the normal 1.33:1 image. This degrades your image and makes it appear "soft," or out of focus.

- Similarly, do not use the popular low-budget video softening technique of putting a net stocking in front of the lens.
- Before committing to shooting in the Canon XL1's frame movie mode, consult with your video-to-film transfer company. Some companies strongly advise against it, while others recommend it.
- Always number and label tapes clearly to keep them organized and avoid accidental erasure.

Recording Good Audio

If there is one common factor that screams low budget film, it's bad audio. No matter how good the story, camera work, and acting may be, poor audio will not allow a viewer to appreciate it.

Many filmmakers fail to recognize that sound recording is a very precise art. While the basic concepts are easy to learn, the craft is truly learned while working in a variety of diverse set situations.

Inexperienced people frequently believe that good production sound is where everything in frame sounds good, when in fact . . .

The main goal of the sound mixer and boom operator is to record clean dialogue that has the proper perspective relative to the picture and is well isolated from background noises.

At some point during principal photography, every film encounters situations that make it a challenge to record clean audio. But, experience can make a difference in a small challenge becoming an insurmountable problem.

Making an unprepared person the production sound mixer and/or boom operator is equivalent to trusting an inexperienced person to light and shoot for you.

Although you may not be able to hire a seasoned pro to record sound, try to find an ambitious boom operator or a TV news sound mixer. But, even more specifically, look for an audiophile who is a true stickler for quality sound. The best sound mixers are very detail oriented.

Rob Shire, my sound mixer on *Hacks*, had been the boom operator on *Detention*. And although he had never been a sound mixer on a film shoot, he primarily worked as a field audio mixer for television and video shoots.

However, I became convinced Rob was the person for my shoot after he revealed the extensive amount of research he had done since my initial conversation with him. In just a couple of weeks, he had consulted with veteran sound mixers about the type of audio situations that were unique to my script.

When he presented me with diagrams and a list of necessary equipment, I knew he could do the job. A few months after the shoot, an Academy Award®-winning sound mixer viewed the film and commented favorably on how well the audio was recorded.

Set high standards for your film's audio and find a person who is willing to hustle to meet them. If you treat audio as an afterthought, you will certainly regret it later.

The DP and Sound Mixer Relationship

Your DP, sound mixer, and if you have one, boom operator, have to develop and maintain a very close relationship that is considerate of each other's requirements.

This can be difficult sometimes because in order to capture the best sound, the boom operator must get the microphone as close to the talent as possible without having it in the shot.

While supervising the lighting team and working with the director to compose shots and choreograph camera movement, the DP must also communicate to the boom operator the proper *frame line* for the current set-up. A frame line is the point at which the microphone begins to appear in the shot.

A good boom operator recognizes that the DP is coordinating many different tasks, and accordingly knows the proper time to remind the DP to provide a frame line. Usually, it is determined during a rehearsal with the talent as the mixer sets recording levels.

Know Your Microphones

It is important that your sound mixer and boom operator know the unique characteristics of the microphones they will be using. There are two major characteristics to be familiar with—the microphone's sensitivity and the pickup pattern.

The microphone's sensitivity determines its effective range. This is important to understand because it allows the boom operator to know the minimum distance the mic must be placed from the talent in order to pick up clean audio. This distance can vary significantly from one microphone to another.

For example, the low priced Audio Technica AT835b short shotgun microphone can pickup top quality dialogue from a distance of 1.5 feet to 2.5 feet when boomed from overhead, while the more expensive Audio Technica AT4073a has a range of five to six feet.

In addition to aiding in microphone placement, the sound mixer will want to understand a microphone's sensitivity in order to know how it responds to various sounds. Some microphones are very sensitive to low bass frequencies, while other respond well to higher frequency sounds.

Similarly, pickup patterns can vary greatly between mics. A microphone's pickup pattern is based on the angles from which sound waves can strike the microphone and still be sufficiently recognized by the mic.

The strength of shotgun microphones are their highly directional patterns that can respond to the sounds the mic is pointed towards, while blocking out sound from other directions. The narrower the pickup pattern, the more directional the microphone is, and the more important it is that the mic be aimed towards talent at the correct angle.

Conversely, lavaliere mics typically have broader pickup patterns that respond to sound coming from many directions.

Booming Techniques

In most normal recording circumstances you will be using a shotgun microphone mounted on a boompole to record your sound. With an understanding of the microphone's range and pickup pattern, the sound mixer and boom operator will know how the mic must be positioned to pickup the best sound.

Shotgun mics are usually most effective when hung from overhead and angled down towards talent. The distance the microphone is held above the talent depends on the mic's sensitivity.

The angle of the mic is determined by the mic's pickup pattern, the number of people being recorded, and their various voice levels. Generally, the angle should prevent the microphone from being directly pointed towards anything in the line of site that could be a source of background noise. Ideally, this angle should end at the ground.

An understanding of the pickup pattern also aids when recording multiple people in a scene by allowing the boom operator to favor the angle towards weaker voices with the confidence that the stronger voices are still being picked up.

The boom operator suspends the microphone above the talent using an adjustable length, eight- to fifteen-foot boompole. The microphone is protected by a springy shock mount that absorbs the boom operator's handling noise while a foam windscreen reduces the potential for noise from strong breezes blowing across the mic.

Using both hands, the boompole is held high in the air but parallel to the ground. The operator keeps his/her arms close to the head with elbows locked at angles instead of fully extended. The rear arm is used to control the microphone by using the front arm as a pivoting point. This position offers the boom operator the most control with the least fatigue.

There are occasions, such as low ceilings, where the scene most be boomed from below as opposed to above. Again, in these situations attention should be given to the line of sight with efforts towards keeping clear of noisy backgrounds.

Plant Mics

There are other situations where it is not possible to boom the mic at all. These circumstances might require the use of plant mics, microphones that are hidden in the scene. In fact, the name comes from the tendency to hide the mics in flower pots and floral arrangements. The specific type of mic used (shotgun, lavaliere, etc.) depends on the requirements of the scene.

For example, a significant number of scenes in *Hacks* were filmed in moving cars with space limitations and simultaneous dialogue between people in the front and back seats. In these conditions we could not boom the mic or successfully use the narrow pattern of the shotgun mic.

However, while doing his research, Rob Shire (soundman for *Hacks*) learned that by taping a small Tram lavaliere mic to a square of cardboard, its pickup pattern could be changed to emulate that of a more expensive PZM boundary mics. These very responsive flat mics can be laid on a floor or table to pickup audio of an entire surface.

Rob taped the lavs to cardboard, then taped them to the front visor and rear ceiling of the car. Although they were well hidden, the pickup pattern they provided allowed the audio of everyone in the interior of the car to be picked up at the same degree of sensitivity. This arrangement even worked excellently for an a capella singing performance. By the way, Rob was crammed in the car's trunk with the Nagra tape recorder. I tell you, dedicated people make the difference.

Using Body Mics

Sometimes you will have to mic talent using cabled or wireless lavalieres inconspicuously attached to their body. This is common in shots that are too wide for your shotgun mic to get close enough to talent without getting in the frame.

The sound mixer often has to become creative while attempting to rig the mic on talent in a manner where it is not seen, but still picks up good audio. This most frequently requires the mic to be hidden under clothes which creates an additional concern about noise generated by the clothing hitting the mic.

This problem can be reduced by using pieces of cotton balls to protect the mic capsule. Additionally, small pieces of tape can be used to hold in place any clothing that may be rubbing the mic.

When using a wired mic, the cable should be taped at various points on the body to keep it secure. And the XLR connector should be readily accessible should you need to change the cable.

When using wireless body mics, pay attention to the antenna to ensure that it is not being crushed or buried so deep in clothing that it is not properly transmitting.

Monitoring Audio Levels

In addition to the proper selection and placement of the microphones, the sound mixer's job also includes the important task of monitoring audio recording levels and adjusting them as necessary to record sound clearly and undistorted.

This is accomplished by riding (adjusting) gain levels to attenuate (lower) the level for audio that is too loud or boost the level for audio that is too low. Although automatic gain control is an acceptable feature on most DV cameras, manual control offers the flexibility to tailor the audio for your specific situations.

In the best scenario, the sound mixer will have mics plugged directly into a portable field mixing unit featuring VU meters that visually represent the level of each mic. Based upon readings from these meters during rehearsal, and any necessary sound checks afterwards, the sound mixer will be prepared to ride the audio levels while recording.

A good pair of headphones provide extra protection by allowing the mixer to listen for unexpected noises. For lower priced audio mixers without VU meters, these headphones are crucial to monitor levels by ear. This is another area where experience is really important.

The audio will then be run from the mixer to the camera's mic input using any necessary mic input adapters. The camera will have been manually preset to a mid-level or set to automatic gain control.

The alternative set-up is less than ideal, but still an option. In this arrangement the mic is plugged directly into the camera, again using an adapter if necessary, and audio levels are monitored using headphones plugged into the camera and the camera's built-in audio meters. The levels are adjusted using the manual level controls.

This arrangement can be awkward, because it requires the mixer to be right next to the camera, which at times can be inconvenient for the camera operator and the mixer, particularly, when there are camera moves.

However, this is still preferable to the least desirable situation of the DP also monitoring audio. When this responsibility is added to the DP's responsibilities for proper lighting exposure, shot composition, correct focus, and camera movement, you can bet that at some point something is going to be compromised. With most DP's being driven by a passion for the visual images, don't be surprised if sound gets the stepchild treatment.

Recording Room Tone and Sound Effects

Every time you finish recording a scene, be certain to remember to record at least a minute of room tone or ambient sound, the natural sounds that are present in that setting.

Although you may not always be aware, every setting has a particular sound created by the acoustics of the setting and background noises. There could be the presence of subtle sounds, such as a refrigerator motor from a kitchen, or more explicit sounds such as traffic off in the distance.

Typically, after completing a scene, the sound mixer will call for everyone to settle down as he records room tone. When in closed spaces, room tone is recorded before people leave and equipment is taken out because their presence affects the room's acoustics.

A good sound mixer will also remember to individually record isolated sounds and sound effects that might be helpful in post-production. These sound elements become critical when preparing your film for foreign distribution where they will dub the audio and have to recreate all of the natural sounds that are a part of the scene.

This includes obvious things such as a door closing. However, it also includes less obvious sounds. In *Hacks*, we recorded all of the various sounds made by the different cars, everything from the horns, to the doors being opened and closed, to the engines revving at different speeds.

And just as important as the recordings themselves were the notes kept by Rob that detailed these audio takes. These notes have been invaluable when editing.

Taping a Scene

After running around in a frenzy of preparation, now comes the time to slow down and be sensitive to the important, subtle details as you record your scenes. It's the attention to these details that can separate your film from the others.

Walk Through the Scene

While talent (your actors) are getting dressed and having make-up applied, you should do a *walk through* of the scene on set with the DP, sound mixer, and gaffer. By now, your production designer and team should be well on their way in arranging any set decorations or props that are to be a part of the scene.

During this walk through, you will discuss the basic range of actions and select a camera position for the first shot. Based on this information, the DP and gaffer begin lighting the scene, usually using stand-ins for the actors. If you have adequate resources, this step can be done in advance to allow the lighting crew to pre-light the set prior to the cast and primary crew's arrival on set.

Block the Scene

When the talent arrives, you should do a walk through of the scene to let them know their actions and movement on set. This provides the DP and sound mixer an opportunity to adjust their equipment to better shoot the scene or record audio. These adjustments can be brief, or they may be substantial, in which case you may take talent to the side to rehearse, or have them ushered back to a safe comfortable place.

Rehearse the Scene

After major lighting and sound adjustments are made, the talent return to the set for a rehearsal. During rehearsals, the DP and sound mixer will continue to make small adjustments, while you focus on reviewing shot composition and helping the actors with their performances. At this time the DP and grip will be practicing any camera, dolly, jib arm or Steadicam movements.

Get Your Shots

After you receive a thumbs up from your DP and sound mixer, and once you and your actors are ready, it is time to record the shots that will make up the scene. You take your place at the monitor and slip on a pair of good headphones so that you can watch and hear what is being recorded through the camera.

A PA or camera assistant runs in and holds a slate in front of the camera at a position specified by the DP. Since audio is recorded with the video, the slate does not have to be clapped to create a sync point as it would for film. However, this slate will have information about the date, scene number, and take number that will be helpful when reviewing tapes later.

The AD calls out, "Standby!" which is echoed by other PAs positioned around to lockup the set and ensure that no one can enter and disrupt the recording.

Once everyone has settled, the AD calls out, "Roll camera!" to which the DP starts the camera and shouts "Speed!" This lets everyone know that the camera is rolling. The PA or camera assistant will shout the scene number and take number, creating an audio slate, before quickly exiting the shot.

The DP makes some minor adjustments, then says "Camera ready." You or the AD then call out, "Action!"

Once "action" is called, talent pauses a beat, then begins their performances. At that time your full attention should be on what you see on the monitor. Everything you have worked for so far—writing and re-writing the script, planning, pre-production, all of the hundreds of details—all culminate at the moment you record these individual shots.

This is your moment, baby! The time at which you have to put up or shut up and transition from a soon-to-be director to a real director. As a director watching that monitor, you should be scrutinizing:

- The camera work. Is everything in focus and properly exposed? Are there unacceptable shadows? Did the boom mike enter the frame? Is the camera movement smooth? Does the composition of the shot work for the action of the scene? Did the DP give you the shots you requested? How is continuity, will these shots inter-cut with others?

- The actors' performances. Are lines being delivered as you intended them to be delivered? Are the performances convincing and natural? Is the tone and pacing of the dialogue and action correct? Is the body language as it should be? Were lines skipped over, mumbled, or flubbed?
- The audio. How is the audio sounding to you? Did you hear a plane in the background that the sound mixer didn't catch? Are two people near each other being evenly miced or is one far louder than the other (when they should be sounding the same)? Are there any pops and hisses from body mics or line interference?

If you are unhappy with any of these issues, immediately call, "Cut!" and communicate the problem or make the proper changes. Sometimes, it helps people to review the shot by playing it back on the monitor, but this can quickly become a habit that can slow down the pace tremendously.

Once the corrections are understood, everyone should reset and return to their starting positions to begin recording the shot again. The camera assistant, sound mixer, and script supervisor should make notes on the take, and the slate should be changed.

Move On to the Next

If the shot was recorded as you intended, let everyone know and prepare to move on to your next camera set-up as you gradually accumulate coverage of the scene.

This is where the director really sets the pace for the production. You must be able to move from set-up to set-up, as quickly as possible, as you get the different shots you will ultimately assemble together to create the edited scene. And once you have covered a scene, you must be ready to start the next one.

You have minimal time to relax casually between different takes or different scenes, even if the previous scene was very demanding. A good AD will help you, the cast and the crew maintain the pace.

But Remember, We Can't Afford to Fix It in Post!

If time constraints have closed in, and you are behind schedule, you have to begin the prioritization process to determine which of the masterfully crafted shots you have to toss out or even worse, what scene you can compress or eliminate.

On big budget shoots, this pressure often makes people compromise by settling for less than perfect audio or camera exposure. Under these circumstances people like to say, "We can fix it in post," meaning that audio can be re-recorded, and the film's exposure can be adjusted when the film is printed. The studios might not like it, but they will come up with the cash if a film goes over schedule or over budget.

Low budget productions do not have this luxury. Re-recording, or looping, dialogue through automatic dialogue replacement (ADR) is a costly process that is difficult to reproduce on your home editing system. When done improperly, the results look and sound like a poorly dubbed karate movie.

Your desktop editing system will allow you to make some adjustments to the video's color and exposure. However, these adjustments can affect the video quality. Additionally, since the new images must be rendered, they can require a lot of patience and time to experiment with the various settings.

Therefore, the best bet is to get the audio and video correct on location, to avoid extremely expensive post-production. Even if it means you have to spend more time on fewer set-ups, and shoot less coverage of the scene. It is preferable to have a well acted, good looking and good sounding master shot, over a scene with a lot of visually and audibly flawed shots.

Wrap It Up

And so, the process continues for the entire shoot. Slowly and hopefully steadily, your film is built scene by scene. Sometimes everything will seem perfect as things fall right into place almost effortlessly. Occasionally, they end up even better than you had planned. Other times, it will be grueling work that has you reconsidering that career in the computer industry.

But once you successfully make it through principal photography, it is certainly a victory that everyone involved should be proud of, even if a couple of folks can't stand each other anymore.

Things to Remember About Principal Photography

- You are always on the clock.
- Good pictures, good sound, and good acting must be priorities.
- Everyone is under stress.
- Give the respect that you demand.
- Feed people good food frequently.
- Preparation is crucial, but . . .
- The ability to adapt is a must . . .
- And after it all, life goes on.

8

■■■■■ DV Editing Options

Desktop editing has become very common in the last five years as the cost of video capture cards and hard drives has steadily decreased. However, DV editing takes quality and affordability to a whole other level.

There are several ways you can go about editing your DV film. Interestingly enough, the more expensive editing systems do not necessarily produce the best results. Available options listed from most preferable to least preferable are as follows:

- FireWire Nonlinear Editing
- Digital Linear Editing
- Non-DV Native Nonlinear Editing
- Non-Digital Linear Editing

A FireWire nonlinear editing system that will never convert your digital signal to analog or to another digital format will indisputably provide the best quality. However, if you are unable to gain access to a DV editing system but have access to one of the other editing options, then make use of what you have.

Regardless of your editing system, there are a few important things to keep in mind throughout the editing process.

When Editing DV . . .

- Protect the integrity of your video and audio signals by using the best connections possible and performing non-digital dubs as little as possible.
- Remember that every time you convert from digital to analog and vice versa you are potentially adding subtle digital artifacts and noise to your video.
- If you must dub your DV footage to another format, never use the composite video output from your camera or DV camera or deck. Use the better quality S-VHS Y/C connectors.
- Or even better, have your dubs made at a professional facility that can do a true component transfer to Betacam SP.
- Or have digital copies made to Digital Betacam using the Serial Data Interface (SDI).
- Use your master DV tapes only when necessary. The narrow width of DV tapes makes them a somewhat fragile format that under frequent starting and stopping can become susceptible to tape stretching. This can cause noticeable smearing of your video images.

FireWire Nonlinear Editing Systems

DV In . . . DV Out . . . Digital All The Way

While the introduction of DV cameras represented a technological breakthrough, the convergence of emerging DV technology and maturing computer technology created digital editing systems that have brought DV into its own as a superior production format.

The basic components of the FireWire nonlinear editing systems are:
- A computer. New computers offer more processing power for less money.
- An IEEE-1394 (a.k.a. FireWire or I.link) card for digitally transferring DV in and out of the computer.
- Media storage. Durable hard drives that economically provide reliable DV storage; and an optional data back-up system.
- Additional hardware. Monitors, speakers, and device controllers allow for professional monitoring and control when editing.
- Computer software. Editing and graphic programs optimized for the DV allow you to make the most of the format.

- A DV player/record device. Required to playback and record your DV tapes.

Combined, these tools make it possible to affordably shoot digital and stay digital throughout the post-production process. Let's take a look at the details of the components that you will use to assemble your DV editing system.

As with all of the specific references to technology in this book, there are probably newer or less expensive versions of the hardware and software referred to in this section. You can always find information on the newest developments online.

Computer Requirements

Processing video on a personal computer requires tremendous computing power. Every time an image is displayed, or manipulated, it requires the computer to perform millions of calculations. A typical DV editing system will be handling over three million bytes of information per second! The rate at which the system is able to consistently move information between devices is called the *sustained throughput.*

Any weak link in the system will lower the sustained throughput. The result is unacceptable video recording and playback quality or an unstable system that crashes frequently. Your computer's processing ability is determined by:

The type of microprocessor and its speed. The microprocessor is the heart of the computer. New models and faster processors are introduced every few months, but you don't need the latest model to have a good DV editing system. Processor speed is measured in megahertz (mHz), the higher the number, the faster the computer is able to compute the information.

The microprocessor usually has a set of computer chips that aid it in performing its functions. This *chip set* is mounted onto a main *motherboard* to which other devices are added. Newer microprocessors will often work with older chip sets. However, they require newer chip sets for optimum performance.

The amount of *random access memory* (RAM). The price of memory chips has plummeted in recent years, making it much more affordable to load up on memory. More memory allows the processor and software to operate faster.

The type and speed of the internal bus system. Components inside the computer communicate with each other using an electronic pathway called a *bus*. Some computers use an older type of bus that operates slower than new versions. The PCI bus is currently the industry standard for most add-on devices.

The capabilities of the video graphic card. Quality graphic cards are required to meet the demands of rapidly displaying the high resolution video images. There are many customized cards that are designed primarily for this purpose. Additionally, in some instances special overlay features are required to mix video with computer generated images, such as text from a titling program.

Graphic cards have their own RAM, so they do not have to take any from the processor. As with the main system RAM, the more video RAM, the better. Many new graphic cards use an advanced bus system called *accelerated graphics port* (AGP) that was designed to provide high speed 2D and 3D graphics.

The operating system and supporting software. Operating system software, such as Windows 95 or MAC OS, control your computer's basic functions (i.e. the keyboard, disk drives, CD player etc.). This software must be kept up to date using small files called drivers. You want to be certain to use versions of an OS and drivers that are compatible with the DV hardware you are using. Windows NT is becoming increasingly popular for high-end DV editing systems because of its stability.

Windows PC or Apple PC?

The long standing Windows PC versus Macintosh debate has continued on into the desktop video world. The major issues are still the PC's lower cost and broad software base compared to Apple's ease of use and maturity as a graphic-oriented platform. Although they are not nearly as different as they used to be, each argument continues to have merit.

On the next page is a comparison of a low-end Windows PC system suitable for DV editing, and a comparable Mac system. You can actually set up a good editing system on less powerful computers in both categories if you already have the computers. But if you are buying a new system these currently represent excellent value for the money.

As you can see, the Windows PC is more than half the price of the Macintosh. But, in comparing prices, it is important to understand the highly competitive manufacturing market that keeps Windows-based PCs so inexpensive, is also what creates complications when building a Windows PC-based editing system.

Because video processing is so demanding, every component in the system must be compatible and properly synchronized with each other

WINDOWS PC	**APPLE POWER MACINTOSH**
Intel Pentium II 500 MMX	G4 450
32 Meg RAM	128 Meg RAM
4 Meg PCI Graphic Card	
4 Gig System Hard Drive (Not for video storage, for computer programs only.)	4 Gig System Hard Drive (Not for video storage, for computer programs only.)
24x CD	24x CD
17" Monitor	15" Monitor
Misc.: Sound card, speakers, 56k modem, mouse, keyboard	Misc.: 56k modem.
Approx. $850	**Approx. $1,800**

to prevent timing conflicts. Windows PCs use a set of variables called IRQs to keep track of timing between devices. Traditionally, every device is allocated a unique IRQ or, if predetermined, shares an IRQ.

Moreover with hundreds of companies competing to create new computer chips, cards, and software, often with their own standards and hardware requirements, you end up with components that frequently work better under some circumstances than others. So you can have a graphics card that works beautifully in one computer, but poorly or not at all, in another.

Far worse, there can be inconspicuous IRQ conflicts present in your system that are not obvious under normal circumstances such as using a word processor or surfing the Net. However, as soon as you add the DV FireWire card and a high speed disk drive, your system is straining to get all the speed it can. And, if it can't get it because of IRQ conflicts, then your video editing equipment will not perform correctly.

Windows 95's promise of plug and play capability was to address these issues by allowing the computer to recognize new devices "plugged" into it. It would then make the internal IRQ and other adjustments necessary for you to "play" the device without having to worry about these issues. Unfortunately, in many cases this process simply confuses the computer more, especially if you are frequently adding and deleting components from different manufacturers.

So, how do you avoid this potential headache? Well, many people would respond to this by saying . . . get a Macintosh.

From its inception, the Macintosh was touted for its powerful but very user friendly software and hardware. The early Macs were the first consumer PCs to feature: high resolution graphics; the mouse as an input device; the point and click *graphical user interface* (GUI); and the first laser printer.

Initially, these progressive features came at the expense of a closed system architecture that did not allow the machines to be easily opened and upgraded. Additionally, the devices that could be used with the machine were very regulated by Apple to ensure compatibility.

The evolution of Mac software was similarly controlled. The built-in graphics capabilities led to the computer being embraced by users doing graphic-intense work such as desktop publishing. Recognizing this user base, Apple and other software manufacturers working closely with Apple, developed more of these graphic-based applications. Most of the popular graphic, desktop publishing, and video editing programs used in a Windows environment started on the Macs.

By the time Mac did evolve into an open system that could easily be upgraded, its software and hardware standards were already well established. Many of them continue to be important today. For example, QuickTime is an Apple-developed computer video format that has kept the Mac ahead of Windows PC for video production and now has a growing significance in the Windows PC software market. Likewise, FireWire is actually an Apple trademarked name for the IEEE-1394 interface that has become the common name for this interface.

The Macintosh's hardware and software maturity is clearly reflected in the graphics and editing packages available for it. With the newest Macintosh models, the FireWire ports are built into the computer and software is preinstalled to help you capture and edit digital video, so you can start with a completely integrated system. Once you get beyond the cost of the basic computer system, additional Mac hardware and software offers better performance at a lower price than Windows PC based products.

When running Windows, you also have the advantage of a tremendous base of other software that is currently available. This may be a real consideration if you plan on using your computer for functions other than just editing.

If you have the budget to choose, determine which editing system you want to use, then purchase your PC or Mac based on the requirements for that hardware and software.

Likewise, if you are on a tighter budget or simply decide to go with a Windows system, then you should also begin by carefully researching the system requirements for the selected editing package. Many DV hardware vendors list compatible systems on their websites.

Find out every detail you can—the recommended motherboards, processors, support chip set, memory, specific graphics cards, and operating system. Use this information to build, or have your system built, around these requirements, paying special attention to IRQ and system settings to ensure optimum performance.

If you are price comparing pre-built systems, don't just base it on price, but also a comparison of the components inside of the different systems. Be certain to communicate with the salesperson that you will be using your computer for video production and that the system must be able to sustain a throughput of 3 megs+ per second.

If you currently have a computer that you want to edit on, be prepared to toss a few old parts and/or upgrade it if necessary. Memory and graphics cards are the most common upgrades.

Again, learn details about what your system is currently composed of, and what you will require to get it up to speed for the editing hardware and software you will use. To avoid disappointment with performance once your system is up, always try to exceed the manufacturer's minimum system recommendations.

Finally, if you ultimately decide that these technical details are more than you'd care to learn about at the moment, you do have the option of finding a *value-added reseller* (VAR) experienced with desktop video systems. A value-added reseller is a computer manufacturer that builds and sells complete, pre-configured turnkey editing systems.

Most companies choose to specialize in a couple of particular editing systems which allow them to develop expertise when setting-up up the systems and dealing with customers problems. While you may spend more than you would building the system yourself, you also will gain the benefits of customer support should problems arise. In the middle of editing your project, this help could be greatly appreciated.

Several established VARs that ship internationally are listed in the resource guide of this book. Whether you choose a local or national VAR, always seek references from customers before you spend your money.

Apple Computer's iMac and G4 introduced the low-cost iMac DV in the fall of 1999. Featuring a built-in monitor, FireWire port and Apple's iMovie software, the system is truly a "plug and play" editing machine. While the small monitor and limited expansion options are a liability, the system is still an excellent choice for anyone looking to get started editing quickly and economically. Apple's Final Cut Pro software can also be run on an iMac DV. If you require more editing power, the more expensive G4 computer also features built-in FireWire ports and dual processors, offering tremendous processing power.

IEEE-1394 (FireWire, I.link) Cards

IEEE-1394 is a high speed data transfer format and interface developed by Apple Computers in the late '80s. Apple trademarked the name "FireWire" and submitted the technology to the Institute of Electrical and Electronic Engineers (IEEE) which approved it as an industry standard. Sony later trademarked I.link as its own version of IEEE-1394, however, they are the same technology. For the sake of brevity, I'll use the name FireWire.

Why FireWire?

Although, FireWire has been around for awhile, it was the introduction of the DV format that spawned engineers to recognize its potential as a transfer protocol. FireWire proved to be naturally suited to DV for several reasons.

First, current FireWire standards have a transfer rate and bandwidth of up to 100 megabits per second (Mbps), which means that it can transfer 100 million pieces of computer data per second! And the IEEE specifications will allow it to go up to 400 Mbps. To put this in perspective, even with its high resolution video and CD quality sound, DV only requires 25 Mbps!

Second, FireWire supports two types of transfer modes. Asynchronous transfer is a two-way communication protocol commonly used with devices such as printers and scanners. Asynchronous devices feature unfixed, variable timing as bits of data go back and forth, while the devices try continuously to send information as fast as possible. With timing issue being critical for the proper display of video data, asynchronous transfer is unacceptable. However, the second FireWire transfer mode is isochronous, operating at a constant data rate with fixed timing. Again, a natural for DV.

Finally, the third advantage of FireWire is that it is hot-pluggable, meaning that is can be easily attached and detached to, and from, devices while the devices are powered up. So you can plug a cable into your camera, and then into your FireWire card without having to turn either of them off.

The FireWire cable is a thin, lightweight cable, quite unlike the bulky cable used for many other bus systems (like your printer cable). The cable is comprised of six wires; two of which send and receive data, and two which handle control information (timing and error checking), and the last set can provide power to devices.

FireWire's integration into consumer electronics began when Sony introduced the VX1000 in 1995 with the FireWire interface built-in. However, it was nearly two years later before the introduction of the first FireWire card for a PC that would allow users to transfer DV in and out of their computer. A new industry was launched by manufacturers realizing that these inexpensive little cards had big potential.

The first generation of FireWire cards left some people disappointed by its shortcomings, such as the failure to allow the camera, or editing deck, to be controlled from the computer. The second generation of FireWire cards rectified many of these issues and provided solid editing capabilities.

However, even as newer cards continue to add features and offer more functionality, IEEE-1394 ports are becoming a standard feature on desktop and laptop computers such as Apple's iMac DV and G4 computers and Sony's Vaio series.

How Do You Use Them?

FireWire cards simply plug into a slot inside your computer. After configuring the card, you can plug your DV camera or deck into the card using the cable that has usually been supplied.

Then, using a DV capture and playback program on the computer, also shipped with the card, you can digitally transfer the video and audio from the camera or deck, to your computer's hard drive. Once there, you can edit the video using an editing program. After you complete your editing, the FireWire card will send your video and audio back out to your recording device.

During this process the DV information always remains digital. However, it does undergo a process of *compression* and *decompression* required by the DV format to show DV on a TV or video monitor. This is accomplished using a sophisticated computer program called a CODEC (COmpression DECompression). All DV camera and decks have hardware CODECs built in that perform this process while recording and playing back video.

FireWire cards fall into two categories, *software CODEC cards* and *hardware CODEC cards.* Although they both provide the same function of bringing DV in and out of the computer and they both have the same video quality, their performance while editing can vary greatly.

Software CODEC FireWire Cards

Inexpensive FireWire cards use software CODECs that rely on your computer and the hardware CODEC in your DV device to perform compression and decompression when playing DV from your computer's hard drives. This keeps the cost of software CODEC FireWire cards low by tremendously reducing the amount of processing the card must perform. Many of these cards also include high speed hard drive controller cards to shorten the path of the DV data from the FireWire card to the hard drive. The benefits of this depend on the decisions you make about your video storage hard drives.

The disadvantage of software CODEC FireWire cards is that the speed at which they operate is heavily dependent on the processing power of your computer. A computer that just meets the minimum system requirements might be agonizingly slow to operate.

Additionally, most software CODEC cards require you to keep your DV device connected to the system in order to play your video from the hard drive out to a video monitor. You can view the video on your computer monitor, but it may or may not be full sized, full resolution, or at the full frame rate, depending on the editing software you use and the computer's processing power.

This marginal video quality may be acceptable for basic editing, but the ability to *scrub video* (playback on your video monitor at full resolution) is critical for evaluating how your final project will actually look. Fortunately, as computer processing speeds continue to climb, the performance of software CODECs also continues to improve.

Hardware CODEC Cards

The alternatives to software CODEC FireWire cards are hardware CODEC cards that incorporate the same type of computer hardware found in DV cameras and decks. This additional hardware adds substantially to the cost of the cards. However, it allows you to transfer DV to your PC, then detach that device (and use it for better things) while still being able to play your footage from the computer and view it full screen on a TV monitor. Additionally, depending on the computers processing power, the hardware CODECs can work with software CODEC to calculate transitions such as dissolves and fades faster than software CODECs alone.

Hardware CODECs also offer the advantage of allowing you to input and output analog video and audio directly to and from your computer. For example, if you have some Hi-8 video you would like to add to your program, using the right card, you can run a cable from a deck directly to a connector on the FireWire card. These connections are often made using a stand-alone breakout box that connects to the FireWire card but allows the convenience of having the connectors nearby as opposed to at the rear of the computer.

With the Hi-8 deck connected to the breakout box, the footage is captured via the FireWire card, and converted into DV by the hardware CODEC. Once in the computer, it can be mixed with your other DV footage. Of course, the other option would be to dub your Hi-8 tapes using a DV deck.

Media Storage

Recording and playing back DV to and from your computer requires large hard drives that are capable of reliably sustaining the high speeds necessary for the fast rate at which the DV information is transferred. It is wise to purchase as much hard drive space as you can afford. However, even with limited media storage space you can still edit your project in small segments.

One gigabyte (gig) of hard drive space can store 4.5 minutes of DV footage. While this may seem like quite a bit of space for a little bit of video, comparable quality video captured using non-DV capture cards will only offer roughly two to three minutes per gig. This is one of the benefits of the fixed data rate and compression method used by DV.

However, DV still requires high speed drives. If the hard drives are too slow while recording, video frames will be dropped. These lost frames will be very noticeable during playback, making segments of the video unusable.

Some FireWire cards have a feature to compensate for dropped frames by going back and re-transferring these segments until all frames have been properly transferred. However, the benefits of this feature are useless if your hard drive is unable to sustain the speed required to playback the video smoothly.

Hard drives record streams of data on a rotating disk. The faster the disk revolves, the more data that can be recorded in the same amount of space. Recording video requires thousands of *revolutions per minute*

(RPM) to pack the data on the disk. However, as speed increases, so does the disk's susceptibility to errors as it records and reads information. To compensate, disk controllers use error checking processes that cause the disk's speed to fluctuate.

This was not a problem for early computer applications, since the hard drives where only accessed with periodic bursts of activity. However, video requires that the hard drives be operated for long periods of time at a speed that does not fall below the minimum acceptable rate for video. If you playback a forty-minute video program, your hard drive will be running consistently for fory minutes. This creates a problem for many low-cost hard drives.

While many inexpensive drives are capable of reaching the high rate required by video, they are not physically designed to sustain that rate for long periods of time. As stated previously, DV has a data rate of 25 Mbps, however, hard drive data rates are expressed in megabytes per second (MBps). DV data is 3.6 MBps, but requires hard drives with the ability to sustain a rate of around 6 MBps.

Inexpensive hard drive components such as the motor and magnetic recording platter do not have the durability to consistently and reliably maintain the sustained throughput required for DV. The drive may work for a little while but before long, begins to fail.

Similarly, the standard low-cost hard drive controllers (such as IDE, EIDE, and most recently, UDMA) used by most computers to regulate the flow of data, were not designed to sustain these high speeds. Their error checking and control mechanisms just cannot keep up.

AV Drives and ULTRA SCSI

When desktop video was first introduced, these problems were addressed by the creation of hard drives designed specifically for audio and video. These relatively expensive but durable AV (Audio/Video) rated drives are controlled using high speed controllers such as the popular Ultra SCSI Controller. Today many upper-end SCSI hard drives meet the specifications of being AV-rated without having that designation. When used with Ultra SCSI controllers, these drives can spin at 7200 RPM or faster, providing a throughput of over 8 MBps, much higher than the throughput required by DV.

When evaluating a hard drive, sustained rate and RPM are important factors. Additionally, you must be certain that the drive supports Ultra SCSI controllers. You must also be sure that you have the correct controller card in your computer.

While SCSI (pronounced "scuzzy") was not developed by Apple, they were the first to implement it as a device controller for personal computers. It allowed for high speed communication between devices, with the benefits of being able to "daisy chain" devices–connect them in sequence using one controller.

Over the years, different versions have evolved based upon the transfer speed supported and the number of pins on the connector. These variations often create problems when purchasing SCSI controllers and devices. You must carefully read the specifications of your FireWire card to be certain what type of SCSI it supports.

Additionally, depending on the age of the computer's motherboard, it may or may not be able to support the controller required by your hard drive. This may also be the case for SCSI controllers included on your system's motherboard, such as those found on most Macs.

Ultra SCSI is the SCSI format used by most hard drives suitable for the demands of DV. But be aware that Ultra SCSI also has two variations, Ultra Wide and Ultra Narrow, depending upon the number of pins used in the connectors.

The onboard SCSI controllers featured on many software CODEC FireWire cards helps to eliminate some of this confusion. These controllers are most often an Adaptec 2940 UW (ultra wide) which is becoming an industry standard, at least for the moment. Most FireWire card manufacturers list recommended hard drives and controllers in their spec sheets and on their websites.

Recently, there has been the introduction of a viable but less expensive hard drive system for video production.

Video RAID Systems and Ultra ATA Drives

Video RAIDS are built from two or more identical drives matched with customized high speed controller cards that allow the computer to use the drives as one big, high speed drive. Traditionally, these RAIDS were made from SCSI drives. However, recent progress now allows for particular models of low-cost EIDE controlled hard drives and UDMA (a.k.a. Ultra DMA or Ultra ATA) controlled hard drives to be used.

RAIDS can be purchased pre-assembled and pre-formatted. A California-based company, Medea Corp., has been at the forefront of this technology. They offer affordable internal and external VideoRAID hard drives that range in size from 6 gig (about thirty minutes of DV) up to 75 gig (nearly three hours of DV). The installation is very easy and usually requires minimal manual reconfiguration of hardware or software settings on your computer.

Ultra ATA drives for DV are also becoming popular with value added resellers. Companies such as ProMax Technology, now incorporate EIDE drives and proprietary controllers into their turn-key systems for video storage.

Adventurous techies can install their own Ultra ATA drives for even less money. Promise Technology Inc. has a product for Windows PCs called the Fasttrack that is an inexpensive disk drive accelerator and controller card when used with two or more recommended hard drives. Sonnet Technology offers a comparable card for Macs. These cards offer the sustained throughput you will need for your DV system.

The Fasttrack and Sonnet cards sells for less than $150, and a 40 gig hard drive can be purchased for less than $200, offering you nearly three hours of DV storage for less than $400! However, be aware that these controllers require proper technical knowledge to set up and use.

Contact information for Medea, Promise Technology and Sonnet Technology is listed in the Appendices.

Backup Devices

Once you have DV stored on your hard drive or more likely, after you have finished editing a project, you will often want to save these media files on a backup storage device to avoid having to recapture them from the computer. This is important for finished projects that you may want to modify later. But, it is also important for protecting your completed work from potential hard drive failures that can wipe out your project.

Low capacity backup devices, such as inexpensive recordable CD-ROM drives or the 2 gig removable disk of Iomega Jaz drives, can be used to backup small video segments. However, longer projects will have to rely on the more expensive high-capacity DAT or tape cartridge backup drives.

These devices can hold 4 to 50 gigabytes of data, allowing you to dump (transfer) your entire project to one DAT or tape cartridge. The low priced units, such as the HP Colorado Tape Drive, cost under $300 and can store roughly 5 gigabytes of data, while the more expensive Sony SDT 900 DAT Drive costs around $1,000 and can store up to 24 gigabytes on a single $10 DAT.

The problem with these backup devices is that transferring data is very slow. Backing up the huge amounts of data for even a thirty-minute program can take hours! Most people using these drives for long projects have to perform backups overnight. There are drives that can do it much faster, but they cost $2,000+.

There is an alternative to backing up all of your media that is common on high-end editing systems, and is now becoming available on some DV systems. This involves the use of time code to recreate projects. I'll elaborate more on this in the next section.

Additional Hardware

There are a few other pieces of hardware you will require to complete your DV editing system. Good monitors and speakers are a must, while an optional device controller provides manual device control comparable to professional edit controllers.

Monitors

Your editing system will utilize an RGB computer monitor and a video monitor. The quality of both components is important. Purchase the largest, highest resolution RGB monitor you can afford. Top of the line 19" and 21" monitors can cost as much, or more than, your computer. But, when editing for hours at a time, you will appreciate being able to position yourself a reasonable distance from the monitor, and still clearly view the numerous details that will be on the screen while using editing software. View Sonic produces a line of affordable RGB monitors.

A good quality, high-resolution video monitor is crucial for accurately viewing your video footage throughout the editing process. This is particularly true if you are using editing hardware that does not provide full screen playback on your computer monitor.

Additionally, computers offer a far wider range of colors than allowed by the standards for broadcast video. Colors outside this range are not considered "legal colors." When viewed on televisions or video monitors, the effects of illegal colors can render a video program unwatchable. Although most computer programs can be set to limit colors to a video legal palette, a good, properly calibrated monitor also helps alert you to this problem.

A video monitor is preferable over a television because monitors provide better resolution and overscan/underscan modes that allow you to see important details that may be obscured on a normal television. Small studio monitors like the 14" Sony PVM14N1U ($460) or the Panasonic CT-1386Y ($300) will do the job.

Speakers

Just as monitors are important for viewing your footage, a good set of speakers is crucial for reviewing and editing audio. Keep in mind that if you intend on transferring your project to film it could potentially be projected using state-of-the-art stereo systems. The speakers must be able to help you prepare for that process.

The little speakers provided with most computers are suitable for video games, but not the high quality audio you will be striving for. Fortunately, quality speakers are available from respected audio manufacturers like Bose (Model MM) and Altec (ADA 305) for less than $175.

Device Controllers

Professional editors use an *edit controller* that provides them the ability to control functions on their playback and record device. Forward, play, and rewind are operated using a rotating jog/shuttle knob. When pushed, the knob allows the operator to quickly switch between slow (jog), which allows frame by frame advancement, to high speed (shuttle) playback modes. Using this device, the editor can shuttle to rapidly move about entire tapes, and yet still use jog to precisely select an exact frame.

Many editing programs have adapted the popular Microsoft IntelliMouse ($40) for this purpose. Instead of having three buttons, the IntelliMouse has a small wheel positioned between two buttons. This wheel can be used to control the direction of the playback device, while one of the buttons is used to switch between jog and shuttle speeds.

Stand-alone control boxes such as the JL Cooper Media Control Station ($200) and Videonics Command Post feature true jog/shuttle knobs and programmable buttons. Both are supported by most major software packages.

DV Editing System Software Requirements

Despite the demanding task FireWire cards perform, the technology in itself is not that complicated, especially for the software CODEC cards. The unique features and limitations of various FireWire cards are directly tied to the software used with them.

In fact, several manufacturers utilize the same hardware for their cards, but offer far different performance based upon customized software. This software basically falls into three categories: supporting software, DV capture and playback software, and nonlinear editing (NLE) programs.

Supporting Software

All computer programs are built upon the basic functions performed by the operating system. Tasks such as displaying text, or creating sounds, are accomplished by the small programs that comprise the operating system. Computer programmers use these programs to create the complex software we use everyday.

DV software relies on the operating system for the internal processing of your DV footage once it is in the computer. Consequently, your computer's editing abilities are strongly tied to the way this media is handled by the system.

On a Windows PC, Microsoft Video for Windows is a long established standard for audio and video files. Using a file format called Audio Video Interleave (AVI), audio and video information is combined into a single file. Combining the data theoretically helps keep audio and video synchronized.

However, in many AVI applications synchronization drifts have proven to be a problem for long files, especially as the data was edited and manipulated. Additionally, a limitation in the Windows operating system did not allow a single AVI file to be larger than 2 gigs.

Despite these shortcomings, until recently, nearly all Windows programs using video and audio were built around Video for Windows. Microsoft has plans to replace Video for Windows with a media system called DirectShow.

Meanwhile, years before Video for Windows, Apple had incorporated its QuickTime Video format into the Mac operating system. From its introduction, QuickTime was heralded for its efficiency in video and audio processing. Subsequent versions continue to improve upon this strong foundation.

The latest version, QuickTime 4, is available for Mac OS and Windows. It incorporates support for DV format video and audio and plays a significant role in the latest video editing software on Mac and Windows PCs.

There are also other types of support software that help your hardware and software perform optimally: device drivers, software patches, plug-ins, and upgrades.

Device drivers allow you to update your operating system to make use of new devices. Drivers are usually included with the hardware.

With true plug-and-play devices the installation of these drivers is very easy.

Software patches are small bits of computer code that correct problems or add minor features to your current computer programs. Most vendors offer software patches for free, often downloadable from their websites.

Plug-ins are computer programs that integrate with and extend the functions of a major software package. They are created by individuals and companies who may or may not be affiliated with the main program's developer to fulfill the needs of a specific group of users. Specialized plug-ins are sold separately.

Upgrades are major changes in the computer software that usually incorporate significant improvements. Users usually have to pay for upgrades. However, it is not as much as they would pay to purchase the new version.

By making use of the most compatible and most recent support software, you can be certain that you are getting the best performance possible from your computer, FireWire card, and editing software.

DV Capture and Playback Software

Initially, most FireWire cards were designed for use with established editing software. DV capture and playback programs were created to control the cards and provide a bridge between the card and editing program.

Simple capture programs provide the basic function of allowing a user to record and name video clips, then save them in a file format, such as AVI, so that they can be used by the editing package. In many cases, the same program must also be used to transfer the edited project back out to the DV device.

The specific features offered by the capture and playback programs are the first line of distinction between various editing systems, particularly among software CODEC cards.

Some of the possible features present in the capture and playback software include:

- Device Control
- Time-Code and Frame Accuracy
- Automatic Tape Scanning
- Clip Logging and Media Management
- File Size Limitation Solutions
- Audio Level Monitoring
- Audio Format Options

Device Control—Allows the DV camera's or DV deck's playback and recording functions to be controlled manually by the user, with a mouse, a stand-alone control box, or control panel-like software, on the computer monitor. The software can automatically control DV devices while performing certain task.

Time-Code and Frame Accuracy—Using the DV format time-code recorded on all DV tapes, the software can consistently return to a specific video frame on a tape.

Automatic Tape Scanning—The software uses frame accurate device control and plays the tape from start to finish while automatically detecting the beginning and ending of each scene. The program creates a log, often with a small picture representing the scene, that can then be used to make decisions about which scenes to load.

Automatic Batch Capture—Once a list of scenes is marked by automatic tape scanning or manually entered by the user, automatic batch capture goes back and transfers the selected footage into the computer.

Clip Logging and Media Management—After the clips have been captured, logging options allow you to add notes and other information that will aid you during the editing process. Media management tools help you add, delete, and arrange clips in a manner that keeps them manageable in complex projects.

File Size Limitation Solutions—Software that overcomes the 2 gig limitation of AVI files to allow users to input longer clips.

Audio Level Monitoring—On-screen VU meters depict the levels of incoming audio.

Audio Format Options—Some of the possible options for recording audio include unlocked and locked audio support, the number of audio channels to be recorded, and the sampling and bit rate. Because the audio standard for AVI files is the 44.1kHz, 16 bit format, some programs require audio to be re-sampled from 32 kHz, 12 bit or 48 kHz, 16 bit. This can periodically result in undesirable audio pops and clicks. Fortunately more programs are moving towards support for the native DV audio format.

Gradually, many of these options are being incorporated into versions of popular editing programs optimized for specific FireWire cards.

Nonlinear Editing Software

Once your DV clips have been transferred to your computer's hard drive, the audio and video information is now ready to be digitally assembled and manipulated with the aid of a nonlinear editing program. Just as word processors liberated many writers and desktop publishing programs empowered publishers, desktop video editing programs are expanding the creative and communication possibilities for many people.

Desktop video is a rather mature market, following the success of video editing hardware and software on late-'80s Macintosh and Commodore Amiga computers. However, the advent of DV and FireWire cards challenged the capabilities of industry standards, such as Adobe Premiere, and led to the introduction of entirely new, feature-packed DV editing software such as the highly rated Radius EditDV and Canopus RexEdit.

Today, Adobe Premiere and Ulead Studio Pro have been completely redesigned to accommodate DV specifications while adding features more oriented towards long form projects. Additionally, higher-end programs such as In:Sync's Speed Razor also offer DV support.

These established programs and more recently developed software packages such as Apple's Final Cut Pro, compete heavily to keep up with the evolving hardware. This greatly benefits the user by providing some of the most economical and most powerful video editing software ever.

However, the increasing number of video editing programs can make it complicated to pick the program that will best suit your needs. This is especially true given the customization that some manufacturers are using to improve the performance of their FireWire cards. In this scenario, you can have two similar hardware cards relying on Adobe Premiere as their primary editing software. However, they have much different features.

For this reason, as you compare video editing packages remember that it is important to keep these comparisons in the context of the other components of the system. A great editing program can be handicapped by a poor DV capture and playback program.

Apple's Final Cut Pro is quickly becoming the preferred package for serious DV filmmaking. The program incorporates many of the best features of the high-end system (such as Avid), as well as the best features of graphics programs (such as Adobe After Effects). While the $1,000 price may deter many low-budget producers, the program offers unsurpassed versatility and power. For those working on simple projects or short films, Apple's iMovie program may suffice, despite its limited features.

The Linear Lineage of Nonlinear Editing

Most nonlinear editing programs operate using an interface modeled after a traditional *linear editing* system. On linear systems, one or more videotape player machines operate as a *source deck* that is connected to a videotape recorder that serves as the *record deck*. The source deck and record deck are both connected to monitors. Since the final program is assembled on the tape in the record deck, the monitor attached to it is called the Program Monitor.

In a minimum configuration, the decks are manually controlled, while most systems use an edit controller to control the source deck(s) and the record deck.

To perform an edit, the tape is fast forwarded or rewound as necessary to find the desired scene. Once the scene is found, the tape is cued to the specific point at the start of the shot that is to be added to the program. This is called the *source in point*.

Similarly, the point on the record deck where the shot is to be recorded is called the *record in point*. An *out point* that designates the point at which to stop recording the shot can be set on the source deck and/or the record deck.

The editor also has an option of selecting whether the video and one or more channels of audio are recorded on the record deck; the video is recorded without audio; and one or more channels of audio is to be recorded without video. Editing systems using multiple video players, called A/B roll systems, can also designate the type of transition, i.e. dissolves, wipes, fades, etc., that will be used between shots.

After these decisions have been made, the editor actually records the edit. Once it is complete, he/she can review it on the program monitor to determine if it meets his/her expectations. If it does, then on to the next edit. If not, then the editor can reset the in points and out points, using a trim function to slightly cheat the points one direction or another until the timing is just right.

The nonlinear editing programs in use today incorporate these concepts. Instead of a source monitor, most programs use a source window. The DV clips you carefully select, name, and organize using your capture program will be arranged in a computer folder or window, usually called a bin, that is close to the source window. A clip can be dragged to the source window where it can be viewed and trimmed to select just the right portion for the correct length of time.

Then, instead of a record deck to edit to, nonlinear software uses a timeline that allows you to sequentially arrange your clips to build your program. A selected video and/or audio clip can be dragged from the source window to the timeline where it can be inserted at any point in the program.

Nonlinear editing derives its name from this ability to non-sequentially create a project by easily adding, deleting, or reordering scenes at will, unlike linear editing, which requires tremendous pre-planning because a program must be gradually built in order, scene-by-scene. This is because it is very difficult and compromises quality to insert a scene between others already recorded on tape.

Once you have assembled your clips and selected transitions between them, the work-in-progress and finished program can be viewed in the program window.

Nonlinear Editing Software Features

The list of features offered by video editing programs changes steadily. However some standards have evolved. Many were adapted from high-end editing systems in recognition of the closing performance gap between them and the low-cost systems. Among the most common features of NLE software are:

- Multiple Track Timelines
- Programmable Transitions
- Special Effects
- Titles (a.k.a. Character Generator)
- Audio Editing Functions
- Standardized Keyboard Shortcuts
- Multiple Levels of Undo
- Project Management
- Edit Decision List
- Plug-In Support
- Timeline Playback

Multiple Track Timelines—Projects can be assembled using multiple audio and video tracks which can be played back simultaneously. This allows you to build complex soundtracks or layer tracks of video to combine and create composite images.

Most programs allow for dozens of tracks, with some systems only limited by your computer's capabilities. Variables can be set to control the relationships between tracks. Management tools allow tracks to be named, grouped, and prioritized.

Programmable Transitions—Once you have laid clips on the timeline, you can select the manner in which they will transition from one to another. In addition to the common transitions found on linear editing systems, nonlinear editing programs offer a vast, diverse assortment of customizable transitions. Additional transitions are also frequently available for purchase as plug-ins.

These can range from a simple *page turn* where one clip appears to be turned like a sheet of paper to reveal the next clip, to advanced 3D *digital video effects* (DVE) that allow clips to transition by flying, twisting, and zooming about the screen.

Since these effects are created by the software, before the transition can be viewed, the computer must first *render* it by performing all of the calculations required for every video frame that is being changed and/or combined. Rendering can be a very time consuming process that is not very conducive to experimentation.

Most editors assemble their program then go back and add transitions later. Some editing programs offer an option to spend less time by rendering test transitions at a lower resolution, then at full resolution before recording onto tape.

Special Effects—In addition to providing computer-generated transitions between clips, nonlinear software also allows for video clips to be modified using a variety of special effects. Most video effects offered by your video camera can be reproduced in the editing software. Other commonly found effects allow you to perform useful functions like:

- Color correction to modify the color attributes of a video clip or the entire program.
- Contrast and brightness changes to balance exposure differences.
- Chroma keying or luminance keying of video to allow for the solid color background of one clip to be replaced with video images.
- Compositing video and graphics to combine video clips with computer-generated graphics such as animations.
- Picture-in-picture to shrink a video clip down and display it over another clip.

Special effects can also come in the form of optional additions to the software, called *filters*, which can be used to modify characteristics of the video in a predetermined pattern. Filters can be used to perform effects such as blurring video or creating artificial lens flares or more sophisticated *organic effects* that use patterns which mimic the characteristics of nature such as rain, fire, and snow.

As with transitions, the special effects are only limited by the creativity of the programmers and the computer's processing speed.

Titles (a.k.a. Character Generator)—Computer-generated titles and simple graphics were one of the earliest applications of computers in video production. Nonlinear editing software usually includes a program that allows you to enter lines or pages of text, then specify how it appears on the screen, either over a computer generated background or superimposed over video.

The manner in which the text transitions on and off the screen, or to other text, can be set. Text attributes such as the typestyle or font, color, shadows, and translucency can be easily specified.

Additional fonts can be added to the software and many programs now allow you to use the wide range of True Type fonts freely, which are available from many sources.

Another important feature of titling programs is the ability to anti-alias text to reduce the jagged, digital looking lines and curves that frequently plague computer generated text. This problem is very common in text with a lot of fine details and thin lines. Anti-aliasing uses high resolution variations in color to smooth text, often making a substantial difference.

Audio editing functions offer the benefits of the nonlinear environment to allow you to perform a variety of audio manipulations, such as:

- Adjusting volume levels, based upon VU meter readings, either in real-time during playback or while making changes on the timeline.
- Panning speakers to produce surround sound encoded programs.
- Mixing audio tracks to combine them and/or adjust their relative levels.
- Applying filters to change the sound characteristics and create special effects in audio clips. These can be used for everything from eliminating background noises to creating mechanized voices.
- Waveform editing allows audio clips to be displayed as visual graphs that can be used for very precise editing.

As mentioned previously, support for native DV audio formats is another important feature used to avoid resampling audio which can cause periodic distortions. Additionally, if you are shooting DVCAM or DVCPRO, support for locked audio is also a must.

Lastly, you should be aware that as with special effects and transitions, many audio effects must be rendered as well.

Standardized keyboard shortcuts have trickled down from high-end systems, most specifically the industry heavyweight Avid Systems.

In the high-priced world of hourly editing rates, speed and accuracy are priorities for editors and their clients. The evolution of keyboard shortcuts is from the realization that despite the simplicity offered by using a mouse to control editing functions and manipulate elements on the screen, keyboard commands substantially improve efficiency.

The availability of these shortcuts on your system will aid your editing with these programs should you have Avid experience or if you choose to work with an editor comfortable with an Avid. And if you are not experienced with an Avid, the shortcuts will help prepare you for future use of the system.

Multiple levels of undo offer the flexibility of trying out various arrangements of your clips, with the confidence that you can go back many steps and undo changes.

While this may at first seem like an insignificant function, it is actually one of the most liberating features of NLE software and is very conducive to creative experimentation.

Some programs allow you to name various levels of undo so you can quickly jump between them to compare different versions of a scene.

Project management tools in your editing software become very important as your project grows to include scenes featuring hundreds of clips arranged on multiple tracks. This includes tools for:

- Arranging clips.
- Selectively deleting portions of video not used to free up extra hard drive space.
- Making notes on various versions of the project.
- Backing up files, including important automatic save functions.
- Customizing setting per project.
- Customizing settings per user.

Edit decision lists (EDL) are data files that contain information on every critical aspect of the project including the arrangement, duration, and transitions between all of the video and audio elements. This list is assembled based on the time-code of these elements and the sequence of events.

This file allows you to easily recreate your project in your computer without having to back-up the huge video and audio files. The editing program simply reads the EDL, then prompts you to load specific tapes so that it can reload the required video and audio. Once the media has been reloaded, your project is reassembled on the timeline.

Some editing programs also export EDL files in industry standard EDL formats. This allows you to use the file in a professional editing suite, saving you time and money since you have already made your editing decisions on your computer.

Plug-in support allows you to expand the features of your editing software and customize it to better meet your needs. Software lacking support for plug-ins must rely on the manufacturer's responsiveness to frequent users' requests to make changes or additions to the software.

Timeline playback—While nearly all editing software allows you to play your timeline and display your project on your computer monitor, some systems do not allow you to simultaneously view the video on your video monitor. These set-ups require that your project first be sent to the DV capture and playback program.

Additionally, some systems do not allow you to playback your entire video from the timeline without first using a *make movie* command that lets the computer know to prepare for this process. This step includes rendering transitions, special effects, titles, and audio effects.

In recognition of many user's desire to *preview* a program before investing time to fully render, some software packages offer the option of playback with partially rendered transitions.

Other Useful Software

Nonlinear editing software performs many functions. However, sometimes your software may lack features or the integrated features are not enough to meet your specific requirements. In these situations you may need to use a specialized computer program that offers more professional features, greater control, and more precise functionality. Some of the most frequently used software includes titling programs such as Crystal Graphics 3D Impact Pro ($99) and TitleDeko ($200). These offer far more fonts, transitions, 3D movement, and special effects than found in the titling programs included with editing software.

Graphics compositing and special effects programs are used for extensive manipulation of video and motion graphics. Adobe After Effects is undoubtedly the leading compositing software package. While it is an expensive program, and mastering it takes a substantial investment of time, After Effects provides unparalleled flexibility when combining and manipulating video and motions graphics. In addition to being a powerful program on its own, After Effects is supported with an incredible array of plug-ins from dozens of other companies.

Many companies offer outstanding special effect plug-ins for the major editing packages. Low cost plug-ins such as Pixelan Software's Video Spice Rack add hundreds of 2D transitions and effects, while more costly programs such as Boris FX Pro and MetaCreations' Final Effects add top quality 3D effects.

Animation programs allow you to create 2D or 3D graphics and special effects that you can incorporate into your projects. Many of the top packages such as Kinetix 3D Studio Max, Softimage 3D, and Newtek's Lightwave cost thousands of dollars and require very powerful computers.

However, there are less expensive programs that are still quite functional on the average PC or Mac. MetaCreations Infini-D has some features comparable to the high-end software. And programs such as Ray Dream Studio combined with Ray Dream Studio 3D provide a good introduction to 3D animation.

If you have an interest in 3D character animation, the MetaCreations' program Poser provides complete sets of 3D models and parts with pre-programmed motion characteristics that can be combined to create characters with natural, realistic movement.

Audio editing programs compensate for the shortcomings of your editing software by allowing for even more precise audio monitoring, editing, and effects. Expensive programs like DigiDesign's Pro Tools cost several thousand dollars and are used for the complex sound editing required for the hundreds of audio tracks used in studio feature films.

In the hands of a skilled operator with a keen ear, lower priced software like the tremendously popular program, Sound Forge from Sonic Foundry, provides professional-level sound editing that can be used to salvage poor production sound and/or create elaborate multi-tracked dialogue, music, and sound effect tracks.

Incredibly, one of the most popular Windows audio editing programs is a shareware program called CoolEdit. A full-featured trial version is available for download from several websites. For a $50 registration fee a version with more features is offered, while a ($300) professional version provides for up to 64 tracks of digital recording.

Use the Internet as your resource for free software, shareware, or trial versions of popular applications. You can find hundreds of valuable editing programs, special effects filters, royalty free music and sound effects, and storyboarding tools by visiting some of sites listed in the appendix of this handbook.

DV Player/Record Device

With your computer hardware and software in place, the final element of your DV editing system will be the DV camera or DV deck that you will use to play and record your DV tapes. As previously mentioned, software CODEC FireWire cards will require a DV device to be connected to view video from the computer on a video monitor.

The Camera as a Player/Recorder

Many people rely on their DV camera as a DV player/recorder during editing. While this option works fine for short projects and saves on the cost of purchasing or renting a DV deck, it presents several disadvantages that can potentially become serious inconveniences or problems. This is especially true when editing for many weeks and months.

First, is the basic inconvenience of having to keep the camera attached to the computer, thereby making it unavailable for other uses. However, even more of a practical concern is the fact that DV camcorders cannot be used to record programs longer than eighty minutes. If you have a ninety-minute program you will be required to record it on two separate tapes, then later edit them together in an editing suite.

Another, less obvious problem is that the mechanics of consumer DV cameras were not designed to meet the demands of editing environments which require more frequent fast forwarding, rewinding, playback, and recording of short segments. Editing places much more wear and tear on your camera than normal recording conditions.

Also, because of concerns about piracy and commercial tape duplication, many early DV cameras do not allow you to input analog video. If your project requires you to use footage shot in a non-DV format, you will be required to utilize some other means of transferring your tapes to DV.

As long as you are aware of these issues, you can undoubtedly use a player/recorder for editing, but if you plan on doing many projects, you may want to consider a more durable and more flexible DV or DVCAM deck.

DV and DVCAM Decks

DV and DVCAM decks are available as small portable units and full-sized studio decks. Most portable decks have a maximum sixty-minute capacity with mini-DV or forty-two minutes with mini-DVCAM tapes.

While this is a liability in many situations, portable decks are very useful for editing on location, especially the several models that have built-in color monitors. However, if you are producing a feature film or a documentary running longer than sixty minutes, a full-sized DV or DVCAM deck will provide you the means for completing your entire project at your desktop.

Full-sized decks can playback and record mini-DV tapes without adapters. Full-sized tapes can be used that offer up to 4.5 hours of recording time. DV decks can record on DVCAM tapes, but not playback DVCAM video. DVCAM decks can playback DV and DVCAM tapes.

The Sony DHR-1000 was the first DV editing deck available. In addition to the I.link (FireWire) interface, it also features analog input, a detachable editing tray with a jog/shuttle knob, built-in editing capabilities, and a Control-L port to interface with other video equipment.

The Sony DV Walkman GV-D900 and model GV-D300 are portable DV decks that can be battery-operated. The GV-D900 has a built-in color LCD monitor and speakers. A comparable DVCAM model, the DSR-DV10, is also available. All three decks feature I.link interfaces and analog input and output.

Full-sized DV and DVCAM tapes can be used in DVCAM decks, such as the very portable Sony DSR-20, the DSR-30 with its built-in editing panel, and the DSR-80 which is designed to interface into component editing suites. With the benefits of the DVCAM format, the DSR-20 and DSR-30 actually represent a better value than the DHR-1000.

If you are using a hardware CODEC FireWire card, you also have the option of using an internal DV transport card that fits into your computer like a floppy disc drive or CD-ROM drive. When used with these cards, the Sony DRV-100 ($1,300) DV tape drive and DRV-1000 ($1500) DVCAM tape drive can playback and record mini-DV and mini-DVCAM tapes. While limited by the record time of the mini tapes, these drives provide a completely self-contained DV editing system.

Using Analog Video with DV Decks

If you have archives of analog footage that won't work with your digital camcorder or DV deck, there is a way to transfer that footage via FireWire to your desktop editing software. There are several products, most notably Sony's DVMC-DA1 Media Converter, which ingeniously converts incoming analog audio and video into a DV-compressed stream. The $500 converter box contains input and output connections for serial cables, composite jacks, and FireWire. This means you can connect your old video camcorder to the DA1 converter box by a serial or composite cable, then attach a FireWire cable to your PC or DVcam and begin the export in real-time. The converter box also sends digital signals to analog devices, and has the ability to mix several sources—so you could plug in a digital voice track with analog background sounds, then output a combined signal of 16-bit, CD-quality audio.

Selecting a DV Editing System

With a thorough understanding of the components that make up a DV editing system, and a pre-determined budget, you can begin the process of determining which system will best meet your needs. Hopefully, by now it is apparent that this will require you to scrutinize the entire integration of the hardware and software for a particular system, as opposed to generic answers about the strengths and weaknesses of individual parts.

The manufacturers, models, features, and prices listed below are to serve as a starting point for your search. As with the other references in this book, take time to explore the latest information for yourself.

Since most FireWire cards are shipped with DV capture/playback and editing software, begin your search by reading the spec sheets from various FireWire card vendors. Request demo videotapes from companies that offer them. Seek input from mail order companies, such as The Electronic Mailbox (www.videoguys.com), which have liberal open-door policies for answering questions.

As you narrow your selection based upon a comparison of features, begin to seek feedback from current users. Again, the Internet mailing list, newsgroups and message forums are a great place to start. Additionally, you can contact local vendors and value added resellers to seek referrals to current customers.

If possible, visit retailers to seek a demo, or even better, ask for an opportunity to use the system for an hour or two. And finally, as you prepare to purchase your system, be certain you understand the company's customer support and return policy in case you should have difficulty with your system.

Digital Linear Editing

The creative and technical advantages of nonlinear editing systems have rapidly established nonlinear editing as the first choice for many editors. However, linear editing, particularly digital linear editing, continues to be a technically viable option. However, the lack of careful planning can result in digital linear editing costing thousands of dollars to complete.

About Digital Linear Editing Systems

Digital editing equipment first became popular in professional editing suites in the early '90s. The top of the line D-1 video format, with the benefits of digital component video, was particularly suited for creating multi-layered and computer effect intensive projects. While the less expensive D-2 format used composite video, but still offered the advantages of minimal image degradation from one copy to the next.

The introduction of the digital Betacam format allowed digital to become practical for field recording. And in the editing suite, digital Betacam offers component video at a lower cost than D-1.

Digital editing systems built around this professional editing equipment can cost hundreds of thousands of dollars. A single D-1 recorder alone can cost close to $100,000. But the fact is, for projects recorded in the DV or DVCAM format, the audio and video quality offered by a $3,000 DV nonlinear editing system is technically on par and, in some cases, superior to editing DV on these far more expensive digital systems.

The DV system may lack the speed and functionality found in high end digital systems, but the ability to edit in the native DV format is an important advantage.

DV Device to DV Device Linear Editing

DV linear editing systems are also available. In fact, many DV cameras and decks feature built-in editing functions which, in a worst case scenario, you can use to edit via FireWire from one DV device to another. This option will only allow you to perform cuts from one shot to another. However, if you plan properly, you can use the in camera effects to create fades, dissolves, and wipes commonly offered in A/B roll editing suites.

Sony offers the DSRM-E1 edit controller which offers a limited amount of memory to record editing decisions and control DV devices without built-in controllers. The control-L connector on most DV devices allows them to be controlled by a number of compatible edit controllers.

This editing arrangement is less than ideal for long projects. It does not offer the precision and features required for elaborate projects. Additionally, there is the risk of damaging your DV source tapes, particularly given the fragile nature of DV tapes that make them prone to stretching and curving when used in linear editing.

One way to reduce this risk is to use your source tapes as little as possible. This can be accomplished by making VHS copies of your footage that can be used for review and basic editing decision purposes. This will reduce the fast forwarding or rewinding of the DV tapes to find your next shot when editing. Additionally, you should always create backup copies of your source tapes.

When to Use a Digital Linear System

Concerns regarding damaged source tapes are just one reason to consider editing in a professional digital linear suite, other reasons include:

- When mixing DV footage with digital Betacam;
- If you have access to a digital linear editing suite or if you are able to negotiate a good deal with an editing facility;
- If you currently own or have access to a 3/4", S-VHS, or Betacam SP linear system, but want to create a high quality digital master tape; and
- If you currently own or have access to a non-DV nonlinear editing system, and you want the best digital master tape possible.

Editing DV Footage on a Digital Linear System

With digital linear editing suites costing hundreds of dollars per hour, it is of the utmost importance that you properly plan for the steps involved as you edit your project. Otherwise, you could end up spending far more than you planned or anticipated.

The basic process of editing your DV tapes in a digital linear editing suite is as follows:

- Select Your Digital Editing Facility. Solicit their feedback early in the process.
- Digitally Copy Your DV Tapes to Digital Betacam. Be certain the dubs are done using the SDI connector. Most editing facilities have added professional DVCAM or DVCPRO decks to their digital linear editing suites. However, in most cases you will have more protection for your source tapes by dubbing them to digital

Betacam, a more durable editing format that uses standard SMPTE time code.

- Create Time Coded Window Dubs. Dub the digital Betacam tapes to VHS and the tape format (S-VHS, 3/4", or Betacam SP) you will be using for the offline edit prior to going into the digital editing suite for the online edit.
- Review Your Footage on VHS. The VHS tapes allow you the luxury of logging and reviewing footage at home.
- Offline Edit Your Project. Use a linear or nonlinear system to create a version of the project that represents all of your editing decisions. If possible, use a system that generates an edit decision list in a file format compatible with that used by your digital editing facility. If not, use a logging program such as Abbate Video's Video Toolkit ($280) to manually enter the edit points to create an EDL file. Or as a last option, create a detailed written EDL by sequentially listing the in point and out point for every shot in your program.
- Online Your Project. Take your digital Betacam tapes and your EDL file, or written EDL, to the facility and watch the meter start running as shots are edited from the digital Betacam source tapes to the digital Betacam master tape. Titles will also be added at this time.
- If you have prepared properly, the process will be nearly automated. If not, watch your allocated time and/or money slip away.
- Color Correct the Onlined Video. Create a new master tape from the completed digital Betacam master, adjusting color, brightness, and contrast between shots and scenes. Since you are working in digital, this important step does not degrade the image quality.
- Create Copies of the Onlined Video. These 3/4", Betacam SP, or digital Betacam copies, will be used during sound editing, depending on the arrangement. Some sound editors will copy the audio to DAT.
- Edit Sound. Sound can be digitally edited as outlined in the next chapter.
- Copy Mixed Soundtrack Back Onto Master Tape. Use the original time code. If everything was monitored properly during the sound edit and mix then sync should not be a problem.

With this final step completed, your DV footage will have been successfully edited on a linear digital system.

Non-DV Native Nonlinear

Next in the hierarchy of DV editing solutions is the option of completing your project using one of the many non-DV native nonlinear editing systems now available. The selections available range from a stand alone editing machine to low-cost, professional video capture cards and high end nonlinear systems.

Non-DV Native Nonlinear?

Most nonlinear editing systems rely on some form of compression to reduce the size of video files down to make them more manageable. Prior to the introduction of the DV format, a compression scheme called MJPEG (Motion JPEG) had become the standard for nonlinear editing systems.

Derived from JPEG (Joint Photographic Expert Group), a still photo compression standard, MJPEG allows for scaleable compression that provides a means to vary compression rates and image quality as required for your project. A low compression rate offers high quality video but consumes a lot of disk space, while high compression rates significantly improve storage capacity at the expense of video quality.

VIDEO QUALITY @ VARIOUS MJPEG COMPRESSION RATES		
Video Quality	Compression Rate	Minutes of Video/Gig.
VHS	11:1-8.5:1	12 min.
SVHS	7:1-5:1	7 min.
Betacam SP	4.8:1	4 min.

MJPEG is currently used in nearly all non-DV native nonlinear editing systems. To edit DV format video using these systems you must either:

- Digitize your video footage using the analog output of your camera or deck connected to the analog input on the edit system;
- Dub your DV to Betacam SP and digitize from a Betacam SP deck; or
- Use a FireWire card to transfer the DV into the computer. However, before the DV can be used, the system must first convert it to MJPEG.

Although all three methods are frequently used with success, they do result in the conversion of your digital data. And as previously mentioned, every conversion from DV to analog or another digital format can add artifacts or noise to your video. With this in mind, let's take a look at some of the popular MJPEG-based systems you can use to edit your project.

Stand-Alone Editing Machines

The Casablanca, by Draco Systems Inc., is an incredible stand alone, broadcast-quality nonlinear editing machine featuring three tracks of audio, a character generator, and an assortment of special effects. The unit is slightly larger than a VCR and not much more difficult to set-up. All you do is plug it in, attach it to your television, connect your camera or VCR, set a few settings and you're ready to start editing using a trackball to control the menu driven options.

Your footage can be input into the Casablanca via the SVHS connectors or using the optional FireWire card. However, the system still converts the DV to MJPEG to edit. While the Casablanca software can be upgraded using the built-in floppy disk drive, the unit is dedicated to editing and cannot be used for other computing purposes. This make the machine unsuitable for people seeking to use some of the popular editing or graphic programs.

However, the Casablanca's simple set-up, ease of use, and excellent video quality, make it very appealing to people desiring to spend minimal time getting a system up and running or learning to use a complex editing program.

In the Los Angeles area, the Casablanca can be rented for as little as $675 per week, far less than the cost of other nonlinear systems.

Video Capture Cards

There are numerous low-cost video capture cards, which when used with the right computer, hard drives, and software, can provide broadcast quality video recording and playback of analog video. These cards are very popular with event and wedding videographers, as well as small to mid-sized production companies producing local cable ads.

If you own or have access to one of these systems, it can also be used to edit your project. However, again there will be some compromise in video quality as a result of using the SVHS video inputs.

The lower priced cards such as the Truevision Bravado 2000 and the Pinnacle Systems Miro DC-30plus can provide good results. However, the higher priced cards like the Miro DC-50 and DSP Perception PVR offer substantial improvements in video quality and the benefits of component output so you can record your videotape master on digital Betacam or Beta SP tape. This will result in a much higher quality video master than using the SVHS out offered by the less expensive cards.

If you are using one of the lower quality capture cards, you may want to consider simply using your system to create an offline cut of your project. Then take your tapes into a professional editing facility and edit them, creating your video master on a digital or analog linear editing system.

High-End Nonlinear Editing Systems

With the abundance of systems available, especially in major metropolitan areas, you can often find good deals on an Avid or Media 100 nonlinear editing system. For example, in the Los Angeles area an online quality Avid can be rented for about $1,200 per week. Or even better, you might find an editor with his/her own system.

Whether renting an editing system or working with an editor, you will still be on another person's time and should be fully prepared. At the least, you should have reviewed VHS dubs of your footage and made notes about select shots and scenes.

For more thorough preparation, check with the editor about an optional logging computer program, such as Media Logger, that might be available, to allow you to log footage on your home PC. With the computer file generated by a program like this you can save substantial time in your editing sessions.

Once in the edit suite, you will maintain the best video quality by using a DVCAM or DVCPRO deck to digitize your video footage. If that option is unavailable, then your next choice is to dub your DV tapes to Beta SP (a component transfer if possible) and then digitize from the Beta SP tapes.

If hard drive space is limited, edit at a lower video resolution, then redigitize the final program at the highest resolution possible. In fact, if you are able to find a better deal on an early model Avid that only has offline resolution, you can use that system to edit offline, then take a disk with your EDL to another facility to redigitize the finished program at online quality.

When your online video is ready, record the final edited program on to digital Betacam, if at all possible. Digital Betacam decks cost several hundred dollars per day to rent, but the expense is worth it to have a top quality master tape. And in most cases, your program will have to be transferred to digital Betacam prior to a video-to-film transfer.

Of course, if your budget doesn't permit the luxury of a digital Betacam master at the moment, then a Beta SP master tape will do.

Analog Linear Editing

As a final option, you can complete your project using a traditional Betacam SP A/B roll editing suite. Given the popularity and availability of nonlinear editing and digital editing suites, linear editing rooms can often be booked at excellent rates.

If the editing suite has DVCAM or DVCPRO decks, you will be able to use your source tapes directly. But before you do, be certain to make FireWire backup copies of all of them in case there should be any problems with the machines. The last thing you want is for your months of work to be chewed up by a dirty deck.

If DVCAM or DVCPRO decks are unavailable, you will need to transfer your DV tapes to Betacam SP as specified in previous sections. You will also need to create VHS dubs for logging purposes, as well as 3/4" or SVHS dubs if you decide to create an offline cut.

Additionally, there are a couple of issues to keep in mind about editing on an analog linear system. First, and most importantly, you must remember that linear editing systems create dissolves and certain transitions by switching from a shot on the tape in deck A to a shot on the tape in deck B. However, you are unable to create transitions between shots that are on the same tape. Two shots on tape A can be cut to tape one after the other, but they cannot transition in any other way.

To get around this, you will be required to create additional copies of select shots for the B deck. When making these copies, always be certain to make them from your original DV tapes.

Along the same lines, always remember that every time you make a copy of an analog tape you are losing a generation of video quality. If the quality of the original footage was noisy, then any subsequent copies will become noticeably more deteriorated. This problem is the reason for going digital in the first place.

9
■■■■■ DV Film
Post-Production

Congratulations, you've made it through principal photography and you are now almost a filmmaker! Post-production brings about a whole new set of exciting possibilities and frustrating challenges. However, given the affordability of DV editing equipment, there is an exciting new scenario for feature film post-production.

In the not so long ago days of film editing on film (as opposed to computers), filmmakers would rent huge motorized editing machines then spend weeks or months physically cutting and *splicing* (taping) their film together. While they could edit like this independently, throughout the process they were dependent on various expensive lab services to advance from one stage to the next.

Today, with the hardware and software specified in the last chapter, an understanding of the post-production process, and a self imposed standard of excellence, you can sit alone at a desktop computer in the comfort of your own home, and professionally complete every post-production step necessary to finish your DV film, with the exception of the video-to-film transfer. And there are even a couple of innovative filmmakers experimenting with that.

Plus, as an added benefit, if you own your equipment or have access to equipment, you can do like the big boys in Hollywood and go back and re-shoot or rework scenes as necessary!

But we're getting ahead of ourselves. Let's take a look at an overview of the steps you will have to take to turn those hours of footage into a cohesive story.

DV Film Post-Production

Organize Your Post-Production Team

↓

Log Your Footage

↓

Edit Your Rough Cut

↓

Preview Your Rough Cut

↓

Edit Your Fine Cut

↓

Add Titles & Lock Picture

↓

Create and/or License Your Music

↓

Edit & Mix Sound

↓

Create Your Master Tape

↓

Reproduce Videotapes or DVD or
Treat Video To Look Like Film or
Prepare For Video-to-Film Transfer

Editing Your Own Project

While the availability and powerful features of DV nonlinear editing systems offer you the option of working alone to complete your film, your project will probably benefit from the creative input and experience of an editor.

Among many novice filmmakers, editing is probably one of the least respected aspects of the filmmaking process. The common school of thought appears to be that as long as everything goes right during principal photography, editing is just a matter of connecting shots and scenes as per the shooting script.

However, the reality is that even on the best managed shoot, not everything goes smoothly. Scenes are cut out or compressed, coverage is limited, audio is ruined, lines are flubbed or missed, or many other unexpected difficulties.

The job of the editor is to take what is provided and work with the director to shape it into a story that represents the director's vision as refined by the realities of principal photography. But a good editor is more than just a technician performing the mechanics for the director. The editor is also an artist offering the director a fresh, expanded perspective of the many hours of the raw footage in the context of the whole story. This is the benefit of working with someone else to edit your project.

Often when editing our own projects, we lack the ability and willingness to detach ourselves and objectively rethink scenes, or in some cases, the entire story. An editor you trust and with whom you can communicate well can provide this for you. I have seen incredible improvements in films that have been re-edited by a professional.

Even if you should choose to edit yourself, an experienced editor can offer suggestions on your rough cut that can challenge you to rethink your approach to a scene.

Your Post-Production Team

Just as you built a team of talented collaborators for principal photography, you can also assemble a post-production team to accent your personal strengths and weaknesses. Among the most important post-production personnel are the:

- Editor—Operates editing equipment and constructs scenes from select shots based upon an understanding of the director's intention and the story.
- Assistant Editor—Provides administrative assistance to the editor and director such as logging footage and keeping track of notes.
- Online Editor—Operates the high end editing suite that you may or may not use to create your video master. The online editor can also be a colorist, who is skilled with adjusting color, brightness, and contrast of images.
- Sound Editor—Edits and mixes existing dialogue, sound effects, and music tracks while also building new tracks as necessary.
- Music Supervisor—Coordinates all creative, technical, and legal aspects of any music used in the project.
- Composer—Creates original soundtrack elements to accent visual action on screen.

Selecting an Editor

As with the other people you worked with during principal photography, an editor must be selected based upon talent, availability, and compatibility. Your search for an editor can begin while you are still seeking to fill your other crew positions.

By involving your editor early, you gain the benefit of being able to consult him/her about the way you intend on shooting a particular scene. Additionally, it is advantageous for the editor to become familiar with the story and characters.

Although you will not be under pressure to fill this position prior to principal photography, you should still include it when listing your other available crew positions in advertisements and on the Internet. And as always, networking will also generate leads.

As candidates respond, ask to see a reel of their work. As you review the reel, look past fancy editing and effects to try to identify a person with an obvious familiarity to the concepts of storytelling structure.

One of the unfortunate realities as a result of the accessibility of editing systems is that many people are now learning how to operate the equipment, without having an understanding of important editing concepts like continuity, pacing, and structure. Editing a fast-paced, thirty-second commercial or a music video is much different than editing a two-minute scene properly paced to be engaging, while still allowing for dramatic subtleties to unfold.

It is also important to work with an editor who feels genuinely connected with your story and characters. Provide prospective editors with a copy of your shooting script and notes on changes made during the shoot. Then listen attentively to comments to gauge his/her interpretation without your input.

When considering an editor who has never worked on a long form project, be certain to reiterate that between completing a rough cut and the fine cut, the editing timeline can extend for many weeks. It's great to work with a person who is very enthusiastic, but you want to be certain that energy can be sustained for the long haul.

Once you find an editor you want to work with and you come to an agreement, make sure you create a contract that outlines the terms.

Assistant Editor

If possible, allow your editor to select an assistant editor, since they will be working very closely together. The assistant must be well organized to efficiently manage and keep track of the numerous videotapes and paperwork such as script notes, tapes logs, and sound reports.

Additionally, an assistant editor should develop the ability to anticipate the needs of the editor and director. Ultimately a synchonicity must develop between the director, editor, and assistant editor.

If you find yourself in a situation where you have finished your shoot, but have not yet found an editor, you may want to bring in your own assistant to help you during the logging process.

Online Editor

You will require an online editor if you and/or your editor offline edit your project, then take it to another editing facility to create the master tape. This person will most likely be designated by the editing facility. However, this should not create any problems since you will not be making editorial changes to your project at this point. In most circumstances the online process is nearly automated.

The skill of an online editor is more relevant if the editor is also doing color correction on your final program. Color correction requires a person with a good eye for subtle visual details and the knowledge of the relevant color characteristic required to be changed to make shots match.

Prior to committing to an online editing facility, visit various shops and have potential colorists review select scenes to gauge their feedback. Also, seek referrals from other editors and directors of photography.

Sound Editor

The sound editor picks up where your production sound mixer leaves off. His/her job is to take all of the synchronized and wild sound elements recorded during principal photography and combine them with sound effects and music to create soundtracks that accentuate the visual images.

Sound editing is also a very precise and highly detail-oriented task. Like a production sound mixer, a good sound editor can discern sounds and noises that initially get past most of us, but could be very noticeable in a theatrical setting.

Just as important as having a good ear, is the sound editor's knowledge of the equipment and techniques required to eliminate problems and make audio sound the best as possible.

You can find sound editors by contacting post-production sound facilities. You can also solicit referrals from experienced production sound mixers.

Selecting a Music Supervisor and Composer

For individuals unfamiliar with the creative and legal aspects of music production, rights, and licensing, a music supervisor can be an important link to ensuring you legally have the best music possible for your project. Similarly, a composer can be crucial for creating music specifically tailored for the mood and themes of your story.

A music supervisor works with the director to determine the musical requirements of the film, once again based upon the director's vision for the story. The music supervisor helps translate this vision into specific genres of music, then begins the process of seeking recording artists and/or a composer to fulfill this need.

From the business perspective, a music supervisor will work with an attorney and use his/her knowledge of the music business to help negotiate the appropriate rights for music for the films and/or soundtrack. Music supervisors can come out of the business or artistic side of the music business.

It is often difficult to find an experienced music supervisor willing to work on low budget projects without distribution in place because many recording artists and record labels are only willing to work with films that have distribution deals. However, if your story is strong enough, you can network to find former record label employees or independent producers with an interest in music supervising.

One of the most important issues to look out for when considering a music supervisor is to be certain that you connect with a person who's agenda is you and your story. It is not at all uncommon to encounter individuals that primarily see your project as an opportunity to further their own agenda.

For an artistically inclined music supervisor this may mean that he/she wants to produce most of the music you will be using, even if it is not the most appropriate. Business oriented music supervisors may have loyalties to the label or artists they bring to you. These agendas will begin to become obvious as you spend an increasing amount of time and effort in trying to keep a person on track with your desires.

The contract between you and your music supervisor will probably be one of the most complicated as there are a number of directions in which the relationship and business arrangement can go, especially where soundtrack deals are involved. Have your lawyer create a contract that protects you and your film from overly ambitious, unethical music industry people, while rewarding those who take a chance, should the film become successful.

Composer

If your film's soundtrack is largely comprised of a musical score, you might want to forego a music supervisor and work solely with a composer. While the same concerns about music rights are relevant, you will only be negotiating with one party, which greatly simplifies things.

As with everyone else involved in creative aspects of the film production, you must work with a composer who has a clear understanding of your vision for the film. And you both must possess the ability to clearly communicate with each other. Unlike a typical musician, a composer for films must have the ability to think musically and visually. And he/she must be able to create music timed to the visual events, whether a ten second transition or a five minute opening sequence.

There are many novice and veteran musicians seeking to score quality film projects. You can contact local music symphonies, conservatories and organizations in order to obtain referrals. And now, many composers post sample works on the Internet which you can also review.

Carefully, evaluate demo audio and videotapes listening for musical ability and diversity. If possible, ask candidates if they would be willing to create a short piece for a sample scene.

Once you have selected a composer and you have agreed on the terms of your working arrangement, have a contract drawn up before beginning any work together.

Logging Your Footage

In the early stages of post-production, there is an incredible sense of accomplishment as you sit down in front of a tape deck and video monitor with a box full of tapes representing the fruits of your labor thus far. However, unless you take steps to organize the material and properly prepare for editing, you will almost certainly find yourself overwhelmed by trying to keep track of all the details. How will you find that beautiful five second sunrise shot among hours of footage?

When using your own editing system you have the luxury of sorting through tapes to find shots as you require them. This is not the most efficient way of proceeding, but you do have that option. But if you are editing on someone else's system, then you will need to create a log of your footage that will help you make the best use of your time in the editing suite.

Logging tapes is the process of viewing tapes and creating a record of every shot, noting the unique tape number that was assigned during principal photography, the shot's position on the tape, details about the technical quality, and other notes such as the actor's performances. Many of these details replicate information from daily script notes taken by the script supervisor and sound reports from the production sound mixer. Note that they are not a substitute for viewing tapes and logging footage. Although sometimes tedious and time consuming to create, a good log ultimately saves time and money.

Paper Logs

The most basic manner of logging footage is to view time-code window dubs of your video and create a handwritten paper log. The typical log page header and column headings are as follows:

TAPE LOG			
Production Title: Hacks **Director/Producer:** Maxie Collier **Tape Number:** 2		**Date:** 5/5/97 **Camera:** T. Schnaidt **Page:** 1 of 2	
In TC: 00:00:00:00 *Out TC: 00:00:00:00*	*Scene#-* *Take#*	*Description*	*Notes*
In: 02:01:43:15 *Out:* 02:02:20:27	13a, # 1	Ext. Gas Station. WS-Gil pumps gas.	Good until gets in car.
In: 02:02:55:08 *Out:* 02:04:01:00	13b, # 4	Ext. Gas Station, Pickup, CU, Gil.	Lines flat. Good reaction.

In the above example, the header is pretty much self-explanatory. The in time code is the point at which the scene begins and the out time code is where it ends. In situations where you are unable to get a time code dub of your footage, you can log using the VCR's tape counter. For this to work, you must rewind the tape to the beginning, then reset the counter and log footage from start to finish without resetting the counter or changing tapes. This method is not nearly as precise as time code, but it will provide you a rough log.

The scene and take number, along with the description refer to the shot's position in the script. The notes provide comments you and/or the editor will refer to prior to digitizing or cueing up the shot.

One thing to keep in mind is that it is important to log ALL of the footage, not just what you consider usable. In many cases you can use a bit of the images from a take with bad audio, or bits of the audio for a take with visual problems.

Computer Logging

The process of logging tapes can be greatly expedited by the use of computer logging programs and the automatic tape scanning feature found on many nonlinear editing systems.

Basic computer logging programs run on your home PC and replace your pencil and paper to allow you to type in the same information you would be writing in a paper log. However, upon completion, you have a computer file that can be used by the editing system you will be working on. The file will allow the editing system to automatically batch digitize your clips and add the short descriptive names and notes you entered with the time code.

There are also logging programs available that include a controller card which connects your DV camera or deck to the computer and allows you to create a log by capturing time code directly from your videotapes. Videonics Video Toolkit ($260) is available for PCs, while E-trim ($595) by Eidria, Inc. operates on a portable PalmPilot computer to allow for logging to be performed on set or other locations outside of the editing room.

Automatic tape scanning greatly simplifies tape logging. You just pop your tape in, start the software, then return later with the starting and ending points for every shot neatly listed. Some programs also capture a still photo from the start of each shot and the end of each shot.

Next, you can go through the list and designate which scenes you want transferred to your hard drive, while at the same time naming clips and adding notes. Once this is complete, you can have the system batch capture the clips as well as save a file containing the log. You can also print the file for a quick reference during editing.

Editing Your Rough Cut

With your footage completely logged, you will be ready to begin editing a rough cut of your film. As the name implies, a rough cut is a preliminary version of the film that basically assembles all of the scenes together in order without taking a lot of time to refine specific scenes. A rough cut is typically much longer than the final cut of the film will be. In a painting analogy, the rough cut is the broad strokes that create an outline of the image.

Your rough cut may also be the offline version of your project if you are using a low resolution nonlinear editing system or a linear editing system with plans on later completing a higher quality online version.

Capturing Clips

To begin editing, you will need to provide the editor or assistant editor with the information necessary to capture all of the clips required for the scene. If you are using a paper log you will provide the time code for select takes.

If you are using a computer logging program, then use the file created by the software to have the DV or video capture program digitize the proper clips. Or perform automatic tape scanning as necessary to select and transfer the desired clips. When all of the clips required for a scene are in place on the editing system hard drive, it is time to become a craftsman and build your scene, and ultimately your film, shot by shot.

Assembling a Scene

There are three ways in which you can go about assembling a scene: using master shots, editing sequentially shot by shot, or editing to music or narration.

The traditional method is to record a master shot that covers all of the action in the scene. Once this shot is laid into the timeline or onto your master tape, you then go back and cut other shots such close-ups and cut-away shots into appropriate spots in the master shot. If you shot master shots for all of your scenes, you can quickly assemble your first rough cut by laying one master shot after the other without editing the individual scenes. This technique works well for providing a solid overview of the story, however in most cases the timing of the story will be significantly changed as you more finely edit individual scenes.

The second method is to assemble a scene sequentially by selecting each shot and laying it in order based upon your own and/or your editor's understanding of the available footage, the intentions of the scene, and scene's role in the entire story. This technique will help you create a rough cut that more accurately represents the correct length of scenes and the final film. However, it locks you into a specific pacing and structure more than starting with master shots. Rough cuts created in this manner must frequently be re-edited from the beginning in order to allow for radical changes.

The third method is to lay down an audio track such as music or narration, then go back and lay down the appropriate video clips in time to the audio. This method is often used for editing live music performances, music videos and montages.

You will probably use all three of these methods at various points in editing your rough cut. As you work on scenes for your rough cut, do not spend a lot of time trying to refine individual scenes. However, do begin to compile a list of scenes you may need to re-shoot or additional pick-up shots you may need to record to make a scene work better.

Basic Editing Concepts

The primary goal while editing is to arrange shots and scenes in an order that allows the story to unfold and characters to develop as per the director's intentions. This goal is accomplished by motivated edits, the continuity from one shot to another, the tempo created by the pace at which shots are edited, the compression and expansion of time, and the transitions used between scenes.

Motivated Editing

Every edit in a film should be motivated by the content of the scene. With so many of us influenced by the fast-paced editing of music videos and commercials, it is easy to forget that narrative storytelling is an entirely different structure. While people may be entertained by a rapid succession of abstract images for the short duration of music videos and commercials, most folks cannot endure these images for the ninety plus minutes of a feature film. Even abstract expression in narratives should be motivated by the story, character, plot, and theme.

This is not to say that the motivation for a specific cut must immediately be apparent to the audience. In fact, suspense is often created by the director concealing the reason he/she chose to draw attention to a specific image.

Continuity

Continuity is consistency from one shot to the next. Discontinuities distract the viewer by drawing attention to the fact that a scene is actually comprised of various shots recorded at different times. The primary areas of concern about continuity are:

- Continuity of action between shots is what allows you to cut from one angle to another and have the viewer perceive the action as being continuous. Performing a cut during continuous actions can help.
- Continuity of details relates to items such as the actor's appearance and props that must be consistent.
- Continuity of direction is when subjects are moving or facing the same direction between shots.
- Continuity of location is consistency in light levels, settings, and backgrounds.
- Continuity of audio is consistency in audio levels and more importantly the sound characteristics between different shots.

One of the most powerful aspects of editing is the ability to vary the context of a scene based upon the continuity or discontinuity of action between shots. Juxtaposition is the relationship between a shot and the shot preceding or following it.

By juxtaposing shots you can create entirely different perceptions of the meaning of a given shot. A classic example is how a close-up of a person looking surprised can either be perceived as a look of delight or a look of horror depending on the shot following it.

Similarly, discontinuity can be used to surprise the viewer or catch them off guard by presenting them an unexpected shot that was completely discontinuous with the previous shot.

Tempo

Tempo is the rhythm that develops based on the timing at which cuts are made and the duration for which shots are held. Variations in the tempo can drastically affect how action plays out on the screen.

Scenes with a tempo that is too fast do not allow the viewer enough time to absorb important information about the story. A tempo that is too slow does not maintain the viewers interest.

The tempo of a specific scene depends on what is being expressed at that time. Chase sequences cut with a slow tempo will not have the same impact as the same scene cut as at a faster tempo. Likewise, a moment of intimacy will most likely be well served by a slower tempo.

Compressing and Expanding Time

Juxtaposition and tempo can be used to compress and expand the time in which actions occur or are implied to occur. This allows the editor to speed events forward or stretch them out as required.

Compression of time and events is very frequently used in films. It is not uncommon for a character to mention going somewhere, then in the next shot is shown at that location. Experienced editors know that the viewer will fill in the incidents that occurred to allow the transition to happen.

Expansions in time can also be used to build suspense by extending the duration of events. This allows you to create those moments where the viewer waits with anticipation to see the resolution of a sequence of events.

Time and events can be compressed and expanded by inter-cutting scenes, the use of montages, and through accelerated motion (rarely used) or slow motion (frequently used).

Transitions

The transitions you select to use between scenes also affect the way a viewer is introduced or taken out of a scene. While most editing programs offer a multitude of computer generated transitions, you should stick with the ones commonly used in cinematic productions.

The main reason for this is that many graphics intense effects do not translate well when transferred to film. But nearly as significant is the fact that excessive usage of novelty transitions appears amateurish.

The most common transitions used in cinema are:
- Fade From Black and Fade To Black provide a strong feeling of beginning and closure.
- A Cut provides a sense of continuity from one scene to the next.

- A Dissolve. Images from one scene gradually fade out while blending with an image fading in from another scene. Creates a sense of a passage of time.
- A Wipe. One image is revealed in a pattern that replaces the image currently on screen. Less abrupt than a cut but a greater sense of urgency than a dissolve.

Additional Editing Tips

Other suggestions to consider while editing include:
- Only hold on a shot as long as required to communicate its purpose.
- Cut on action to help improve continuity.
- When cutting on a person exiting one shot and entering another, cut as the person's eyes exit the frame. Then cut in the next scene about six frames before the person's eyes enter the frame.
- Use cut-away shots to cover jump cuts.

Assembling the Rough Cut

Whether laying down master shots or building scenes shot by shot, your rough cut will slowly begin to evolve as you add scenes. It is at this point that the strength of nonlinear editing is appreciated as you spend time rearranging scenes to experiment with the order of events.

If your editing system has adequate hard drive space and supports long form projects (over one hour) you can assemble the entire rough cut on the system. Once it is complete you will need access to a DV or DVCAM deck to output the project to videotape.

If you don't have access to a deck, you will have to record the program on two sixty-minute DV tapes, then take them to an editing facility and have them edited together to create a master copy. However, since you do not require top quality for your rough cut, you can also connect a VHS or SVHS deck to your camcorder analog output and then record the program from the editing timeline directly onto VHS or SVHS.

Likewise, if you do not have enough hard drive space or your editing program does not support projects over an hour, you can build your rough cut in small segments and individually record them on separate DV tapes. You can then later combine these tapes at an editing facility or in a worst case scenario, combine them by editing from your DV camera to your VHS or SVHS deck.

Previewing Your Rough Cut

With your rough cut complete, for the first time you will be able to watch your story from beginning to end. Sure, there are certain to be slow moments or scenes that don't play right, but that's why it's called a rough cut. With this rough cut you can begin to solicit much needed feedback on the film and plan your re-shoots.

Showing Your Project to Industry People

Sometimes in our anxiousness to solicit additional funding or production assistance, we prematurely show our project to individuals and companies in the film industry hoping that they will see the potential of our little diamond in the rough. Unfortunately, with the high competition in the marketplace a half-finished work-in-progress may get you a few nods, but in most cases people will want to see the finished project prior to committing to become involved. In the worse cases, viewing the incomplete work may turn them off to the point that they have no interest in seeing the project once it is complete.

This reality is even more of an issue with your project being shot on video. Although industry people are slowly beginning to accept video as a production format, especially for documentaries, there is still a very high bias against it. Your best bet is to not show your work-in-progress to industry people but instead focus your efforts on completing the film.

Soliciting Feedback

Before you head back to your isolated laboratory to begin your fine cut, you may want to share your work-in-progress with a select audience. This can be a simple screening on a wide-screen TV with a few honest, unbiased people you trust, or a semi-private video projected screening before an audience of carefully recruited strangers.

In either case, your goal is the same, to solicit blunt critical feedback on elements of the film that can still be changed during the editing phase. So while you should be open to all comments, you should pay particular attention to comments about pacing and structure of the story.

One way to encourage this is to create a survey form that polls viewers about:

- Scenes they liked
- Scenes they didn't like

- Memorable moments in the film
- Boring moments
- Suggestions for improvement

Even more useful than the survey is to note viewers reactions as they are watching the film.

It is nerve racking showing any film, much less a work-in-progress. There's always a desire to interrupt and express your plans for music or missing shots that will fill in holes in the story. But it's more important that you let the viewer derive his/her own opinion from what is presented on the screen.

Your preview screening will require you to have a thick skin, but think of it this way—would you rather hear unfavorable comments while you can still change some elements of the film, or after you have spent much more time and money to commit your opus to film?

Pick-ups and Re-shoots

Armed with your own notes from editing, and comments from the preview screening, you may need to shoot pick-up shots for footage you are lacking or even completely re-shoot some scenes.

Pick-up shots are common on most films while re-shoots are very common on big budget films. Especially when a film has not tested very well at preview screenings. For many of us the prospect of re-shoots is a dreadful thought. The technical, financial, and managerial aspects of assembling the crew, cast, and resources required are much more demanding than editing.

To successfully make the mental shift back to a production mindset you must view re-shoots as a progressive step and as an opportunity to improve the film. However, do not fall for the extremism of trying to remake the entire film based upon the new directing insights you gained from principal photography and editing.

Budget, schedule, organize and record your pick-up shots and re-shoots with the same, if not more, focus than principal photography. Even a one day shoot with a small crew requires proper planning.

Editing Your Fine Cut

So, a room full of people told you that they don't know how they were able to sit through your dreadful film. Take their comments with a grain of salt and move on with the knowledge that the film they viewed still had a long way to go.

With your new footage from your pick-up shots and re-shoots, and a new perspective of the film gained from the rough cut and feedback, you and your editor (if you are working with one) are now prepared to begin the process of adding those fine, delicate strokes to the picture created in the rough cut. You begin the meticulous process of making every cut count.

Many necessary changes were probably very obvious, such as radically shortening or completely eliminating a scene. Other changes may require more scrutiny, such as exactly when to enter a scene and when to cut out. Additionally, transitions between scenes become more significant as you discover that two scenes that cut together terribly, dissolve together very effectively. Or that a fade to black provides the proper sense of closure for a scene.

You will also now find it necessary to begin performing more audio editing functions like adding voice-overs, creating overlapping dialogue as multiple characters speak simultaneously, or grabbing a good audio take and using it when a character is off camera to add a line that may have been missed in another take.

During this stage you might also choose to experiment with music for your scenes. Some directors like to add *temporary tracks* of music to their rough cut early in the process, while others prefer to wait until scenes have been edited more.

While editing your fine cut you will be reviewing scenes repeatedly to determine how they play individually and with other scenes. This refinement is a cyclic process as you finish a new cut then review it thoroughly again, before starting from the top to make more changes. You may also have screenings of various cuts of the film to solicit additional input.

Adding Titles

As you near completion of your fine cut, you will probably want to add titles and credits to your film. Since you still have more people to involve in post-production, the end credits will probably be one of the final steps; however opening credits can now be added.

While your editing software and additional titling software may offer you numerous special effects for titles, the most effective titles for video-to-film transfers will be solid colors on solid backgrounds with minimum movement.

Classic white text on a black background is very effective, especially when anti-aliased. However, avoid large blocks of reds in text or in the backgrounds as they have a tendency to smear. Additionally, text superimposed over video also commonly smears and suffers from digital, jagged edges, even when anti-aliased.

Titles that fade in and out or cut on to the screen work well. But, rolling credits are discouraged as the smooth movement is lost during the transfer process, potentially resulting in jerky movement and smeared graphics.

Also, avoid very fancy typestyles with a lot of fine details that may also be lost during the video-to-film transfer. Be certain to keep titles within the aspect ratio you intend for your final format so they will not be cut off. If uncertain about the final format, stay close to the center third of the video monitor.

Locking the Picture

At some monumental moment, after many blurry-eyed hours in front of the computer monitor and many different cuts of your film, you, your editor, and assistant editor will turn to each other and jubilantly declare the picture as *locked*. After this point no additional changes can be made to the picture without creating substantial and potentially costly expenses down the line. The only exceptions are opening and closing credits, as long as they are not inter-cut with scenes.

Letterboxing Your Project

If you composed your shots for 35mm or simply desire the letterbox look, there are a couple of points at which the letterbox can be added.

Some directors prefer to add the effect prior to editing scenes. The problem with this is that the effect must be rendered on all of the clips you require for a scene. Waiting for the rendering can greatly slow you down in the early stages of editing. The other option is to complete your editing then apply the letterbox effect once the picture is locked.

To create a letterbox effect you can apply black bars to the top and bottom of your film using a partial wipe transition or a matte effect in your nonlinear editing software.

Creating a Locked Picture Master Tape

With your picture locked you will now want to create your locked picture master tape by recording the final cut on a DV, DVCAM, DVCPRO or Betacam SP tape (using component out from the edit system).

As mentioned in the last section, if your project is recorded on several DV or DVCAM tapes you will have to edit the segments onto the master tape (using FireWire if possible). When creating the individual tapes, try to ensure that there are no transitions between two segments on different tapes.

Your master tape should be fast-forwarded to the end then rewound to repack the tape. Then the tape should be set-up as follows:

- Record 1:30 of color bars and tone. Most editing programs can generate this.
- Next, record a :20 slate detailing the program's title. Specify that it is a locked picture copy. Also include the program's length, the date, director's name, producer's name, and the editor's name.
- Record an :08 countdown followed by :02 seconds of black.
- Record your program from this point.

Once you have your locked picture master tape, create a back-up copy. Since this back-up master will be made via FireWire, you don't have to worry about image deterioration. Put that back-up master tape away somewhere safe.

Creating Time Code Dubs

Make several VHS time code window dubs of your locked picture. These will be used for reference extensively during sound editing.

Your composer may also require 3/4" or SVHS window dubs with time code also recorded in an audio format on one track. Talk with him/her about what type of tapes you should provide.

Creating and/or Licensing Your Music

Selecting the appropriate music for your film is just as important as casting the right actors. Music can be used to add life to a slow scene or draw attention to key moments in a scene.

When used effectively, music establishes moods, atmosphere, and rhythm that stimulates viewer's emotions on an entirely different level than the images on screen. Combined, music and images can work in harmony or at odds with each other to create the emotional impact you desire.

Whether you choose to work with a music supervisor or go at it on your own, you should allow yourself sufficient time to create and/or license the music required for your film. There are places you can to acquire music for your film:

- Major Labels
- Unsigned Artist and Independent Labels
- Original Recordings
- Library/Buyout Music
- Public Domain Music

Before we explore these further, let's examine some basics about music rights and licensing. As with all copyright and ownership issues, music rights and licensing can be a very complicated matter that benefits from the knowledge of an experienced attorney.

About Music Rights and Licensing

When you license music rights from an individual or company, you are receiving permission to use the designated music under specific circumstances. In the simplest situation, you will require synchronization rights to include a pre-recorded song in your film. This gives you permission to use the song in the context spelled out in the license such as in a scene, during credits, and/or in promotional material like a trailer or commercial.

However, while synchronization rights allow you to use the song in your film, you will also require performance rights that give you permission to include the song as part of a public exhibition. And the exact type of public exhibition must also be stated. It is not uncommon to receive performance rights that are only for a specific situation, such as film festivals. Additionally, theatrical performance rights commonly have different conditions than television performance rights.

If you plan on producing a separate CD or album soundtrack, you will require an even more complicated set of licensing contracts such a mechanical license that gives you access to the master recordings of a song. In addition to the licensing fees, the important issue of royalty terms must also be negotiated.

To acquire the rights to use a particular recording you must first establish contact with the music's publisher—the person or company that controls the rights to the music. This may or may not be the author, and in many cases more than one entity is designated as the publisher.

ASCAP and BMI are two companies that have established themselves as the music industry's leading clearinghouses for music publishing. They act as administrators for music publishers by maintaining ownership records, collecting fees, and distributing payments to the publishers. You can contact ASCAP or BMI to find the publishers of songs for which you are seeking rights.

Licensing from Major Labels

Once you have found the publisher of a song you wish to use, contact them to find the specific information they will require from you to provide a quote for the licensing fee. Many record labels have a division or a staff person that primarily focuses on music licensing and special markets. This is especially true in light of the increasing significance of soundtracks in low budget feature films. These people are often very receptive to people who approach them with an understanding of what is involved in the process of licensing music for film.

Typically they will ask you to provide a written request for a quote that includes the following information:

- Title of song
- The author
- Duration of the song to be used
- Performance outlets, i.e. U.S. theatrical, festivals, home video.
- Whether or not it will be used in trailers and advertisements.
- Description of the scene. Maybe script pages or clips from the film.
- Use of existing recording or re-recording.
- Length of license.

From this information you will receive a written quote that more than likely will blow you away. However, you can often renegotiate various facets of the license agreement. For example, it is now very common for people to license the rights to use a song for little or no money as long as the film is only shown at festivals. Rights can be upgraded to full theatrical rights later, hopefully after a distributor is on board to pay for them.

If you use this arrangement, be certain to determine the upgrade fee as part of your initial contract. You will be in a much weaker position to negotiate once your film has become a festival hit.

Another alternative that may interest a label is for you to use a song by one of their unreleased artists or one of their underperforming artists. The inclusion of the song in your film will provide free publicity for the song and artist, while you benefit from having a top quality production. And if the artist or song later becomes popular you benefit even more.

Keep in mind that when dealing with labels, despite their volume of business and high profile, they have a surplus of artists and music that need outlets. So while you may have to pay a premium to use popular songs by the top acts, there are a whole lot of up and coming talent that may serve your purpose much more economically.

Unsigned Artists and Independent Labels

If you are willing to invest the time, you can also find some very talented unsigned recording artists or artists signed to small, independent record labels. In both cases, you can frequently license good music for next to nothing if you find people who can see that the arrangement is mutually beneficial.

You may want to start your search locally, especially if your film is a very regional story. You can spread the word by faxing notices to local recording studios, independent record stores, nightclubs, and radio stations, particularly college stations. You can also contact labels directly. Additionally, you can open up your music search to an international audience by again turning to the Internet. You can post messages in newsgroups, websites, and at some of the many music related e-mail newsletters and online organizations.

Hacks features a very strong reggae music element. By soliciting music on the Internet, I have received reggae music from all over the world, including places that I never imagined, such as New Zealand!

Of course, when soliciting music in this manner the quality of the material can vary tremendously. But with patience and diligence you can uncover some excellent music. The ears of a good music supervisor or audio engineer also come in handy during this phase as you try to determine if the song you love so much is musically and technically tight.

In all of your notices and solicitations you should be honest and forthright about the fact that there will be deferred payment or no payment in return for the rights to use the song in your film. However, emphasize that you are not seeking exclusive rights and that you are only looking to include the music in the film.

If you plan on creating and selling a soundtrack, most recording artists or labels will, rightfully, request an advance payment against any future royalties. That arrangement takes you into the music publishing business and requires significant legal and financial planning.

However, for basic synchronization and performance rights your lawyer can draw-up a simple contract that will properly secure the rights for you while protecting all parties involved.

Original Recordings

Original recordings provide you with an opportunity to create music specifically tailored for the needs of your film. And as an added benefit, original recordings can prove to be a less complicated option than licensing music from other people. Although you will incur the expenses of studio time and salaries for musicians, performers, and engineers, you can walk away with music for which you fully own all of the rights.

Work-for-Hire

The most common situation for this is when working with your composer. If you can afford to hire him/her outright then the job can be considered a work-for-hire contract. You would also hire any vocalist and/or musicians under a work-for-hire contract. In this arrangement you can maintain all publishing rights. However, if the composer or any of the musicians are in a union such as the American Federation of Musicians, you may still be required to pay additional royalties.

If your composer is working for deferred payment then the copyright and publishing terms must be individually negotiated. Some composers may demand all of the publishing and copyrights, while agreeing to license you the music for no money, particularly if he/she is providing equipment or facilities. By maintaining publishing, they can make royalties from the work by licensing it to others or selling copies of the sheet music.

Working with Your Composer

Although you may provide your composer copies of select scenes or various cuts as you edit, the true work begins when you deliver a time coded window dub copy of the locked picture.

The first step in creating the score is for you and the composer to have a *spotting session* where you sit down together and determine the points in the film that require music. While you may have used temp tracks for various scenes as you edited, during a spotting session you identify every music cue, from the short stingers used to accent a specific event, to background music and underscore for entire scenes.

As you establish the music cues, you and the composer should also discuss your intentions for each scene. You must express what the music should contribute to the tone, action, and theme for the scene, making references to other films and musical recordings as necessary.

You and your composer will have to develop the ability to communicate in common terms. And it is critical that clear communication be maintained. Composing is a process far too time consuming for the composer to put hours of work into a piece, only to discover you didn't see eye to eye on its purpose.

Conversely, many composers do not like extensive input while in the process of writing a composition. It is during those moments that the composer will draw upon information discussed during the spotting session, while tapping into his/her individual creativity and personal artistic expression.

Live Instruments vs. Synthesized Music

The decision about whether to use live instruments or rely on keyboards and synthesized instruments depends heavily on your budget and personal aesthetics. The rich, cinematic sound of a full orchestra performing a well written score can create many memorable moments in a film. Unfortunately, those rich sounds come at the high price of expensive studio time and musician fees.

Additionally, you will have to find a composer who has experience writing, organizing, and conducting live music for scoring sessions. But, if you are fortunate enough to attract a composer with this type of experience, you may also be able to tap into his/her network to gain access to musicians and recording facilities.

However, if your composer must rely on synthesized instruments, do not despair because the sound quality of many professional instruments is outstanding. By carefully selecting instruments and spending some time in the recording studio an impressive multi-layered score can be created much more economically than live recording sessions.

Library and Buyout Music

Library music and buyout music are pre-recorded compositions of various styles and lengths that a producer can license to use for a flat rate. The music is typically offered on CD sets grouped by musical styles and themes. Each set features several compositions with each piece offered in different lengths, from a few seconds to several minutes.

The advantage of buyout music is that it is inexpensive to purchase and easy to use. Plus once you pay the license fee you can use it as often as you wish.

The disadvantage of buyout music is that a lot of it sounds pretty bad—like the demo tracks on a cheap keyboard. There are several companies such as Sound Ideas and Music Bakery that offer high quality music. However, you must remember that the same music is being used by many other producers and will pop up in other productions.

Creating Your Own Music

One outstanding alternative to buyout music is provided by a company named Sonic Desktop which offers SmartSound ($195), a computer program that allows you to create customized soundtracks by assembling pre-recorded blocks of music to create semi-original sounding compositions. The program is shipped with a library of sound blocks and the company consistently offers new CDs with additional musical themes and styles.

You do not have to be experienced with music production because the software offers suggestions as you build tracks and adjusts attributes of the music to ensure that the blocks work together. Using the program's soundtrack editor, you can easily create a score timed to you picture.

Another program with similar functions is Acid from Sonic Foundry ($400). Although not as musically diverse as SmartSound, Acid allows you to easily create professional sounding music by building tracks of looped audio samples.

Like SmartSound, Acid helps music novices with the tracks timing and transitions. Acid is very useful for creating contemporary sounding music such as house, reggae, and hip-hop tracks. The program includes over 500 samples and additional CDs are also available.

If you are more musically inclined, then you can use MIDI (Musical Instrument Digital Interface) devices and computer software sequencer programs like Cakewalk ($300) to create complex multi-tracked musical arrangements. Midi is a device-independent communication standard and data format for music that revolutionized music production much as FireWire and DV is doing in video production.

Midi songs are programmed using sequencers to designate instruments, arrange notes, change pitch, and specify other musical attributes. Because Midi is a data format, even complicated multi-tracked songs do not require large amounts of memory or hard drive space. The exact quality of the playback is contingent upon the quality of the device on which the file is played back.

Most professional sequencers also allow you to add recorded vocals or instruments. And many programs also can create sheet music from Midi files. With the right hardware, software, and talent you can create very professional recordings.

Public Domain Music

Public domain music is comprised of compositions and recordings which are not copyrighted, or for which the copyrights have expired allowing them to be freely used. There are many great Broadway, jazz, folk, blues, swing, and ragtime songs that you can re-record or adapt for your own use. There are even some songs by the great composer George Gershwin.

You can start your search for public domain music using books like the annually published Directory of Public Domain Music ($99) or Public Domain Music Bible ($577). The monthly newsletter, The Public Domain Report, highlights public domain music, art, film, literature, theater, and children's works.

You can also perform your own copyright searches at the Library of Congress and Copyright Office website. Or you can hire companies such as the publishers of The Public Domain Report to perform copyright searches for you.

When researching copyrights, be certain that you are looking for the original copyright status and not a derivative work, a reproduction of a work later copyrighted by another company or individual. For example, if you create a new version of a public domain song, you can copyright your own version.

There are many websites that feature Midi files of public domain music, including original compositions and reproductions of classical compositions that the Midi composer makes available for public use. Before using any of these files, contact the composer for permission.

And be cautious because there are thousands of Midi files that are illegal reproductions of copyrighted songs.

Editing and Mixing Sound

While your composer is at work on your score and your music supervisor or attorney is busy haggling with record labels about licensing fees, you and your sound editor should be busy editing your dialogue and sound effects tracks. If you are doing your own sound editing, you must now be prepared to shift modes from visual to auditory as you learn the audio editing nuances of your nonlinear editing program.

In most cases, the current versions of the leading nonlinear editing programs provide enough audio tracks and features for you to do your sound editing. However, in complex situations or for certain audio effects you may have to turn to Cool Edit or Sound Forge.

If you work with a professional sound editor, he/she will use a digital audio workstation like Pro-Tools or Opus that uses time code to synchronize a video tape player to playback the picture as the audio tracks are edited in the computer.

Editing Dialogue Tracks

Although you may have performed some basic dialogue editing while editing your picture, during sound editing you will perform many more manipulations of the dialogue to ensure that it has the quality and rhythm you desire. This is accomplished by tools available in your editor to:

- Balance audio levels between takes;
- Adjust various audio frequencies to equalize the sound characteristics between takes;
- Add ambient sound as required to match takes;
- Remove extraneous dialogue and noise by filtering them out or replacing them with ambient sound;
- Add effects to ensure that the dialogue is in the proper perspective with the picture, i.e. distant sound for wide shots, fuller sound for close shots;
- Sync dialogue from other takes or dialogue recorded by itself with a shot;
- Record, edit, and arrange narration and voice-overs; and
- Record, edit, and arrange automatic dialogue replacement (ADR) as required.

ADR is one aspect of post-production that is difficult to replicate on home editing systems. Poorly recorded and edited ADR can look out of sync with the picture and have a very noticeable artificial sound quality. Even professional ADR requires a lot of recording and editing time to look and sound natural. Additionally, many actors have difficulty recreating the performance given on set, adding to the problem.

If you require a substantial amount of ADR for your project and you are editing on your home system, you may need to use a professional post sound facility for those segments of your film.

Building Sound Effect Tracks

Sound effects are another means for adding realism to your film or, if desired, enhancing the level of surrealism. Building sound effects tracks is a serious craft. The excessive use of inappropriate sound effects creates an amateurish tone that can jeopardize the viewer's connection with the entire film. Conversely, the lack of sound effects can leave the viewer with an indiscernible feeling that some important film element is missing.

The subtle use of sound effects can help a scene feel natural while a heavy dosage of carefully selected sound effects can work with the music to establish an infinite variety of atmospheres including fantasy, horror, romance, and adventure.

Sound effects can either be *on frame sound effects* that are synchronized with actions occurring on the screen, or *off frame sound effects* that are not associated with anything visible on the screen.

If you properly planned ahead, then your production sound mixer should have recorded sound effects on set at every opportunity possible. But even if this was done, you may still be required to record new sound effects and/or turn to sound effects libraries.

Recording Effects

The beautiful thing about recording sound effects is that your primary focus is that the sounds serve their desired purpose, regardless of how they were produced. This fact is what makes creating sound effects such an art. Professional sound effects recordists develop an understanding of the sound characteristics of many different objects under various conditions and most importantly, they have a knack for understanding the potential cinematic application of these sounds. Likewise, you should experiment to identify items that can be used to create the sound effects you desire.

You can record sound effects on location or in a studio, as necessary. A good stereo mic and your DV camera will work fine, but you can also use Hi-8 cameras, mini-disc recorders, or portable DAT machines. And once you have recorded sound effects you can use your audio editing program to radically modify them in many different ways.

Foley Effects

We previously discussed the importance of unidirectional mics that allow you to isolate and record dialogue that is free of background noise. But many times some of those same background sounds relate to basic actions occurring on screen, such as doors opening and closing, footsteps, the rustle of clothing, etc. In our final edited scenes, the absence of these sounds can lead to the scenes feeling staged and artificial. *Foley effects* are the numerous on camera sound effects that may have to be added or enhanced to correct this problem.

Traditionally, foley effects are created on a *foley stage* which features a booth where the *foley artist* can view the film projected on a screen and use a variety of prop items to create sound effects in time to events in the scene.

Fortunately, you can use your nonlinear software to edit such sound effects directly into your program properly synchronized to the picture. You can also use the sampling feature of some music keyboards to sample a sound effect, then record it into the editing system as you play it back synchronized to the picture. This process feels more natural to many people because you can do it in real time, as opposed to the manual cut and paste technique required to synchronize it in your editing software.

Sound Effects Libraries

Sound effects libraries are available on CD for buyout use, much like buyout music. In fact, many of the same companies like Sound Ideas, Music Bakery, and Sonic Desktop also offer sound effects CDs. Other companies offering quality sound effects CDs include F7 Sound and Visions' Concept: FX CD series and the ten CD Platinum Sounds for the 21st Century Collection from Hollywood sound designer Frank Serafine.

The sound effects are available in CD audio format as well as AIFF and WAV computer file formats that allow them to be taken from the

CD and dropped right in to your editing program. Once there, they can be manipulated as you desire. Most of the companies allow you to preview the sound effects on their website or via sampler CDs.

Sound effects should be built in layers designed to increase the dramatic impact of certain moments. Allow yourself sufficient time to experiment with the individual sounds and layers that you will have to create for your scenes.

Music Tracks

As your music tracks begin to arrive from the composer, usually on a CD-R (Compact Disc Recordable) that can be used in any CD player or DAT (Digital Audio Tape), you will need to transfer them into your editing system.

You can achieve very acceptable quality recording from the CD or DAT machine's analog output to the analog audio input on your editing system. However, for the best quality you will want to digitally transfer the recordings directly into the editing system. In many cases you can do this from a CD by using your editing system's CD-ROM drive, or from DAT using a DAT interconnect card such as Canopus Corporation's DATPack ($500).

In some cases you may also record music directly from the composer's keyboard into your editing system, although you have to be careful to watch for conflicting audio line voltage levels that can distort the music. Additionally, it is always good to have a stand alone version of all of your music tracks should you later need to re-mix your audio.

Once the tracks are in the editing system you can begin to match them to their corresponding scene. You can also experiment with various audio level settings, although you will do most of those adjustments in the final mix.

The Mix

After many hours of editing dialogue, building sound effects tracks, and arranging music tracks, you will end up with several dozen tracks that must be combined together with every track set at the appropriate level in relationship to the other. This process is called the *mixdown*. At this time you will also perform audio effects to create stereo and surround sound.

Prior to actually mixing the tracks, you and your sound editor will go through the entire program and create a *cue sheet* that contains notes about where to adjust tracks and what adjustments of effects are to be applied.

The actual mix can be performed in real-time with the sound editor using an on-screen representation of an audio mixing panel to make adjustments as the program plays back, with the ability to easily stop, back-up, and resume at any point. Depending on the capabilities of the editing system and the number of simultaneous audio tracks used in the project, the mix may have to be performed in several passes, sub-mixing groups of tracks down to single tracks.

Most nonlinear editing systems and audio editing programs also allow you to perform mix functions graphically by marking notations on the tracks that represent various audio changes and effects.

As you are performing your mix, you will also want to create a sub-mix of your music track and effects track by themselves. These M&E tracks allow your film to easily be dubbed in another language. This is done by re-recording the dialogue in the desired language, then re-mixing the new dialogue with the M&E tracks.

The mixdown is one of the most exciting moments as you realize that you are finally nearing completion. Still, care must be taken to ensure that the proper balance is found between the tracks. Otherwise, you might end up with the dialogue being overrun by music and effects or having music so low that it fails to make its full impact.

Stereo Sound and Noise Reduction Processes

If you mix your project using some of the high end editing programs or in a professional post-production sound facility, you will have several options for stereo surround sound and noise reduction.

Stereo surround sound is the process of controlling the levels and balance between separate channels of sound, based upon various speakers arrangements in the playback system.

Dolby Stereo is perhaps the most well known system. Dolby Stereo is created by mixing audio tracks into four channels (left, right, center, surround) then running them through an encoder that combines them as per the Dolby Stereo specifications. There are similar processes such as Ultra Stereo that do not use Dolby equipment but serve a similar purpose.

Dolby AC-3 is a stereo surround sound format based on five channels and speaker positions. This format is used in DVD, digital satellite programming, and high definition broadcasting.

Noise reduction processes are filtering, encoding, and decoding methods used to reduce common noises that are introduced during audio recording, mixing, and playback.

Laying Audio Back to Picture

If you edited your sound in a nonlinear system, then you are ready to proceed to color correcting the final master tape. However, if you edited your audio in a digital audio workstation or a multi-track tape system, you will need to output your mixed audio track to tape. This audio will then have to be re-synced in your nonlinear system or on you videotape master.

If you correctly maintained the time code from your locked picture while editing audio, then the time code on the audio tape and in your editing system or video tape master should synchronize, allowing you to lay the new audio back to picture with no problems. If not, you might be faced with terrible synchronization problems that may require a completely new sound edit or mix. This is another benefit of completing your picture editing and audio editing on the same system

Your Master Tape

Your project is just a few steps from completion. These last few steps help you prepare and secure your program master tape.

Color Correction

With the picture and audio complete you can now go through and color correct the entire film, shot-by-shot. This process will allow you to even out the color, brightness, and contrast difference between shots. This can be accomplished in varying degrees in most nonlinear editing programs. However, it can be performed professionally if you have a digital Betacam master tape created from your DV, DVCAM, or DVCPRO master tape.

Professional tape-to-tape color correction can cost hundreds of dollars per hour, especially when using digital Betacam. Additionally, it typically takes roughly four times as long as the length of your program. For example, a ninety-minute project may take six hours or more to color correct. As you can imagine, it can get very expensive, which is why it is one of the final steps, but with a good colorist the results can be outstanding.

Color Correction on Your Computer

Although you will not have the degree of image control available when using professional systems, you can still make substantial corrections to video. The most important requirement is that you be willing to invest the time and patience required to experiment with the image settings.

The process will require you to make adjustments, then wait as the changes are rendered by the computer. Then, if you are using a software CODEC card, you will need to view the clip on your video monitor to get an accurate representation of the effectiveness of the new settings. If the changes work, then you continue with the next clip, if not, you will have to undo the change and try again. A slow process, but much less expensive.

You can also completely remove color to create a black and white film. But as you adjust the color attributes of your images, be aware that extreme changes can degrade your images or add substantial artifacts.

Backup Master

As a precaution, you should create another back-up copy of your final program master. If you have a digital Betacam master tape, then you should also have a Betacam SP back-up created for those occasions you don't want to pay extra for a digital Betacam machine.

These back-up tapes are especially important because you may be sending the master tape to a duplication facility, video treatment service bureau, or an out-of-town facility for video-to-film transfer.

Shipping Your Tape

Your tape should be shipped in a thick foam-padded envelope or a sturdy shipping box. Do not use the paper padded envelopes as they produce small specks of paper residue that can get in your tape case and damage the tape. Also, do not take a chance with the thin Priority and Express Mail envelopes from the U.S. Post Office. The sharp edges of your tape case can easily tear them. Be certain to always require a signature for the delivery, in case you should later need to trace a shipment.

Using a Video Treatment Process

If you intend to create a version of your project that has been treated with a process such as Filmlook, this step will be performed after the entire project is completed. You could optionally perform color correction at this time, however you would end up with only a color corrected copy of the Filmlook version.

If you are solely planning video distribution then this is acceptable. But if you plan on having a film print made, you will want to do it from you color corrected, non-Filmlooked master tape.

To prepare to use a video treatment process, first contact the service bureau you will be working with to find out exactly how they want you to prepare your order. You will need to specify the video format for your new Filmlooked master tape. Again, digital Betacam should be your first choice followed by Betacam SP.

Typically, the process is applied in real-time, so the time it takes will more or less be the time of the length of the program. However, the process can also be applied with adjustments or special processes applied from scene-to-scene.

If you are having scene-to-scene adjustments made, and you are sending your tape away to a remote service bureau, then you will need to include a note specifying the changes and the time code in and out points. To avoid confusion, request a demo tape of sample effects so that you can communicate clearly in you notes.

If you are using a local service bureau, you will have the option of sitting in for a supervised session to dictate scene-to-scene changes to the colorist applying the process. However, be aware that the hourly rate of these supervised sessions is much higher than normal rates.

Once the treatment process has been applied, your original master tape and the new treated master tape will be returned to you. Again, for protection you may want to create a back-up copy of the treated tape.

Video Treatment on Your Computer

If you choose to perform a video treatment process using software like Adobe After Effects or the DigiEffects Cinelook plug-in, prepare yourself for the substantial time required by the programs.

Having recorded a "clean" copy of your color corrected project on to a videotape master, you can now proceed to start at the beginning of the project. You will have to work your way through, applying the film effect scene by scene, much like color correction. Each application will require being rendered and viewed on your monitor to determine its effectiveness.

Completing the entire program could take several weeks. But, then again, you are saving thousands of dollars by doing it yourself.

Once the process is completed, record a copy of the project on to a new master tape.

Preparing for Your Video-to-Film Transfer

There are several steps you will have to take to prepare your video master to be transferred to film. The exact specifications vary from one company to another. Given this, it is important that you review the written instructions of the company that will be performing the transfer. Be certain to ask questions about any details that are unclear to you.

Additionally, always write down instructions and include them with your order to avoid miscommunications. The information most frequently required includes:

- The desired film format—16mm or 35mm.
- The aspect ratio at which the video is to be transferred. Full screen video transferred at a 1.85:1 (35mm aspect ratio) will have the top and bottom cropped to fit the aspect ratio. However, if you composed your shots for 35mm, this will not create a problem.
- Reel breaks—Transporting a feature length motion picture as one long single strand of film would call for the film to be spooled around a huge reel. Instead, films are broken up into several reels. The length of each reel typically cannot surpass 30 minutes in length and some transfer companies will use even shorter reels. You will be required to specify the time code for the point in your program where you desire your reel breaks to occur.

  Ideally, these carefully selected points should be at a cut in the film that does not have music or overlapping dialogue that could be affected by the breaks. Some companies may actually require you to edit your master tape and create a single tape for each reel. Or they may charge an additional fee to do this for you. Others just require a list of the time code.

- Sound specifications—You must provide details on the specifications for the film's soundtrack. This information depends on how your tracks were recorded and mixed. Some of the options are: mono audio, Dolby stereo, Ultra Stereo, surround sound, and noise reduction.

  If you are required to edit your master tape into separate reels, you may also have to include a visual and audio sync point at the beginning of every reel to ensure that the film negative and audio magnetic tape can be synced when they are combined to create your negative.

10

■ ■ ■ ■ ■ Distribution and
Exhibition

Admittedly, this final chapter is the shortest chapter of the book, even though the topic is one of the most important. After all, why spend so much time, money, and effort to produce a film that is never seen.

Distribution opportunities for DV films are only now beginning to emerge. After years of bias towards projects originating on video, home video distributors, theatrical distributors, and film festivals are finding success with some high profile video projects. Meanwhile, ambitious filmmakers have taken matters into their own hands and made success-ful forays into home video and theatrical self-distribution; while others eagerly prepare for the advent of the Internet as a viable distribution outlet.

As I was outlining this chapter, I realized that the proper treatment of the subject of film distribution and exhibition is a book of its own, particularly in reference to independent film, self-distribution, and emerging technologies such as DVD and the Internet.

But for now, here is a summary of some of the possible outlets for you to distribute, exhibit, and promote your film, including:

- Home Video and DVD
- Markets and Festivals
- Theatrical Screenings
- The Internet

Regardless of the outlet you choose to utilize, the bottom line is that at this point in time, you will have to work nearly as hard at getting your film shown before an audience, as you had to work to get your film made. To be successful you will require determination, resourcefulness, and an unabashedly strong knack for self-promotion.

Home Video

On a small scale, home video is the simplest and most self-sufficient manner for you to distribute your project: you simply dub some VHS copies, slap on some computer generated labels, and ship it to anyone willing to view it. But as you strive to reach broader audiences and generate income from tape sales, the number of obstacles and expenses grow progressively. You may be able to convince a couple of local video stores to carry your film, but without a distributor it will be difficult, if not impossible, to have your film distributed in the national video retail chains like Blockbuster Video.

If your project is a genre film, particularly action or thriller genre, you may be able to attract a small home video distributor interested in the possibilities of foreign sales. However, the profit potential for these relationships is very slim, especially for the filmmaker. The distributor will not become involved unless they believe they will make money off of your film.

The difficulty in attracting video distributors is based on retailers' apprehensions about using valuable shelf space for unknown films. Retailers know that the film will rent much less frequently than the blockbuster films that have the benefits of celebrity drawing power and multi-million dollar advertising campaigns.

Since the profitability of a video store is based upon the ability to generate as many rentals as possible, your little film doesn't stand a chance. In fact, even many independent films that have performed well in limited theatrical, festival, or cable release, have difficulty generating substantial home video sales.

The Cyclic Nature of Genres

As previously mentioned, genre films have a slightly better chance of interesting video retailers. However, a genre film's success heavily depends on the current popularity of specific genres. While action films internationally maintain a pretty consistent interest level, many other genres tend to be very cyclic.

Typically, a new theatrical film or direct-to-video film successfully taps into a new or under-exploited genre, thus drawing attention to the genre. This inevitably results in an avalanche of imitators that eventually saturates the market, killing the genre until its next revival down the line.

This pattern can be witnessed in the current trend of teen slasher films such as the *Scream* series and *I Know What You Did Last Summer*. *Scream* launched the revival which can trace its roots back to the teen horror films of the early '80s and back even further to the teen drive-in horror films of the '60s.

Another example is the current direct-to-video success of urban drama films starring rap musicians. This trend was launched by Baton Rogue, Louisiana-based rapper Master P. Without the backing of a major video distributor, his 1997 direct-to-video urban drama *I'm Bout It*, sold over 200,000 copies at $19.95 and over 1,000,000 copies of the soundtrack! Since then he has produced and released a theatrical film and three more direct-to-video films.

These impressive figures attracted the attention of mainstream companies such as Miramax, which distributed his 1998 theatrical film, *I Got the Hook-Up*, as well as many independent recording artists seeking to mimic his success. While a few others have had moderate success, the youth audience is now growing apprehensive because of the low quality of many of the productions. Additionally, a substantial bootleg market for the films has developed, resulting in illegal copies often being sold on the streets weeks before their release in stores.

The Potential of Niche Markets

Despite the dismal prospects of sales to video stores, there is a potential to generate income by direct and mail order sales of videos of your project if your film is geared towards a very specific audience, and venues exist for the economical marketing and distribution to the audience. For example, there are several small B-movie companies producing T&A heavy horror films on video, then selling them directly to their customers via fantasy and horror magazines, newsletters, and trade shows.

As another example, Master P circumvented video stores and instead choose record stores to sell his film directly to consumers. Video retailers later sought him out because of frequent requests from customers.

The marketing and sales outlets you use can be specialized stores, catalogs, very targeted publications, websites, e-mail newsletters, conferences, expos, and other events that bring your audience together.

Public Libraries and Schools

Several years ago, I wrote a script for a half hour children's film, and as I was researching distribution outlets, I discovered that for certain types of projects public libraries and schools represent a very healthy market. In fact, there are production companies that exclusively produce shorts, documentaries, and features for these markets.

Programs are licensed with an exhibition fee or sold outright. The programs are often packaged with additional learning or study aids. The license and sales fees can run as high as several hundred dollars with study aids costing more. The programs purchased include everything from short educational videos to dramatic feature films.

To have a program considered for purchase or licensing, it must often be reviewed by a panel at the library or school headquarters. Approved programs are usually ordered in quantity. As an added benefit, many librarians and school administrators share lists of approved programs with librarians and administrators in other counties or regions.

Videotape Duplication and Packaging

The cost of duplicating and professionally packaging VHS tapes has never been lower. Even in low quantities (less than 100) a ninety-minute program can be duplicated for less than $4 per tape. Should you be fortunate enough to have a market that merits duplicating higher quantities up front, with an order of 1,000 or more, you can have the same program copied for less than $2 each.

Tapes can be created at local duplication houses or via one of the many mail-order duplication companies. When comparing duplication prices, be certain that the price you receive is for standard play (SP) quality copies. Extended play (EP) is cheaper, but you want your picture to look its best so stick with SP copies.

For packaging, you can turn to companies like Eastco Pro where you can have 2,500 four color, glossy cardboard video sleeves printed for less than $400. This is the minimum quantity at which it is cost effective for the printing process. The price is based upon you providing camera-ready art that is able to be reproduced without any changes from the printer. Additionally, many companies can also inexpensively print posters and fliers from this artwork.

Based upon the specs provided by the printer, you can create camera-ready art using your computer, a graphic program like Corel Draw or Photoshop, and a laser printer. You can incorporate still photos taken during principal photography or grabbed from your video.

If you are not experienced in graphic design, you can economically hire a graphic designer from a local college or even from the Internet, in which case you would send your pictures, logo and text, via e-mail. The designer would create the design and then provide a color printer or color copier proof to you for approval. The final file can be e-mailed or U.S. mailed back to you and in many cases, simultaneously sent to the printer. Many prefer to use select file formats as opposed to working from a printed copy of the design.

However, prior to spending the money to duplicate and package a large volume of tapes, you may choose to just copy a few tapes and create an attractive color cover that can be slipped into the plastic cover of a *slip cover tape case*. These can be very professional when used with a decent design printed on a good color laser printer, such as those at Kinko's, and duplicated on a color copier. The paper must be trimmed slightly prior to placement in the case. You can also purchase VHS tape labels at your local office supply store that can be printed on your inkjet printer to create attractive labels.

All said, on a single copy basis you can copy and professionally package your tape for approximately:

VHS Tape	$2.00
Label	.10
Cover—Color Copy	1.00
Slip Cover Tape Case	1.00
Total	$4.10

This low price makes it economical to only order large volumes when required. In most cases, the turnaround time for duplications is only a couple of days, even in quantities of several thousand. By waiting to invest heavily in inventory, you can apply the money saved towards your marketing efforts.

DVD

Digital Versatile Disc (DVD) is a high quality digital audio/video playback format that is based upon advanced compact disc technology. Since its introduction to consumers in 1996, DVD has become one of the fastest growing consumer electronic products ever.

A new variation called DIVX was introduced in the summer of 1998. DIVX allows program producers to encode a DVD so that it can only be played a limited number of times, after which a viewer must purchase a code to access more viewing or simply toss the disc. DIVX provides an economical alternative to purchasing or renting DVDs. Technically, DVD and DIVX are the same technology.

Like CDs, but much more precise, DVDs use microscopic lasers to read variations in the tracks of data impressed in the DVD. The data read from the DVD is an advanced audio and video compression format called MPEG-2. This format is so sophisticated that it allows the disc to hold ten times as much information as a compact disc, despite the fact that they are physically the same size. This information can be audio, video, data, or a combination of same.

The integration of advanced computing power allows DVDs to offer special features such as dialogue tracks in multiple languages, the ability to change the order of scenes in real-time allowing for different versions of a film to exist on the same disc, multiple subtitle tracks, and much more.

Creating a DVD from a film or video program is called *authoring*. This process involves properly preparing the video, audio, subtitles, and computer graphics. Once prepared, they are *premastered*, a step that combines the elements and creates a master file called a *disc image*. This image is then *mastered* using lasers to create a master DVD. Copies are created using a physical reproduction process that is similar to the old process of reproducing music albums by *stamping* them out of hot wax.

The DVD programs are authored using an authoring system. The cost of such systems currently ranges from $5,000 to $500,000 dollars. The high cost of the authoring system is based upon the advanced encoding and media management they must perform. Video is encoded into the MPEG-2 format, audio is encoded into Dolby Digital, and graphics are created. These individual components are called *assets*. They are linked in the authoring system using a computer program similar to a nonlinear editing package. Once the assets are connected and the program is tested extensively, the file is then premastered.

Because of the high cost of authoring systems, and the expertise required to ensure the process is performed properly, many producers turn to service bureaus to author their program. Such bureaus typically charge $50 to $100 per minute for MPEG-2 encoding and $30-$90 per minute for Dolby Digital encoding. The authoring charges vary greatly, but most companies can quote you a fairly accurate price based upon an evaluation of your program and the features you desire for your DVD.

After the program has been mastered, copies can be created at prices comparable to the cost of reproducing VHS tapes. And in large volumes, DVD is less expensive per unit than VHS.

While fairly costly at this time, the price of DVD authoring equipment continues to fall. In the near future, it will be possible to economically produce DVD on your home computer.

Home Video Distributors

I once received a semi-threatening e-mail following a conference where I referred to home video distributors as "pimps." Well, I'm not one to generalize and since I plan on having a long career in this business, let me clarify my statement:

If you allow it to happen, most any distributor, home video or theatrical, will pimp you and your film.

At this point in time there are many home video companies exploiting the abundance of low budget independent films created by filmmaker's forced into desperate situations.

By pimping, I mean that you did the bulk of the work and sacrificed to produce your film, but they end up with the bulk of the profits. Oh sure, they'll show you beautiful (and often gaudy) color sales materials and tape covers, while telling you how heavily they have invested in your film. But as we saw above, these items can be created inexpensively.

Just how bad can this relationship be? Well, let me share a specific example as related from a close friend who has several films distributed on home video. Some of the information is changed for privacy considerations. Though I'd love to reveal the guilty party, it would serve no purpose because the dynamics of the deal are typical of the industry.

After a year and a half of planning, shooting, and editing, my friend, Filmmaker X, completed her 16mm feature, *The Film*, on video with a total budget of about $40,000 cash plus a good amount of deferred payments due to the cast and crew once the $40,000 had been recouped (we'll get back to this in a minute).

After one of the early screenings, Filmmaker X was contacted by the Excited Home Video Company who shared a gorgeous catalog of nicely packaged films with claims that her film would fit right in. The company representative mentioned the possibilities of selling thousands of copies.

Filmmaker X cordially declined as she continued for several months with numerous minor festival screenings and private screenings for theatrical distributors. And although she received many great compliments on her film, she repeatedly heard comments like "too soft," "no names," "a hard sell."

Meanwhile, her investors began to grow anxious about the possibilities of recouping their money, until one of them pulled out the catalog from Excited Home Video Company. Based upon the average price of $39.95, he figured that even if they only sold a little over 1,000 copies, they could get their money back and get out of the film business forever. With the other investors rallied behind him, he pressured Filmmaker X to inquire about a deal with Excited Home Video. Eventually, she reluctantly conceded.

The representative of Excited Home Video Company forwarded what he called a "standard contract." Filmmaker X was horrified by the terms. In exchange for the exclusive world rights to sell the film, her company would receive a $6,000 advance and 15 percent royalty on the retail price of every tape.

She and her lawyer talked terms with the rep. Eventually he said he might be able to squeeze out a $7,500 advance. With the lead investor encouraged by possibilities of some cash, Filmmaker X signed the deal and handed over her beloved videotape master.

A few weeks later, and two weeks after the specified date, she received the advance payment, which was gobbled up by a few pressing debts and small payments to the investors. The distributor also forwarded a proof of the tape cover which grossly misrepresents her tender romantic comedy as a torrid tale of passion. But, in the contract, she had signed away any rights to approve the final art.

Let's fast forward. Many depressed months later, Filmmaker X received a call from one of the actors in the film who excitedly told her that his cousin in Texas just rented the film on video from the local Blockbuster. He ended the enthusiastic call with a final question: "When am I going to get paid for my role?" Filmmaker X told him she was going to have to check with the distributor.

The next day, she called the previously ever-accessible rep from Excited Home Video Company, but his assistant said he was in a meeting and promised to have him call back. As she hung up, Filmmaker X got another call from another actor who just picked up a copy of the film from the video store on her block.

A few days later, Filmmaker X had heard from the entire crew, the cast, investors, and relatives all over the country congratulating her for getting her film in video stores and making it to the "big time." But she still hadn't heard back from the rep from Excited Home Video Company, despite repeated calls.

Finally, she had her lawyer fax a notice requesting the quarterly sales report and royalty payment that was to have been made several weeks prior. To her surprise, in a few days she received an official looking package from Excited Home Video. She hastily opened the package and saw a computer printout with a figure highlighted, the number . . .

1,434 Copies Sold!

She shouted excitedly, encouraged by the sales figure, and performed a quick mental calculation–1,434 copies at $6 (15 percent of $39.95) almost $9,000! After deducting the $7,500 advance that would be $1,500, not bad for a first royalty check. She looked through the package, but didn't find a check. Certain there was some mistake, she looked at the report more closely and was shocked to discover that her earnings for the copies sold were only . . .

$3,226.50

And that she still owed them over $4,000?! How could that be? An even more detailed inspection of the report revealed that . . .

The 1,434 tapes had been sold at only $14.95!

She was outraged. She called her attorney, who after several moments of silence, sheepishly told her that a retail minimum price was not established in the contract, and that Excited Home Video Company had the right to sell the tape for as little as they desired.

Why would they want to do this? Well, it turned out that Excited Home Video Company sold so many copies of *The Film* by including it as a free tape when video stores purchased a set of more expensive tapes, giving customers more value for their money but greatly devaluing Filmmaker X's film. To add insult to injury, they duplicated the tapes using low-quality EP recording. Worst of all, there was nothing she could do about it.

The phone calls from the cast and crew continued. All they knew was that the video was available at video stores all over the country and that they should be paid. As Filmmaker X tried to explain the economics, issues of mistrust quickly surfaced. Within weeks, several actors joined together to file a lawsuit against Filmmaker X.

The suit was eventually dropped after Filmmaker X paid out-of-pocket for an independent accountant to review the records and prepare a statement for the actors' attorney. But the relationship between the filmmaker and several close friends remains strained.

I know it is a disheartening story, but it's true. After three years, several thousand videos sold, and a couple of small foreign sales, Filmmaker X has yet to recoup the $40,000. I have talked to other filmmakers with similar experiences. On the upside, the film generated enough attention for Filmmaker X that she was able to get money to do another project.

I know that for me to call home video distributors "pimps" displaces some of the responsibility of filmmakers and their attorneys and accountants to check and double-check potential distribution deals. After all, the goal of any business is to find a niche, then capitalize on it.

An established music producer once told me, "In the entertainment business, everyone gets screwed on their first deal." With that in mind, my attitude is to call a spade a spade, and a pimp a pimp, then with this knowledge, try to play the game the best I can, keeping in mind a few basic guidelines:

- Desperate people do desperate things;
- Never sign a distribution contract without a qualified lawyer reviewing it;
- Clearly understand how every clause translates into dollars and sense . . . I mean cents; and
- Research the background of potential distributors. Try to talk to other filmmakers about their experiences.

Markets and Festivals

Film markets and festivals have long been an important means for independent films to receive exposure, in many cases, offering the only time many films will receive an audience. Markets and festivals also have an important role among large production companies and distribution companies seeking new talent and new films.

Film Markets

Film markets are film showcases created for the purpose of bringing filmmakers, sellers, and buyers together. These highly competitive, commerce-driven environments often feature festive atmospheres as people aggressively campaign to promote their products. The leading markets such as the annual American Film Market in Santa Monica, California, and Mifed in Milan, Italy, are responsible for hundreds of millions of dollars in film sales and licensing.

Attending these major markets requires a substantial investment. The exhibitor fees alone can cost several thousand dollars, while travel, marketing, and promotional materials add even more.

The Independent Feature Market (IFFM) is an annual film market held in New York City every fall. It is sponsored by the non-profit film support group, The Independent Feature Project. Hundreds of completed and work-in-progress documentaries, short films, and feature films are screened before other filmmakers, film enthusiasts, and film industry professionals.

Some critics of the IFFM have said that its liberal submission policy panders to desperate filmmakers. Conversely, my experience at IFFM was fantastic. To be certain, the quality of the works ranged from fantastic to unbearable, and there were many overzealous promotional strategies. But, I found that by having networked extensively prior to arriving, I was able to establish excellent contacts that were more fully realized when people were able to meet face to face at the market.

I would highly recommend the market to filmmakers. The odds are very slim of you walking away with a deal, but with proper preparation you can have the benefit of having your film screen in front of an audience and build your network.

Currently, they can screen works-in-progress from video but require prints for features. However, the IFP is a very progressive organization and hopefully will be adding feature screenings from video.

Film Festivals

In their purest form, the purpose of film festivals is to provide a venue for filmmakers to present their work to an audience. Festivals may be geared to a specific audience, region, or theme, and competitive festivals may award prizes, but the emphasis is always on the art of cinematic expression.

Of course, in reality, many festivals are as much about business as they are about art. Million dollar deals are common occurrences at major festivals such as the Sundance Film Festival and the Cannes Film Festival.

Exposure at festivals can greatly increase the value of your film. Fortunately, many film festivals are becoming more receptive to video originated films. The 1998 Cannes Film Festival featured two DV originated films, *The Idiots* and *The Celebration*. Both films were well received, with *The Celebration* being a co-recipient of the Special Jury Award.

In addition to the several high profile film festivals, there are hundreds of other film festivals around the world. A list of major festivals is included in the resources list. Visit the Film Festival Server Website at www.filmfestivals.com to search a list of practically every known film festival.

If you have a short DV film you may want to consider, the D.Film Festival, a traveling film showcase that specializes in short films created using digital tools. The festival travels to cities around the world presenting the works.

Most festivals require a non-refundable submission fee that can range from a few dollars to hundreds of dollars. Additionally, once accepted you most often are required to pay for your own travel expenses. Some festivals pay a small gratuity and/or lodging. And while you don't always have to attend the festival for your film to be screened, most of us long to see how our films play before various audiences.

Between submission fees, travel expenses, lodging, and promotional material, festivals can become rather expensive to participate in.

When evaluating a festival, be certain to review the festival's submission and screening requirements. Some filmmakers have their project treated with Filmlook or a similar process primarily for the purpose of festival submissions. If you are considering lying on an application, be aware that it is not difficult for a seasoned eye to identify treated video.

And for festivals that accept video originated projects, confirm whether they will be able to project the video or if they will require a print. With the growing popularity of video, video projection systems are becoming much more commonplace.

Theatrical Screening

Without a doubt, one of the most significant personal moments for a filmmaker is being discretely positioned somewhere in a crowded theater as the lights go down and *your* film flickers on the big screen. It's a moment that is both nerve-racking and exhilarating as the images that originated in your mind are projected before you and an audience of strangers. It is truly an experience that cannot be replicated on home video or television.

Fortunately there are high quality video projection systems that can provide DV filmmakers the opportunity to have this experience, without the expense of a video-to-film transfer.

Video Projectors

Early video projectors operated by placing powerful lenses in front of a picture tube to project the image. The distance and focus of the projection was controlled by varying the distance between the lenses and the tube. While these devices could project an image a long distance, the image often suffered a loss of contrast and poor color reproduction.

Contemporary video projection systems use high resolution LCD panels to produce the images before projecting them, using precision lenses. The video can be projected over long distances and still maintain sharpness and color quality. In a theatrical setting, lower end units may have to be placed in the center aisle, while the better projectors can be in the film projection booth.

Most major cities have at least one independent theater that has a video projection system. Many of these theaters are receptive to renting their facilities for a screening. In larger cities such as Los Angeles and New York, private screening rooms with video projectors can also be rented. Additionally, many colleges and universities have auditoriums with video projectors.

However, if you are unable to locate a facility with a video projector, you can rent a unit from an audio/visual supply house. Unfortunately, they don't come cheap. A low-end units such as the Sharpvision ($325 per day) can provide very good results in a small theater while the Sanyo PLC900 offers even better picture quality, but at twice the cost ($800 per day).

The Sanyo can also be used with a *digital scaler* ($200 per day) that takes the 525 line video signal and converts it to a 1024 line image. This conversion greatly improves the video quality and effective distance from which the projector can be used.

Top-of-the-line video projectors such as the Barko 8100 and the POWER Displays from Digital Projections are far more expensive to rent, but provide the best video projection quality possible.

If you are renting a system you may also need to rent a Betacam SP or digital Betacam deck for playback. However, most video projectors accept S-VHS video input, so you can use your DV or DVCAM deck if you have a DV or DVCAM master.

Your audio can be patched from the deck into the theater's house sound system. Or you can rent an amplifier and set of powerful speakers such as the Apogee AE5 to set up your own audio system.

From Your Print

If you are fortunate enough to have a print of your film, then you are spared the expense of having to seek out facilities with video projectors or rent a system on your own. If you have a 35mm print, you have the luxury of being able to go into any theater in the world and screen your film.

Finding theaters with 16mm projectors is a little more difficult in the U.S., but most independent theaters have them, as do many colleges and universities. You can also check with local media arts organizations for film screening facilities.

Film projectors, 16mm and 35mm, are much less expensive to rent than video projectors. If you are unable to economically find a facility to screen your print, then you can rent a projector and a screen for just a couple of hundred dollars.

The Internet

Although the quality of video and audio delivered over the Internet is currently limited for computer users operating at slow *dial-up* modem speeds (56k or less), a rapidly growing number of people are connecting at the much higher *broadband* speeds offered by *cable modems* and DSL lines. Experts estimate that full screen, full motion video will be possible for most home users in the next two to five years.

Despite its limitations, the current technology for online video is very accessible and provides a good opportunity for you to promote your film.

About Video Streaming

A web page is typically loaded by a user sending a request to a server computer that hosts the desired page. This server is responsible for sending the requested text, graphics, and photographs to the user, then confirming that it was received. This staggered, back and forth interaction takes place every time a page is requested.

Sending audio and video for smooth playback requires a process that allows computer data to be sent in a steady flow. Streaming is the technology used to accomplish this. With video streaming, a user places a request to view a video clip. This request is received by the server which then begins to send the requested video as a steady stream of data. As this data is received by a media player program on the user's computer, it is buffered, stored in memory, until there is a suitable amount available for playback.

The playback begins as the software continues to receive and buffer new data, the only time during this process that the server stops sending is when it receives a notice from the playback software that there was a problem or that the user has sent a command to perform a function like stop or go back in the clip, in which case the server resends data or responds to the command.

In most cases, the media player is a web browser plug-in such as the Real Player from the video streaming industry leader Real Networks or Microsoft's Netshow Player. However, there are other streaming technologies such as Geo System's Emblaze that do not require a plug-in and allow the video to be viewed directly in the web browser.

Creating Files for Online Playback

When media streaming was first introduced, it required an expensive program to encode AVI and QuickTime files into the streaming format and an even more expensive media server program for the host computer. Today, however, competition in the industry has led to the availability of free or low-cost encoders and has reduced the need for server software. While using a media server program can improve performance in many cases, it is no longer required.

Most nonlinear editing programs include software for encoding files in a variety of streaming formats. One popular program is Media Cleaner Pro, which not only allows for encoding files, but also helps create files that are optimized for online performance. This is accomplished by manipulating variables such as the number of colors, image size, and video frame rate based upon the anticipated speed of Internet connection at which the user will be connected.

Once a file has been encoded, it can be easily added to a web page. Real Networks features several low-cost computer programs to help with the process of publishing and managing web pages with audio/video components.

Internet Film Distributors

As more people recognize the strength of the Internet as a promotional and distribution outlet for audio and video products, *webcasting* has emerged from a novel, techie hobby to a rapidly developing industry. Today there are a rapidly growing number of companies offering online distribution of audio and video programs. Sites like IFILM.com and Broadcast.com feature thousands of hours of films and videos.

These companies, and others, typically offer to represent the film-maker in negotiating distribution deals with television or cable networks, film festivals, airlines, etc. They provide free encoding and hosting of films, and in most cases show parts or whole films to the public from their site. Some of these sites ask for exclusive rights to showcase the films, while others ask only for non-exclusive, non-commercial rights.

Most of films shown currently online are shorts, animated films, or trailers for features. Longer films tend to test the patience of web viewers, and many filmmakers wish to display only teasers to generate interest in their work.

Internet film distributors generate revenue mostly from advertisements. However, many of these sites are beginning to package groups of short films together for theatrical runs, cable programming specials, or compilation DVDs which can be purchased online. In these cases, the distributors usually share the proceeds from the deals among the participating filmmakers. A few sites have also experimented, unsuccessfully, with charging viewers to watch or download films on a pay-per-view basis.

Despite the limited revenue currently generated by Internet distribution, most companies recognize that with the spread of high-speed broadband access and developments in video compression technology, it won't be long until the industry explodes.

When selecting an Internet distributor, take you time to carefully read the contract or submission form explaining exactly what distribution rights you are making available to them. Some distributors seek exclusive rights, including home video, syndicated TV, cable TV, and/or colleges and special markets (such as airlines). Others solely acquire the exclusive rights to stream your film on the Internet. While some companies, especially those seeking to build their catalog of products, seek non-exclusive rights that allow you to also offer your project online at other websites.

Self-Promotion

The ability to make yourself and your project stand out from the crowd can be the factor that determines whether a distributor or your audience embraces your film, or walks on by, drawn by the more enticing pitch of one of your peers. In this scheme of things, it's not just who has the better film, but who can sell their film better.

Of course, that is not to say that the product does not have to live up to the hype. Fame is gained and lost by hype, but a career is built on having the talent to draw attention to yourself and your work, then meeting or surpassing people's expectations

If your personality is more comfortable in the isolated world of an editing suite than standing before a few hundred people fielding questions about your film, then you need to expand your understanding of a filmmaker's job description. Somewhere in the small type is the requirement that a filmmaker must serve as a spokesperson for his/her film.

You can get around this, to some degree, by working with people such as producing partners, publicists, and agents who become your cheerleading squad. But if you do not have these affiliations then you will have to bury your shyness and any self-consciousness you have and learn to toot your own horn.

You can begin on a small scale by seeking publicity from local papers during principal photography. You should also send a production notice to the film trades like the *Hollywood Reporter* and *Variety*. Most filmmaking magazines also feature listings of films in pre-production and production. You'll also find many places on the Internet, such as www.filmfinders.com to announce your production.

Additionally, setting up a simple website can offer a means to provide interested parties with more details about yourself, the cast, the crew, and the production. You can set-up a free website using services like www.xoom.com, www.tripod.com, or www.geocities.com. Even if you have no or limited web page design experience, all three services feature easy-to-use page design programs to get you going in a short time.

If your film targets a very specific market you should also begin promotions to that audience as early as possible. Successful grassroots campaigns are built upon the inter-communications and relationships within specific groups.

Press releases to publications and media outlets can garner some attention. However, the challenge of self-promotion is learning how to time you public announcements.

By introducing yourself and your project in the early stages, you provide an opportunity for people to develop familiarity with you long before your project is released. Of course, this can backfire if your project is delayed, or poorly received, but that's true on the low budget level or multi-million dollar film range.

If you learn to accept self-promotion duties as part of your job as an independent filmmaker, it will provide you with an advantage over many filmmakers who may be equally or more talented than you are.

■ ■ ■ ■ ■ ■ Closing Words

I'm Outta Here … Gotta Go Make More Movies

I type these closing words with the sense of having been on an adventure covering a wide range of diverse but very interconnected terrain. My hope is that I have been able to keep you engaged, even through the less exciting but still very significant technical details.

I learned many things while writing the original version of this book. And I have learned and experienced many, many things since. Fortunately, I've been able to apply this knowledge to my own film projects, including my current project, *Paper Chasers*. In fact, I'm happy to say that *Hacks* is also being completed on my Final Cut Pro editing system.

I encourage you to take the information you've read herein and make it your own—apply it, modify it, challenge it. Regardless of whether you make a $500 DV short three years from now, a $500,000 high definition feature next summer, or a $5,000,000 35mm feature in the near future, I hope that you can close this book having been both inspired and informed. Even more, I hope you close this book and say, "I'm going to make a film…"

Until the next time—envision, create and appreciate.
Peace.

■ ■ ■ ■ ■ Case Study:
Paper Chasers

The DV Filmmaker Files is a collection of case studies from digital film projects by filmmakers around the world. To read other case studies or submit your own, visit: www.dvfilmmaker.com/dvfiles/.

Project Summary

Title:	*Paper Chasers*
Filmmaker:	Maxie Collier, aka Son #1
Residence:	Los Angeles, California
Type of Project:	Feature Length Documentary
Production Company:	Next Wave Films and Son #1 Media
Format:	Mini-DV and DVCAM
For Details:	www.paperchaserstv.com

The Idea

Paper Chasers is a feature length documentary about hip-hop entrepreneurship. The film follows me and eight of my friends, also filmmakers and aspiring entrepreneurs, as we drive across country in a RV interviewing hip-hop entrepreneurs and business owners. Our subjects are all successful in the worlds of music, film, fashion and the Internet.

The First Step

Paper Chasers started as one of twelve film and video projects in my original Year 2000 Business Plan for Son #1 Media. However, after a couple of disappointing months of pounding the pavement, trying to raise funds to fully support all of these projects, I changed my strategy and selected *Paper Chasers* as my primary focus.

Once I committed to the project, I immediately created a short proposal that summarized:

- The concept, including a comprehensive list of people I hoped to interview.
- A tentative schedule.
- The production team required.
- The minimum production funds required.
- A couple of paragraphs about the market and marketing strategy.

While I had spent months working on my detailed, thirty-four page business plan for Son #1 Media, I was not willing to invest that sort of time and effort in the creation of a complex plan for the film. I hammered out a five-page project outline one afternoon in late February.

My interview "wish list" featured high profile people like rapper/CEO Master P, rapper/actor Ice Cube, and the godfather of hip-hop entrepreneurship, Def Jam Records founder Russell Simmons. I also selected potential interviewees geographically, based on their base of operations. We would travel from Los Angeles to Houston, and on to New Orleans, Atlanta, Washington D.C. and New York.

After studying the project more thoroughly, I decided on a May 22nd start date—late spring. I knew I did not want to take a traveling production crew down through the hot Southwest and humid Deep South during the summer months. We would need as much pre-production time as possible to coordinate our schedule with the very busy executives I hoped to interview. I completed the project outline determined to start filming by my start date. I had about ten weeks to raise money, book interviews, assemble my crew and coordinate the production.

Raising the Money

Armed with my project outline and contacts established during my years in Los Angeles, I spent the next few days calling, faxing and e-mailing several film production companies and Internet companies. My pitch was straight and to the point:

"I'm producing a documentary on hip-hop entrepreneurs, people like Master P. The film has excellent soundtrack and Internet potential and I've produced other films. I have a team ready and we begin production on May 22nd. Are you interested in seeing a project summary?"

I originally wanted a relationship with a company with a strong track record for creating products for urban audiences. I had witnessed many urban projects fail due to poor or misdirected marketing campaigns. I had talked with a couple of companies before meeting with Peter Broderick, the founder of Next Wave Films (an Independent Film Channel Company) which provides finishing funds for filmmakers with incomplete projects. I had great respect for Peter and his staff; before starting his company, Peter already had a strong track record in the indie film community.

While Next Wave Films had passed on investing in my first project, *Hacks*, Peter and I had become friends, often appearing on the same panel discussions and at the same workshops. Upon hearing about it, Peter immediately took an interest in *Paper Chasers*. Like many others in the film industry, he was very aware of the success Master P and other rappers had achieved with their low budget direct-to-video and theatrical features.

We both agreed that Next Wave's strong industry relationships, coupled with my knowledge and contacts in the hip-hop community (as a result of my years of employment at Black Entertainment Television [BET]) and our mutual knowledge of digital filmmaking, we could effectively produce an outstanding project.

I pitched the project on March 15th. Peter talked with his people at the Independent Film Channel and we were negotiating contracts by April 3rd. I spent nearly three years raising funds to shoot and complete *Hacks*, but less than a month raising the funds for my third project, *Paper Chasers*. I think the difference can be attributed to:

- **The strong and proven market for hip-hop themed films.** Hip-hop films have repeatedly demonstrated the ability to generate substantial home video sales. Additionally, many of these projects also generate significant revenue from soundtracks and album sales. In my pitches, I was able to reference specific films, such as Master P's *I'm 'Bout It* and Roc-A-Fella Record's docu-drama, *The Streets Is Watching*.
- **New contacts and relationships.** *The DV Filmmaker's Handbook* and The DV Filmmaker's Website created many opportunities for me. While the book has generated modest amounts of cash, the website has been a non-profit and very time-consuming hobby. However, my investment has paid off with the invaluable contacts, relationships and credibility both projects have generated.
- **My demonstrated ability to plan and coordinate a large project.** *Hacks*, with fifty-one speaking parts and many logistical dilemmas, showed that I was capable of pulling a team together to handle the requirements of this cross-country trek.
- **Living and working in Los Angeles.** I fought the move as long as I could, but the contacts and resources available in Los Angeles have made it well worth it.

What advice would I offer the first-time filmmaker with no track record or contacts? Commit yourself to producing something, anything—a script, a short, a business plan, a web page. Something that shows the world you are moving forward no matter what.

As the negotiations kicked in for us, I moved into full pre-production.

Fast but Not Easy: Pre-Production

Pre-production for *Paper Chasers* actually started the day I sat down and wrote my proposal. I created a rough budget and schedule and identified potential crew members and vendors. Directorially, I immediately made it a habit to tape the steps I was taking to pull the production together.

The budget was completely reworked. The original budget called for four of us to travel across country in a mini-van. However, with the funds provided by Next Wave Films, we could now afford to bring additional crew members and upgrade from a mini-van to RV.

Also, we now had to be more concerned about additional expenses, such workman's compensation insurance and a payroll service to properly handle tax issues.

My Production Team

Part of the "hook" for *Paper Chasers* is the fact that my production crew was to be comprised of a group of close friends. Six of the eight crew members were film and television professionals I knew from the Maryland/DC area who had also relocated Los Angeles. Like me, these friends aspire to make films and build successful businesses. My goal was for *Paper Chasers* to be a high profile project that pulled us all together and created new opportunities for everyone involved.

Of course, with a bunch of unique, diverse personalities, it would be a challenge. Hence, the motivation for documenting the behind-the-scenes as well as the interviews with our subjects.

My core production team consisted of:

Yvette Plummer—Producer/2nd Unit Director

Yvette had previously produced and directed a feature titled *A State of Mind*. She was very familiar with low budget production, and her experience and contacts were invaluable. Additionally, she had just wrapped production on a freelance gig with MTV's hip-hop variety show, *Lyricist Lounge*. She was the perfect candidate to document the behind-the-scenes material.

Rebekah Sindoris—Line Producer

Rebekah first worked with me as a production assistant on *Hacks*. By the time she relocated to Los Angeles a couple of years later, she had gained enough experience to help me produce another digital project. She came on board as line producer for *Paper Chasers* and immediately began getting the finances and paperwork in order.

Eric Taraby—Production Coordinator

As the production paperwork piled up, Rebekah brought in Eric Taraby to assist her. Although he had no previous production experience, he had spent a couple of years working in the fast-paced industry of professional sports. He was attracted to the project and was willing to provide support for Rebekah. He would also help with booking and scheduling interviews, particularly once we got on the road and the rest of us were dealing with the interviews at hand.

Hans "Prime" Dobson—Associate Producer/Marketing and PR

Prime and I became friends while working together at BET. He went on to become one of the on-camera hosts of BET's most popular shows, *Rap City*. Blessed with an outstanding gift of gab, Prime is one of those people who can be placed in any environment and an hour later walk out with dozens of business cards and new friends. He was also used to working with temperamental celebrities (although he can be a bit of a temperamental celebrity himself). He used his talents to help book interviews and promote the film while we were on the road. He was also going to be the relief interviewer to fill in when I was conducting other interviews with the primary camera.

Anthony Artis—Associate Producer/2nd Unit DP

Anthony also worked with me on *Hacks*, where he did an excellent job as locations manager. Some of my first experiences with DV were with Anthony shooting on a VX-1000. We reconnected a couple of years later when he moved to Los Angeles. A multi-talented techie with an NYU Film School background, Anthony is a production jack-of-all-trades. Together, he and Yvette would be the 2nd unit documenting the behind-the-scenes activities. He was also critical in the office as we wrote and faxed dozens of letters to potential interviewees.

Eric McClain—Director of Photography

Eric and I knew each other from the D.C. film community. Eric spearheaded a collective of filmmakers known as Black Magic Cinemaworks. The group created several award-winning, low-budget sci-fi shorts. Eric had shot film and video for years. Since moving to Los Angeles, he freelanced as a colorist at major post-production houses such as Hollywood Digital and Riot Digital. His film, video and post experience, along with his low-budget production experience, made him an excellent choice for director of photography.

Marquez "The Greatest" Edmonds—Technical Assistant/Sound

Marquez is a professional comedian and actor. We met in the early '90s when Marquez played a small role in one of my early short films in D.C. After losing contact for a few years, we stumbled across each other at a Los Angeles comedy club. He was taking production classes at the time and expressed an interest in working together on some productions. For *Paper Chasers*, he was responsible for production sound and assisting with lighting.

Roman Gabriel—Still Photographer/PA

Roman is an exceptionally talented photographer and another Maryland refugee. He, Prime and Eric had all been friends for several years. He came to California to attend the prestigious Art Center College of Design in Pasadena. Our budget was so tight (even with the Next Wave funds) that there was no budget for a still photographer. I planned on handing several 35mm and digital cameras to crew members and encourage everyone to take stills. After learning about the project, Roman called and offered his services if the production was willing to cover some minimal expenses. He also had the great idea of us doing a photojournalistic book in addition to my own book. He took initiative and made a deal with Ilford Film to provide us with free film stock.

We also had Production Assistants in the office (Robin J., Brian M. and Yolie R.) and various cities (Jojo, Brian H. and Jeff D.) to which we traveled.

Since most of the crew worked on a freelance basis, they were able to adjust their schedules on short notice and sign on to the production. With the team in place, we got to work seeking potential sponsors, booking interviews and making deals with key vendors, including equipment rental houses, hotels, and automotive and RV rentals.

Looking for Sponsors

While Rebekah got the office together, Yvette and Eric T. started contacting potential sponsors, hoping for some deals or better yet, cash, in exchange for product placement. Recognizing the commercial influence rap music, fashion, and films have had on youth culture worldwide, many companies now marketed directly to this audience by sponsoring everything from concerts to Internet websites.

With us taping hours of behind-the-scenes material, there would be many opportunities for companies to receive exposure. We sought product placement from soft drink companies, clothing manufacturers, hotels, airlines, car rentals and the RV rental. By the end of production we had received:

- Cases of Snapple, Hawaiian Punch, Canada Dry Ginger Ale and more. We drank them around the production office and on the road. This saved us hundreds for our slim craft services budget.
- A discounted rental on a Ford Explorer. This saved us about $1,000.
- A discounted RV rental from Cruise America. In exchange for a credit in the film, we received a 25 percent discount on our rental. This saved us about $1,200. However, had I really considered all of the exposure their RV receives with every drive-by shot, I definitely would have tried for a much better deal.
- Free clothes from Foot Locker and hip-hop fashion designer Ralph Reynolds (RP55). We later interviewed Ralph and RP55 co-founder Ron Perry at their Virginia Beach headquarters.
- Free rolls of still film stock from Ilford Films. Roman captured some incredible photos using Ilford's black and white negative stock.

With time tight, we were not able to cut as many deals as I hoped. But the savings were still definitely worth the effort. In addition, Yvette and Eric's work had the added benefit of introducing the project to the hip hop marketing world. These will be good relationships as the project develops.

Booking Interviews

Anthony and I got to work booking interviews. I knew from working on many music video sets and hip hop shows that it was going to be a challenge to pin down some of these busy hip hop executives and artists, particularly with the start of the summer tour season.

Many of the rap artists I was targeting had reputations of keeping interviewers waiting for hours—or worse, blowing off their appointments altogether. I had worked music videos shoots where artists had kept well-paid crews waiting for hours, causing the video to go over budget by the thousands. So why would they make they themselves available for us?

Our approach was to present the film as a historical documentation that would tell the success stories of some of the hip hop community's key players. We created a pitch that would help the film be seen as an opportunity that should not be missed.

I contracted with another member of our collective, graphic artist Nick Quinn, to produce some stunning four-color letterhead, business cards and promo sheets. It would be crucial for us to present ourselves professionally when our material reached the hands of publicists and agents fielding dozens of interview requests.

I had previously compiled a prioritized list of nearly seventy-five people I would like to interview. We began to research contact information from record labels, websites, and personal contacts.

After creating a form letter introducing the project, we began to work the phones, faxes and e-mails like telemarketers. It's amazing how many people you have to go through to get to a well-known celebrity. First, a record label refers you, if you're lucky, to an ex-publicist who passes you off to a new manager who stands in front of you like a leprechaun watching his pot of gold. And once you get the okay, you still have to spend time going through a personal assistant to schedule an interview time.

Still, we made progress booking the interviews. However, I had a lot of concern about our scheduling. For example, I really wanted to interview Master P. But what if we drove all the way to New Orleans and he wasn't there? Should we go to Atlanta early or stick around?

In those instances, my plan was to still tape as much as possible about the person and his or her hometown, as well as interviewing other, lesser known but in some cases equally impressive, entrepreneurs. This approach actually worked far better than I imagined, although it did require the production to be much more flexible.

After wrapping up his work with sponsors, Eric T. joined us and continued booking guests until the last day of principal photography.

Working without Funds in Place

The production team came together pretty quickly but it took a bit longer to negotiate our contract with Next Wave Films and get the funds flowing. For nearly a month I, with the aid of my credit cards and short-term loans from friends, had to cover mounting production expenses, including payroll. My crew was very supportive, but by the third week of long days, things were a bit stressful. I ignored thoughts in the back of my mind of what would I do if the Next Wave deal fell apart.

My first production coordinator, another young Marylander I had hoped to train on the job, was not able to afford to continue with the project. He could not afford to continue working for the small stipends I was paying until funds became available. Plus, his girlfriend was not too excited about him being away on the road for close to four weeks. Especially not around the world of hip hop groupies we would be encountering. He was out of there . . .

Rebekah brought Eric Taraby in as a replacement. Later, I would be grateful this switch happened before we hit the road. Production was too fast-paced and our team was too small for me to have time to train a person in office skills and production procedures. Eric T. came with a good set of organizational skills and a very people-oriented personality, both of which are job requirements for a good production coordinator. Eric T. was able to deal with the tiny salary we had to offer.

To incentivize the rest of the crew, I offered everyone who made it all the way through production, specifically everyone who made it from Los Angeles through the last day of shooting in New York, points in the project.

When the funds finally came through, everyone became much more focused and at ease, although the work days continued to be long.

Directorially

The momentum began picking up as we got closer to our start date. I was giving more consideration to the focus and structure of the film as well as the visual style.

Other hip hop documentaries, like *The Show* and *Rhyme and Reason*, focused on the history of hip hop music. I was always clear to tell people that *Paper Chasers* was more about exploring the business of hip hop. We wanted to establish personal profiles of each entrepreneur's path to success as well as asking specific business questions about planning, production, marketing and dealmaking.

My goal was to create an entertaining project that educated and inspired viewers with incredible success stories. And I wanted to parallel our behind-the-scenes activities with the day-to-day business experiences of the entrepreneurs we were interviewing.

Visually I wanted to create a clear distinction between the look of the behind-the-scenes footage and our interviews. I wanted the behind-the-scenes material to feel like footage captured by a group of friends hanging out: very gritty and unpolished, very real.

On the other hand, every interview we booked and taped was such a coup that I wanted them to appear radically different. I wanted a very stylized look that used lighting and careful shot composition to dramatically capture the image of these executives in their workspaces. To accomplish this goal we taped behind-the-scenes footage using a low-end single chip camera, the Canon Ultura, and a 3 chip, Panasonic EZU1. For our main camera, we primarily used a Sony DSR-500WS, and occasionally a DSR-300. The images produced by these cameras are far superior to those of the Ultura and EZU1, particularly the DSR-500, which featured true 16:9 capabilities.

Hitting the Road: Production

A lot of our experiences during production are documented in the movie, so I'm not going to elaborate on those details here (see the movie or visit the *Paper Chasers* website). However, I am including our equipment list along with a few notes.

Our Equipment Package

Cameras and Accessories

CANON ULTURA. I purchased this low cost mini-DV camera for about $900. This camera was used to record hours of behind-the-scenes footage prior to our departure. Once on the road, it became the "anyonecam," meaning it could be used at any time by anyone on the crew who wanted to shoot. Every person on the crew shot with this camera at some point in time. It produces great images in daylight and in well-lighted situations, but in low light the images quickly begin to look noisy and pixilated. Just the minimalist look I wanted to contrast with the DSR-500 footage. We also used this camera as a DV deck to create back-up dubs of DVCAM master tapes.

PANASONIC EZU1. Eric owned the Japanese equivalent of this camera. Since the controls were in Japanese, only a few people on the crew became proficient with it. As the primary second unit camera, it was most often used by Yvette and Anthony. This camera produced very distinct images, with a noticeable bias towards reds and greens. It also worked well under low light situations. We frequently shot with an inexpensive wide-angle converter (particularly inside the RV). Unfortunately, midway through the shoot the camera's microphone jack developed an unpredictable short that intermittently wreaked havoc on the audio. Fortunately, we often had the Canon taping also.

SONY DSR-300 AND DSR-500WS. Some of our first interviews were taped with a $12,000+ Sony DSR-300 on loan from a friend and supporter (thanks, Reed R!). This full-sized, shoulder mounted camera produced images that were significantly sharper than the Panasonic and Canon cameras we used.

However, the camera was unavailable for our three-week road trip. Additionally, after using it a few times, I began to play with the idea of shooting our interview segments, concerts, and scenic shots in 16:9 to even further stylize the look. Since the DSR-300 did not feature a true 16:9 chip, I decided to use a more sophisticated model, the DSR-500WS. Costing over $20,000, the DSR-500WS produces images nearly on par with digital Betacam, even under low light. We taped phenomenal concert footage in nightclubs illuminated by disco balls.

While the rental fee was more than the purchase price of some mini-DV cameras, this camera allowed Eric to deliver exactly the look I wanted. He spent a few days prior to our departure becoming used to the camera's many options and quirks (for example, he was forced to open the camera and manually flip a small switch to turn on the camera's 16:9 mode, versus being able to select the option from a pull-down menu).

Audio
SONY ECM-44B LAVALIERE MICS. We purchased a couple from B & H Photo Video for about $140 each. They worked great.

SENNHEISER MKE-300 SHOTGUN MIC. We used this inexpensive mono shotgun microphone with the second unit camera. It performed well and featured a mini-plug, allowing it to easily go from the Canon Ultura to the Panasonic EZU1 without an XLR adapter. However, it was this swapping that eventually lead to the short that developed in the Panasonic camera. In retrospect, I should have purchased XLR adapters for both cameras and gone with a more professional shotgun.

AUDIO TECHNICA 835A. I planned on using this microphone in situations that required mobility (such as walking and talking with an interviewee) as well as group interviews where more than two people would be talking. This low cost mic is very sensitive and works best booming from practically right above the subject. We ended up only using it a few times.

SOUND DEVICES PRE-AMP MIXER. I first saw this rugged little $750 mixer/pre-amp at the National Association of Broadcasters conferences where several production sound people recommended it. It worked fine for us, although it has fewer inputs and it is a bit more difficult to use to monitor levels than some of the more expensive mixers (like the Shure FP-33).

Lights
ARRIFLEX 3 LIGHT KIT. Our camera package rental included a classic, old Arriflex light kit that included three heads (500-650 watts), stands and barndoors packed in a very rugged hard shell case. However, packing and unloading this heavy and bulky kit several times a day became a job that caused a lot of dissension among my overworked crew. Halfway through the trip, I just started hauling it myself. Next time, I'll definitely go with the much, much smaller Lowell three light kit, even though the Lowell lights are not quite as precise and controllable as the Arri kit.

Tape Stock

We used an assortment of tape stock including: Sony Mini-DV and DVCAM, Panasonic Mini-DV, Fuji Mini-DV, JVC Mini-DV and TDK Mini-DV. We found the TDK tapes on sale at Costco (a warehouse club that allows members to purchase in bulk) for the incredible price of three for $21. To be honest, they looked and felt less durable than the other tapes, but we shot with quite a few of them without problems. However, in post-production it became obvious that they were in fact very poorly constructed. We have experienced problems with tape jams and I cannot recommend this stock, despite its low price.

Production Equipment

We had three laptops and four cellular phones for our traveling production office. We were able to connect one of the phones to our laptops to have wireless Internet service (Sprint PCS) that allowed us to conduct research and use e-mail while traveling. This proved invaluable, though the service only worked near mid-size cities.

We also had an iMac DV in the RV. I thought we would have time to use it to log tapes while driving between cities. I also hoped to cut a trailer after a few interviews. However, by the time we hit the road most of our time between cities was spent driving or recuperating from our hectic shooting schedule. The iMac ended up mostly being used to watch DVDs and as an office machine.

Life on the Road

We pulled out in our RV on May 22nd, as planned. We drove 1,400 miles to Houston then hit the ground running and gunning with our first interviews. For the next three and a half weeks our routine was drive, shoot interviews, book more interviews, party, argue and drive some more. It became an adventurous grind that challenged us all—the hot humid Houston days, the cramped RV, cheap hotels, the unpredictable interviews, late night concerts, groupies and more.

It didn't take long for our team to get in a good rhythm during our interviews. Once we arrived at a location, Prime and Eric T. would meet and greet our liaisons while I shifted into interview mode. After meeting our interviewee, I'd walk through their workspace with Eric M. to select an area in which to conduct the interview. We would look for elements of the location that we could accent with controlled lighting to create a dramatic look. After talking through the set-up, we'd unload and get down to business setting-up the shot.

Eric M. and Anthony would set lights and camera. Roman would help them while taking still photos. Marquez would set up his audio gear. Yvette would record the behind-the-scenes footage. Prime would finesse an assistant or breakaway with the anyonecam and shoot secondary interviews with others in the vicinity. Eric T. would be planning for the next interview and Rebekah would juggle the logistics for the next city.

After a few days we were a well-oiled production machine. But behind the scenes was a whole different story. In fact, that is the story and the foundation for the film. That's all I have to say about it for now . . .

Things I Might Have Changed

Looking back, there are a few key items I would plan differently. If I had more money I would have added two more people to the crew (this would have also required a larger RV):

A **Driver**–Driving, on top of our production issues, placed additional stress on us all. Our budget did not allow us to hire a person strictly to drive. However, if I searched the local colleges I probably could have found someone willing to do it for the experience.

An **AD**–I spent countless hours dealing with issues with my crew, particularly as we got further into production. These issues included delegating tasks, making sure people were on time for crew call, disseminating schedule information to the crew, resolving conflicts, and keeping everyone motivated. This was on top of driving, conducting as many as five comprehensive interviews in a day, and putting time in on the phone trying to book interviews. Eric T. helped as best he could, but his time and efforts were best spent planning ahead for the next city. An experienced AD would have had a significant impact on personnel management and served as a buffer between me and the crew.

A less **demanding schedule**–I would have spent more time in each city and planned more days off for the crew. Of our twenty-six days on the road, our schedule allowed us only two days off. This took its toll on all of us.

A **more experienced crew**–One of my goals for this project was to pull together my group of friends and create an opportunity for us all. However, I realize now that the inexperience of several production people introduced unnecessary stress. The production was already challenging enough without having to hear numerous grievances from people learning on the job. On the other hand, it was our different personalities and prior relationships to each other that provided the foundation for the behind-the-scenes drama.

Success

By June 16th, when we wrapped in New York City, we had driven over 4,000 miles, taped fifty-three interviews, and recorded over a 120 hours of footage (by the time we added our pre-production footage and Los Angeles interviews, we had closer to 150 hours of material). We were also successful in generating a buzz in the hip hop community. We accomplished our mission.

Life after Strife: Post-Production

Even as I write this I am deep in post-production for *Paper Chasers*. I'm very happy with the process and love the freedom of editing in my own home at all hours of the night. Critical to all this has been organizing 150 hours of material.

I found some cheap, stackable plastic storage bins at a local office supply store. They were less than $20 and feature a dozen pull-out trays that I have labeled by date and city. Each bin can hold about ten mini-DV tapes. I store the DVCAM tapes on top of the bins, which allows me easy access to all of the material.

In Final Cut Pro, I have created bins and directories that mirror the arrangement of bins and tapes on my desk. I have also kept several notebooks on hand with printed logs. My approach to editing all of this is to completely edit our behind-the-scenes footage without including the interviews, thus making the behind-the-scenes footage serve as the foundation of the film. The interview segments will be added later, based on chronology and subject matter.

I'll have many more post-production notes on the DV Filmmaker's Website once post is complete. But for now, here is some basic information on the editing systems that I'm using for *Paper Chasers* post-production.

- Logging System—iMac DV, 256 Megs. RAM, Final Cut Pro 1.2.5
- Primary System Hardware—Apple Mac G4 (512 Megs. Ram, 27 gig System HD), 60 gig HD added to internal IDE controller, 2 60 gig HDs added using the Sonnet IDE Controller, 30 gig Western Digital External HD, Apple Studio Display 17" Monitor, Sony DSR-20 DVCAM Deck, Sony Trinitron 13" Monitor, Videonics Command Post Controller, Logitech Mouse
- Primary System Software—Mac OS 9, QuickTime Pro, Final Cut Pro 1.2.5

About the Trailer

I have included a short trailer for *Paper Chasers* on the DVD accompanying this book. The trailer was edited in Final Cut Pro. It features extensive use of layering, multi-colored text, mixed aspect rations and wipe transitions that make it a terrible candidate for a video to film transfer. However, I intentionally made it complex in order to test the limits for potential transfer houses. Here are a few notes about the trailer.

First, I created a short musical track using Acid Pro. This great program allows you to easily create tracks using copyright free music elements. I combined these with audio samples from several interviews to create an original track.

Visually, the first shot of me pitching *Paper Chasers* to a couple of guys is from some of the earliest footage I shot for the project. It was taped with the Canon Ultura. As you'd expect, there is a lot of noise from the single chip camera shooting at night with minimum lighting. During this pitch I cutaway to several shots of me with some of the rappers and executives (Master P, James

Prince, and Flava Flav) we interviewed. Those shots where taped with the DSR-500 and DSR-300. This one sequence represents the visual diversity the film will have.

Next, I have a title shot of our RV. This was also shot with the DSR-500.

The next sequence introduces viewers to myself and my crew as "characters" in the film. I used the layering features of Final Cut Pro to add layers of moving landscapes behind shots of my production team to add texture and motion while subtly showing the viewer that the film is a cross-country journey.

The last sequence features sound bites from several of our interviews. In these "talking heads" shots, you will notice how we clearly spent time stylizing our interview set-ups. I even sampled colors from each shot to use for the titles.

Conclusion

So there you have the *Paper Chasers* case study. I've learned quite a bit more about the medium in the months I've been married to this project. I hope you've been able to learn more from these real world notes. To keep up to date about *Paper Chasers*, visit the website at www.paperchaserstv.com.

Now, it's time for me to grab another cup of coffee and get back to editing.

Peace,

Maxie Collier

▪▪▪▪▪ Appendices

References and Resources

Companies listed in this directory are to be utilized at your own discretion. A listing does not represent an endorsement. Research carefully prior to doing business.

Acting & Casting

Acting World Books	(818) 905-1345
Actor's Site	www.actorsite.com
Actor's Source	www.actorsource.com
A-Z Fastcast	www.a-zfastcast.com (818) 377-4444
Backstage Magazine Casting:	www.backstage.com (323) 525-2356
Caryn.com Actor's Area	www.caryn.com/foractors.html
Casting Net	www.castingnet.com
CastNet.com	www.castnet.com (323) 964-4900
Cyber Showbiz	www.cybershowbiz.com
Extracast.com	www.extracast.com
Hollywood Actors Network	www.hollywoodnetwork.com/hn/acting/

Audio Editing

Cool Edit—Software	www.syntrillium.com
Mixman Technologies	www.mixman.com
The Pan Handler Surround sound plugin	www.sbfilmaudio.com/audio.html (800) 681-8671
Samplitude Pro—Software Soundspirations	www.soundspiration.com (214) 298-3472
Sound Forge—Software Sonic Foundry	www.sonicfoundry.com (800) 57SONIC
WAVES Audio processing software.	www.waves.com (423) 689-5395

Camera Support & Stabilization Systems

Cinema Products Steadicam Jr. & DV	www.steadicam.com (800) 311-2463
Crane Construction Plans—Free	www.pacifier.com/~tmnathe/boom.html
Glidecam Industries Camera stabilization system	www.glidecam.com (800) 949-2089
Jimmy Jib	www.jimmyjib.com (602) 493-9505
Steady Tracker Cranes and stabilization systems	www.steadytracker.com (714) 362-3741

Cinematography & Videography

Desktop Video Newsgroup Accessible through www.dejanews.com	rec. video.desktop
Video Production Newsgroup Accessible through www.dejanews.com	rec. video.Production

Crew Sources

Cineweb's Connections	www.cineweb.com/connections/
Creative Planet	www.creativeplanet.com
Crew Net	www.crewnet.com
Film & Movie Crew Job Board	members.aol.com/crewjobs/
Film Biz	www.filmbiz.com/crew/

| IFILM Pro | www.IFILMpro.com |
| Reelmind.com | www.reelmind.com |

Desktop Video

Desktop Video	desktopvideo.about.com
Electronic Mailbox	www.videoguys.com
Multimedia Tools	multimediatools.com

Documentary Filmmaking

| DOX Documentary Film Magazine | www2.dox.dk/dox/ |

Digital Video

DV Central	www.dvcentral.org
The DV Filmmaker's Website	www.dvfilmmaker.com
DV-L E-Mailing List	www.dvcentral.org/thelist.html
Global DVC Group	www.global-dvc.org

DV Cameras & Accessories

Battery Tech. Inc.	(800) 442-4275
Batteries and power supplies.	
Bogen	www.bogenphoto.com
Tripods and supports.	(201) 818-9500
Canon USA	www.canondv.com
	(800) 828-4040
Century Optics	www.centuryoptics.com
Lenses and lens converters.	(800) 228-1254
Hardigg's Cases	www.hardigg.com
Camera cases.	(800) 542-7344
JVC Electronics	www.jvc-america.com
	(973) 315-5000
Markertek Video Supply	www.markertek.com
	(800) 522-2025
NRG Research	www.nrgresearch.com
Batteries and power supplies.	(800) 753-0357
Panasonic	www.panasonic.com
	(201) 348-7000

Sony Electronics	www.sel.sony.com
	(201) 930-1000
Sharp	www.sharpusa.com
	(201) 529-8200
Video Smith	www.videosmith.com
Wondercam shoulder mount.	(215) 238-5050

DVD Authoring

Advance Media Concepts	www.amcmedia.com
	(800) 242-5504
Digital Outpost	www.dop.com
	(800) 464-6434
Digital Video Service Bureau	www.amcmedia.com
	(800) 242-5504
Enterprise DVD	(818) 505-6000
Optibase	www.optibase.com
DVD authoring system.	(800) 451-5101
Video Transfer Inc.	www.vtiboston.com
	(800) 242-3827
Visible Light	www.visiblelight.com
	(800) 569-4494
Vision Wise Inc.	www.visionwise.com
	(888) 979-0473

Editing

Avideditor.com	www.avideditor.com
Avid-LE-mail List	www.itg.uiuc.edu/avid/mail-archive
Mac Digital Video Resources	www.postforum.pair.com
Nonlinear Editing Page	www.nonlinear3.com
Runway Edit's Editor to Editor	www.runway.com/edtoed.html
Zerocut	www.zerocut.com

Entertainment Law & Insurance

D. R. Reiff & Associates	(800) 827-7363
Insurance.	
Harry Tulchin & Associates	www.medialawyer.com
	(310) 914-7979

Mark Litwak, Esq www.marklitwak.com
 Features extensive legal articles. (310) 859-9595

Michael Saleman (888) 222-8959

Robert L. Seigel, Esq (212) 307-7533

The Winogradsky Company (818) 761-6906
 Music creative & legal services.

Festivals & Markets

American Film Market www.afma.com/afm.htm
 Santa Monica, CA (310) 446-1000
 Event: Late Feb.

Berlin Int. Film Festival www.berlinale.de
 Berlin, Germany (011) (49-30) 254-890
 Deadline: Nov. Event: Feb.

Cannes International Film Festival www.festival-cannes.fr
 Cannes, France (011) (33-1) 4561-6600
 Event: May

D.DILM Digital Film Festival www.dfilm.com
 On-going submissions. bcheever@earthlink.net

Film Festivals Website www.filmfestivals.com

Independent Feature Film Market www.ifp.org
 New York, NY (212) 465-8200
 Event: Sept.

LA Independent Film Festival www.laiff.com
 Los Angeles, CA (213) 937-9155
 Deadline: Jan. Event: April

RES FEST Digital Film Festival www.resfest.com
 New York, NY

Rotterdam International Film Festival www.iffrotterdam.nl
 Rotterdam, the Netherlands. (011) (31-10) 411-8080
 Deadline: Late Oct. Event: Late Jan.

Slamdance Film Festival www.slamdance.com
 Salt Lake City, Utah (213) 466-1786
 Deadline: Nov. Event: Late Jan.

South by Southwest Film Festival www.sxsw.com
 Austin, TX (512) 467-7979
 Deadline: Dec. Event: March

Sundance Film Festival www.sundance.org
 Salt Lake City, Utah (801) 328-3456
 Deadline: Oct. Event: Late Jan.

Film and Video Organizations

1394 Trade Association	www.firewire.org
America Cinema Editors	www.ace-filmeditors.org
American Film Market Association	www.afma.com
The Directors Guild	www.dga.org
Independent Feature Project	www.ifp.org
Independent Feature Project West	www.ifpwest.org
The Motion Picture Editors Guild	www.editorsguild.com
	(323) 876-4770
The Producers Guild	www.producersguild.com
Screen Actor's Guild	www.sag.com
Women In Film	www.wif.org
Writer's Guild of America	www.wga.org
	(213) 782-4500

Filmmaking In General

Cyber Film School	www.cyberfilmschool.com
Dov S-S Simens 2 Day Film School	www.HollywoodU.com
	(213) 933-3456
Film.com	www.film.com
Filmmaker Site	www.filmmaker.com
Movie Production Newsgroup	rec. arts.movies.production
Accessible from www.dejanews.com	

Film Reviews & Databases

The Internet Movie Database	www.imdb.com

Financing

Blowup Pictures	www.blowuppictures.com
Next Wave Films	www.nextwavefilms.com
Completion funds for indie films	paradigm@earthlink.net

FireWire Cards

Canopus Corporation DVRex-M1, DVRaptor	www.canopuscorp.com (888) 868-2535
Como USA DV Edit Factory	www.como-usa.com (606) 647-1077
DPS Spark Plus	www.dps.com (905) 944-4000
Fast Electronics DV Master/DV Master Pro	www.fastmultimedia.com (425) 489-5009
Pinnacle Systems Miro DV300	www.pinnaclesys.com
Promax Technologies FireMax Card	www.promax.com (949) 727-3977
Radius Inc. MotoDV	www.radius.com (800) 5-RADIUS
Truevision Bravado DV2000	www.truevision.com (317) 577-8788

Graphics, Animation, Titles, & Special Effects

Adobe Systems After Effects Software	www.adobe.coma (408) 536-6000
Alien Skin Software Adobe Photoshop Filters	www.alienskin.com (919) 832-4124
D ETITLE PRO Titling program.	www.drs-digitrax.com (530) 666-4025
DigiEffects Adobe After Effects plug-ins.	www.digieffects.com (415) 841-9901
ICE (Intergrated Computing Engines) Effects.	www.iced.com (781) 768-2300
Kinetix Animation.	www.ktx.com (415) 547-2000
MetaCreations Animation & effects.	www.metacreations.com (805) 566-6200
Puffin Designs Animation & effects.	www.puffindesigns.com (415) 331-4560
Softimage Effects and graphics.	www.softimage.com (800) 576-3846
Strata Inc. 3D Graphics.	www.strata.com (800) STRATA3D

Technical Animations Inc.   www.techanim.com
  Animation software dealer.   (888) 44-PIXEL

Terran   www.terran.com
  Media Cleaner Pro

Hard Drives, Backup Drives & Controllers

Adaptec   www.adaptec.com
  SCSI Controllers   (408) 262-2533

Cybernetics   (757) 833-9000
  Backup tape drives.

Glyph Technologies   www.glyphtech.com
  DigDAT Backup Tape Drive

Medea   www.medeacorp.com
  VideoRaid systems.   (818) 597-7645

Micronet   www.micronet.com
  SANcube FireWire Drives

Promise Technology   www.promisetechnology.com
  Fast Track Controller Cards

VST Technologies   www.vsttech.com
  FireWire Drives

Independent Theaters

The Independent Theater Search   www.dto.net/indieview/

Internet Distributors

Always Independent Films   www.alwaysif.com

Atom Films   www.atomfilms.com

Broadcast.com   www.broadcast.com

CinemaNow   www.cinemanow.com

Entertaindom   www.entertaindom.com

Eveo   www.eveo.com

ICast   www.icast.com

Icebox Animation   www.icebox.com

IFILM   www.IFILM.com

MediaTrip   www.mediatrip.com

The New Venue   www.newvenue.com

Reelshort	www.reelshort.com
Short TV	www.shorttv.com
SightSound	www.sightsound.com
Sputnik 7	www.sputnik7.com
Studio Next	www.studionext.com
Urban Media	www.urbanentertainment.com
WireBreak Shortz	www.wirebreak.com

Lighting Instruments & Kits

Frezzi Energy Systems	www.frezzi.com
	(973) 427-1160
Kino Flo	(818) 767-6528
Lowel Lights	www.lowel.com
	(800) 334-3426
Mole Richardson	www.homemole.com
	(323) 851-0111
NRG Research	www.nrgresearch.com
	(800) 753-0357
Smith-Victor (call for catalog)	(800) 348-9862

Mail Order Audio & Video Sales

See also Value Added Resellers

ADORAMA	www.AdoramaCamera.com
	(800) 888-2410
B & H Photo/Video	www.bhphotovideo.com
	(800) 221-5743
Berger Bros.	www.berger-bros.com
	(888) 262-4160
Camera Sound	www.camerasound.com
	(800) 477-0022
Digital Video Direct	www.dvdirect.com
	(888) 383-8783
Discount Video Warehouse	(800) 323-8148
Electronic Mailbox	www.videoguys.com
	(800) 323-2325
Vidicomp	www.vidicomp.com
	(800) 263-8216

Music and Sound Effects

ASCAP	www.ascap.com
Music publishing	(323) 883-1000
Beatnik	www.beatnik.com
Music publishing	
BMI	www.bmi.com
Music publishing	(310) 659-9109
Cakewalk	www.cakewalk.com
Music Production Software and Scorewriter	888-CAKEWALK
Cinematrax-Original Music	www.cinematrax.com
The Classical Midi Archives	www.prs.net
Con Tempo Music Library	(888) MUSIC 85
Buyout music.	
Creative Support Services	www.cssmusic.com
Buyout music & Effects	(800) 468-6874
Ethnic & Folk MIDI Files	ingeb.org/home.html
House of Wave	www.houseofwave.com
Buyout music.	(888) 367-5200
Indie Film Composers	www.indifilm.com
Composers network.	(408) 353-3771
Introduction to MIDI	www.eeb.ele.tue.nl/midi/intro.html
Manchester Music Library	(888) 846-3745
Buyout music.	
MIDI Music	midimusic.miningco.com
Mixman Technologies	www.mixman.com
The Music Bakery	www.musicbakery.com
Buyout music.	(800) 229-0313
Musicopia	www.musicopia.com
Buyout music	(800) 622-7723

The 1997 Directory of Public Domain Music
Katzmarek Publishing   members.aol.com/Katzmarek/pdmusic.htm
(320) 558-6801

The Public Domain Music Bible,
dNet Online, $577   www.d-net.com/min/min10080.Htm
(800) 827-9401

The Public Domain Report-Newsletter	www.pubdomain.com
	(800) 927-9401
Sonic Desktop	www.smartsound.com
SmartSound Soundtrack Software	(888) 668-3711

Sonic Foundry   www.sonicfoundry.com
  Acid Music Production Software   (608) 256-7300

Soundtrack Studios   www.soundtrackgroup.com
  Post sound services.   (212) 420-6010

Microphones & Audio Accessories

Audio Technica   www.audio-technica.com
  Microphones.

Azden Corp.   www.azden.com
  Microphones.   (516) 328-7500

Beachtek   www.beachtek.com
  Audio adapters.   (416) 690-9457

Elite Video   www.elitevideo.com
  Adapters and accessories.   (800) 468-1996

Letrosonic   www.lectro.com
  Microphones.   (505) 892-4501

Roland Corp. US   www.rolandus.com
  Music & recording instruments.   (213) 685-5141

Samson Technologies   www.samsontech.com
  Microphones.   (516) 364-2244

Sennheiser Electronics   www.sennheiserusa.com
  Microphones and headphones.   (860) 434-9190

Studio1 Productions   www.studio1productions.com
  Audio adapter box.   (800) 788-068

TASCAM   www.tascam.com
  Digital and analog audio equipment.   (213) 726-0303

Nonlinear Editing Systems & Information

See also FireWire Cards

Avid Systems   www.avid.com
                                         (800) 949-AVID

DPS   www.dps.com
  Perception PVR   (800) 775-3314

Draco Systems   www.draco.com
  Casablanca Editing Machine   (303) 440-5311

The Electronic Mailbox   www.videoguys.com
                                         (800) 323-2325

Fast Electronics   www.fastmultimedia.com
  601 Six-O-One MPEG-2 System   (425) 489-5009

Matrox Video Product Group DigiSuite & Digisuite LE	www.matrox.com (800) 361-4903
Media 100	www.media100.com (508) 460-1600
Pinnacle Systems Miro DC30+ , Miro DC50	www.pinnaclesys.com (800) 4PINNACLE
Truevision Bravado 2000	www.truevision.com (800) 522-8783

Periodicals—Print & Electronic

Backstage Magazine	www.backstage.com
Daily Variety	www.variety.com
Digital Cinema	www.tech-head.com
DV Magazine	www.dv.com
The DV Filmmaker's Report– Email Newsletter	www.dvfilmmaker.com
DVEreview-Newsletter	www.dvereview.com
Film Score Monthly	www.filmscoremonthly.com
Filmmaker Magazine	www.filmmag.com
The Hollywood Reporter	www.hollywoodreporter.com
Indiewire-Email Newsletter	www.indiewire.com
Interactivity Magazine	www.interactivity.com
Movie Maker Magazine	www.moviemaker.com
New Media Magazine	www.newmedia.com
Production Weekly	www.productionweekly.com
RES Magazine	www.resmag.com
Videography Magazine	www.videography.com
Videomaker Magazine	www.videomaker.com

Production Expendables

Studio Depot	www.homemole.com (323) 851-0111

Production Sound Recording

Designing A Movie For Sound
          filmsound.studienet.org/articles/designing_for_ sound.htm
The Movie Sound FAQ   www.moviesoundpage.com

Scripts & Script Writing

The Copyright Website   www.benedict.com
The Craft of Screenwriting   www.wga.org/craft/
Drew's Script-O-Rama   www.script-o-rama.com
Final Draft Script Software   www.bcsoftware.com
The Megahits Page   www.mmsysgrp.com/megahits/
New York Screenwriter   www.nyscreenwriter.com
The Nine Act Structure Home Page   www.dsiegel.com/film/
Screenwriter's and Playwright's Home Page
          www.teleport.com/~cdeemer/scrwriter.html/
The Screenwriter's Homepage   home.earthlink.net/~scribbler/
Screenwriter's Utopia   www.screenwritersutopia.com
Screenwriters.com   www.screenwriters.com
Script Format Style   www.panam.edu/scrnwrit/
The Script Doctor   www.scriptdoctor.qpg.com/
  Script analyst   (818) 505-8525
US Copyright Office   lcweb.loc.gov/copyright/
The Writer's Computer Store   writerscomputer.com
          (800) 272-8927

Television

Alliance For Community Media   www.alliancecm.org
History of TV Technology   www.rcc.ryerson.ca/homepg/writings/
Public Access   www.modpro.com/ual/

Value Added Resellers

Amigo Business Computers	www.amigobc.com
	(516) 757-7234
Digital Video Equipment Co.	www.stselec.com
	(800) 226-7871
Image Machines	(800) 909-7879
Intelligent Media Inc.	www.intelligentmedia.com
	(818) 615-1700
Ocean Systems	www.oceansystems.com
	(800) 253-7516
ProMax Technology	www.promax.com
	(949) 727-3977

Video Duplication, Packaging, & Printing

Custom Video	(800) 380-7339
Darke Video	(510) 465-0181
DPS Video	(800) 638-3876
Eastco Pro	www.eastcopro.com
	(800) 365-8273
ICCA	(800) 624-5940
Karol Media	www.karolmedia.com
	(800) 526-4773
MAI Video Duplication	(800) 987-6440
Postcard Press	(800) 957-5787
4-color promotional material.	
Professional Label	www.prolabel.com
	(301) 570-0774
SF Video	(800) 545-5865
Sterling Video	(800) 705-9850
VAV Fulfillment Service	www.vfsfulfillment.com
	(888) 828-3873

Video Editing & Support Software

Adobe Systems Inc. Adobe Premiere	www.adobe.com

Apple Computer, Inc.
  Final Cut Pro
  iMovie
	www.apple.com

In: Sync Corporation Speed Razor DV	www.in-sync.com (301) 656-1700
Radius Inc. EditDV	www.radius.com (800) 5-RADIUS
Ulead Media Studio Pro	www.ulead.com (800) 85-ULEAD

Video Projection Systems

Digital Projection	www.digitalprojection.com

Video Streaming

Emblaze	www.emblaze.com
GTS	www.graham.com
Microsoft Media Player	www.microsoft.com/windows/mediaplayer
Real Networks Real Audio and Real Video	www.realnetworks.com

Video Tape Stock

American Video Tape Warehouse	www.americanvideotape.com (800) 598-8273
Tape Resources	(800) 827-3462
Tele-Measurements Inc.	(800) 223-0052 x 205

Video to Film Transfers

Canadian National Film Board
  3155 chemin Cote de Liesse Road, T-4
  Saint-Laurent, Quebec H4N 2N4
	www.nfb.ca
	(514) 283-9258

Cineric New York, NY	www.cineric.com (212) 586-4822

Duart Film Lab
New York, NY

www.duart.com
(212) 757-4580

Duboi Digital Effects
22 rue Paul-Vaillant Couturier, 92300
Levallois-Perret, France

www.duboi.com
(33) 01 47 59 89 89

Film Craft Labs
Detroit, MI

(313) 962-2611

Film Team USA
Austin, Texas

www.dvfilm.com
filmteam@uas.net, (310) 362-8616

Four Media Corp.
2820 W. Olive Ave.
Burbank, CA 91505

www.4mc.com
(818) 840-7106

Sony High Definition Center
Culver City, CA

www.spe. sony.com/PICTURES/Hidef/
(310) 280-7433

Video Treatment Services & Software

DigiEffects
Cinelook Software

www.digiefects.com
(415) 841-9901

Filmlook Inc.

www.filmlook.com
(818) 955-7082

Roland House Video (Filmreel process)

www.rolandhouse.com
(703) 525-7000

■ ■ ■ ■ ■ Glossary

1.33:1–The aspect ratio of television, 16mm film, and Super-35mm film. Based on a screen measuring 4 units across by 3 units down.

1.66:1–The aspect ratio of Super-16mm film.

1.78:1–The aspect ratio of high definition and digital television, based on a screen measuring 16 units wide by 9 units tall.

1.85:1–The aspect ratio of 35mm film.

4:1:1–The luminance to chrominance sampling ratio used in DV. For every 4 samples of luminance (video brightness level), chrominance (red and blue color information) is sampled once

4:2:2–The D1 standard video luminance to chrominance sampling ratio. The higher chrominance provides for better color reproduction.

8 Bit–Computer data comprised of 8 elements. Remains in use by older computer software, processors, and accessories.

12 Bit–Computer data comprised of 12 individual elements. The size of digital samples used by one of DV's audio specifications.

16 Bit–Computer data comprised of 16 individual elements, provides more information than 12 bit. The size of higher quality digital samples used by another of DV's audio specifications.

16:9–The aspect ratio of high definition and digital television as expressed in horizontal by vertical units.

24 fps–24 frames per second. The rate at which motion picture film is photographed and projected in the US and other countries.

24p–24 frames per second progressive scan. A video format that records video in a manner similar to a film camera.

25 fps–25 frames per second. The rate at which motion picture film is photographed and projected, and television images recorded and displayed in Europe and other countries.

30 fps–30 frames per second. The rate of images recorded and displayed by the NTSC television system used in the US and other countries.

32kHz–32 kilohertz. One frequency at which audio is sampled in the DV format.

44.1 kHz–44.1 kilohertz. The frequency at which CD quality audio is sampled. Also one of the frequencies available for DV audio.

48 kHz–48 kilohertz. The highest audio sampling frequency for DV audio.

1080i–A high-definition video standard featuring 1,080 lines of interlaced video.

A/B Roll Editing–Editing is performed using two video sources, A and B, and a video switcher or mixer that allows for a variety of transitions between them as they are recorded to a video recorder.

Accelerated Graphic Port (AGP)–A low cost bus system developed to provide high speed 2D and 3D graphics.

Active Pixel Elements–The individual, microscopic light sensitive pieces of a charged coupled device used to convert images to video signals.

AD–Assistant Director

Ad-lib–A spontaneous or improvised performance.

Ambient Sound–The background sounds present in any environment.

Analog Signals–Signals created, measured, and transmitted by variations in electronic frequencies.

Anamorphic–A wide angled lens system that compresses picture information to fit into a small aspect ratio. To be properly viewed must be uncompressed during projection using another anamorphic lens.

Anti-Alias–A technique used to eliminate the digital looking jagged edges of computer graphics and text.

Aperture–Also known as the iris. The adjustable lens opening that controls the amount of light reaching the CCD.

Artifacts–Undesirable, visual imperfections as a result of stray pixels.

Aspect Ratio–The relationship between the width and the height of a picture. Determines a pictures shape. 35mm film is more rectangular than standard video.

Assets–The video, audio, and graphic elements used to author DVD.

Asynchronous–Two-way communications without a fixed timing rate as devices try to communicate at the highest data rate possible.

Attenuate–To reduce the level of sound waves.

Audio Slate–A verbal announcement of take and scene number recorded before a scene.

Audio Video Interleave (AVI)–The established Video for Windows file format combines video and audio information.

Authoring System–A high powered computer system used to encode media files and program DVD.

Authoring–The process of creating DVD.

Automatic Dialogue Replacement (ADR)—Re-recording poor or absent audio by having actors perform their lines in sync with the picture. Also called looping.

Automatic Gain Control—Circuitry that monitors and limits the intensity of audio and video levels.

AV Rated Hard Drives—Durable hard drives designed to sustain data transfer rates required for audio and video production.

Back Light—A light used to separate a subject from the background.

Balanced Line—A professional signal and cabling method that reduces an audio line's susceptibility to noise and interference.

Batch Capture—Automatic digitizing of select video clips from a tape based upon a pre-determined list of time codes.

Betacam SP—Sony's industry standard professional analog video format. Uses 1/2" tapes slight smaller than VHS.

Bin—A computer icon representing a folder or storage space in the graphic computer workspace. Nonlinear editing programs often organize video and audio clips in bins.

Bit—The smallest piece of computer information. Based upon a binary number system that allows it to only have a value of one or zero.

Boom Operator—The person responsible for using a boom pole to suspend a shotgun microphone above talent.

Break Out Box—A stand-alone or mounted box designed to make a FireWire card or video capture card's connectors more accessible.

Broadband—High-speed Internet connections offered via satellite, coaxial cable tv lines, fiber optic cable tv lines or DSL, special high-capacity telephone lines.

Buffered—A method of storing data in memory prior to use by a computer program or device.

Bus—An internal communication channel for computer components.

Byte—A chunk of computer data comprised of 8 bits.

Cable Modem—A high-speed modem that receives and/or sends data over the same coaxial or fiber optic cables that carry television programming.

Camera Picture Tube—A light sensitive glass tube used to scan image information to convert it into electronic signals. Mostly replaced by CCDs.

Camera Ready Art—The artwork from which printed materials are reproduced.

Cardioid Microphone—An omnidirectional microphone with a pickup pattern roughly shaped like a heart.

CCD—See Charged Coupled Device.

CCIR-601—A standard for digital component video, first used in the D1 video format. 4:2:2 sampling rate, 720x486 pixels.

CD-R (Compact Disc Recordable)—A compact disc that can be recorded on one time.

CG—See Character Generator.

CGI—Computer generated images.

Character Generator—A computer based device for creating titles and text for use in video production.

Charged Coupled Device—A light sensitive computer chip used to scan images to convert them into electronic signals.

Chip Set—A collection of customized computer chips designed to support a specific microprocessor.

Chroma Keying—The process of replacing a pre-selected solid color background with other video or graphics.

Chrominance a.k.a. Chroma—The portion of a video signal that represents color information such as tint (shade) and saturation (intensity).

Clapboard a.k.a Slate—Hinged boards snapped together in front of a film camera to create a visual and audible synchronization mark for film.

Claw—The hooked arm responsible for pulling film through a camera.

Closed System—A computer system for which the hardware and software specifications are exclusive to the manufacture.

CODEC—Computer code responsible for providing the compression and decompression of data.

Color Correction—The process of adjusting the color characteristics of a shot to match another.

Color Temperature—A measurement of the color of light based upon the Kelvin scale (K). Higher number are more blue, lower numbers are more red. Daylight=5000°-5500°K, Household lights=2800°K.

Component—A video signal that keeps luminance and chrominance separate for better picture quality.

Composite—A video signal that combines luminance and chrominance, more efficient than component, but lower quality.

Composite Print—Picture and audio elements combined in a single film print.

Compositing—Layering multiple images on top each other.

Compression—Computational processes used to reduce the size of digital information.

Compression Ratio—The relationship between the amount of data before and after compression. The greater the amount of compression, the higher the ratio.

Computer Generated Image (CGI)—Graphics, video, and animation created in a computer.

Conforming—The process of creating a final film negative or master video by reproducing editing decisions made on a lower quality work print copy.

Contrast Range—The camera's ability to discern between the shades of reflected black and white light within a scene. Video's maximum contrast range of 30:1 is far less than film's range of 100:1.

Coverage—The variety of angles and the number of times a scene's action is recorded in full or in part.

Cue Sheet—A listing of significant points in a film or video for which predetermined events, such as sound effects or music, are to occur.

Cued—Setting a tape or video clip at a desired point in preparation of playback or editing.

Custom Presets—Customizable camera settings retained in the camera's memory for quick recall.

Cycle—The timing between peaks of a signal. Measure in hertz.

D-1—The first digital video format and the highest quality format in wide use. Uses the CCIR 601 digital video standard.

Daisy Chain–The ability for computer devices to share a controller by plugging one device into another.

DAT–Digital Audio Tape. A high quality digital audio recording format widely used in music, video, and film production.

Data Rate–The speed at which data moves about between devices or inside of a computer.

DCT–Discrete Cosine Transform. The video compression method used by the DV format.

Decibels (dB)–A logarithmic unit of measurement used for measuring the strength of audio and video signals.

Decompression–Returning a compressed file to its original size by reversing the computational process used to compress it.

Depth of Field–The range between the farthest and nearest points in which all objects in the picture frame appear in focus.

Derivative Work–Music, songs, scripts, stories or other intellectual properties created by modifying the copyrighted or public domain properties of others.

Detachable Lenses–The ability to add or remove entire lens assemblies to and from a video or film camera, compared to undetachable lenses fixed to a camera's body.

Device Drivers–Small computer files that provide a computer operating system with instructions on how to use a particular piece of hardware.

Dial-up–An Internet connection made over a standard telephone line. Legally limited to 53k or less.

Diffused Light–Lighting for which the beams are spread over a larger area, reducing the edges and shadows.

Digital Audio Tape–See DAT.

Digital Betacam–A 1/2" tape, component digital video format evolved from Sony's analog Betacam SP format. Uses compressed CCIR 601 standard video.

Digital–Information represented as computer data.

Digital Versatile Disc (DVD)–A new compact disc media for high quality distribution of film and video programs. Uses MPEG-2 video compression.

Digital Video Effects (DVE)–A stand-alone studio device or computer software program for performing special effects on video.

Digital Video–Video captured and reproduced as computer information.

Digital Zoom–The use of computer processing to enlarge portions of a video image.

Digitize–The process of converting audio or video into digital information.

Direct Draw Overlay–A computer graphic card option that allows you to mix video and computer graphics on your computer monitor. Does not affect video output quality.

Director of Photography (DP)–The person responsible for establishing the visual look of the film by designing lighting arrangements and designating camera settings. On most low-budget films, also operates the camera.

DirectShow–Microsoft Corp.'s multi-media software module and file format set to replace Video for Windows and AVI files.

Disc Image–The final file created once DVD assets have been combined and tested. Used to create a master disc.

Dissolves—A transition where one image gradually fades out as another gradually fades in.

Drop Frame Time Code—A time code format that compensates for true 29.97 frame rate of NTSC video. Matches standard time by dropping two frames of time code every minute (except the tenth minute). Used in broadcast television where it is helpful for the time code recorded with a program to match real time.

Dropout—A tape defect that briefly disrupts the video signal resulting in a speck or other imperfection in the video image.

DSL—Digital Subscriber Line. A high-speed connection over ordinary copper telephone lines dedicated to data. Also, features variations such as ADSL, HDSL, and RADSL.

DVC—Digital Video Consumer format. Features standard size and mini-DV size tapes.

DVCAM—Sony's professional DV format. Same video format as DV but features locked audio and wider pitch for the data track offering greater reliability during editing.

DVCPRO—A professional DV format develop by Panasonic. Also features locked audio as well as an analog audio track.

DVE—See Digital Video Effects.

EBR—See Electron Beam Recorder.

Edit Controller—A device used to control playback decks and a record deck during editing.

Edit Decision List—A list of time codes and decisions for edits performed during the assembly of a program. Can often be saved as a computer file to allow programs to be quickly and easily recreated.

EDL—See Edit Decision List.

EIDE—Enhanced Integrated Drive Electronics. An older controller specification used for computer hard drives and other devices.

Electronic Beam Recorder—A device that uses microscopic electronic beams to draw images onto film. Used for transferring video or computer generated images to film.

Electronic Image Stabilization—Electronic circuitry designed to reduce a camera's susceptibility to excess movement and provide a more stable image.

Electronic News Gathering (ENG)—Field recording of video using portable production and editing equipment.

Emulsion—The light sensitive element of film that is exposed to take a picture.

Exposure—1) The size of a shutter and duration for which it allows light to reach a light sensitive CCD, picture tube, or frame of film. 2) The F-stop setting for the lens aperture that allows light to enter a camera.

Fade—1) Images gradually revealed from a solid color or that gradually transition to a solid color. 2) Gradually raising or lowering audio levels.

Field—Half of a video signal captured during one pass of the scan of a video image. One half of a video frame.

Fill Light—A light instrument used to light a subject from the side and reduce shadows created by the key light.

Film Recorder—A high resolution monitor or laser system used capture video or computer generated images on film.

Film Stock—The light sensitive strips used to capture motion pictures.

Filters—Glass instruments used in front of a lens to modify the attributes of light entering the camera.

Fine Cut—A meticulously edited version of a project.

FireWire—Apple Computers' trademarked name for the IEEE-1394 interface.

Flat Lighting—Even lighting, without shadows, contrast, or highlights. Lacks the depth required for drama.

Fluid Head—A device used to mount a camera to a tripod, while using a specially lubricated joint system to allow for smooth camera movement.

Focal Length—The measurement, in millimeters, from the optical center of a camera's lens to the surface of the film or CCD imaging chip inside the camera.

Focus Control—The ability to adjust a camera's lens to properly focus on an image.

Foley Artist—A person who creates foley effects.

Foley Effects—Sound effects created in sync with action on screen.

Foley Stage—The studio used to record live sound effects.

Font—Stylized text used in character generators, computer software, or print production.

Frame—A single entire film or video picture. Video frames are comprised of two fields of partial picture information.

Frame Line—The boundaries of an image as viewed by a camera lens.

Frame Movie Mode—A recording mode available on the Canon XL1 that records video using progressive scanning to capture entire frames instead of interlacing fields of video.

Frames per second (FPS)—The number of film or video pictures taken or replayed per second.

Frequency—The number of cycles performed in one second. Expressed in hertz (Hz).

Friction Head—A device used to mount cameras to tripods. Uses adjustable screws to regulate tension while performing camera moves. Not as effective as fluid head.

Gaffer—The person responsible for connecting lighting instruments and electrical wiring during production.

Gain—A signal's total effective range. Usually expressed in dB.

Gel—A colored, flame resistant plastic used in front of lighting instruments to color the light.

Gigabytes (gigs)—A measurement of computer data size. Roughly 1,000 megabytes of information.

Graphical User Interface (GUI)—The use of pictorial icons to represent functions and commands in computer software. Allows operation to be more intuitive than text based interfaces.

Gross Profits—The income received prior to the deduction of expenses.

Hardware Codec Cards—IEEE-1394 cards featuring on-board computers with hardware and software to perform video compression and decompression.

Heads—The element of a video camera or audio device that reads and records data on tape.

High Definition Video (HD Video)—A wide screen, high resolution video format featuring up 1,080 lines of video.

Hot-Pluggable—The ability to connect and disconnect devices while powered.

IDE—An older device controller used in computers.

IEEE-1394—A special high-speed bus standard capable of over 100 megabits/sec (12.5 megs) sustained data rate.

Image Stabilization System—1) A lens and sensor system that helps eliminate the effects of camera movement as images are being recorded. 2) A device that isolates the camera from the operators movement to produce stable images.

Incident Light Meter—An instrument that measures the amount of light falling on a subject.

Interlace—The combining of fields of video to create a single frame of video.

Interpolation—The process of adapting computer graphics or video information to another format by using a predetermined formula to compensate for differences.

Iris—The mechanical, adjustable opening that controls the amount of light entering the camera.

IRQ—Interrupt Query. A computer variable used to regulate the internal communication of computer devices.

Isochronous—Two way communication between devices at a constant data rate.

Jog/Shuttle—A controller that provides control over editing decks using a knob that can easily switch from precise frame-by-frame forward and backward movement to high speed forward and backwards movement.

JPEG—Joint Photographic Expert Group. A still photo compression scheme.

Jump Cuts—An intentional or unintentional, jarring transition from one shot to another created by discontinuity between the two shots.

Juxtaposition—The relationship between a shot and the shot preceding and/or following it.

Kelvin—The temperature scale used to define the color of a light source. Expressed in degrees Kelvin, i.e., 2800ºK.

Key Light—The main lighting instrument used to illuminate a subject.

Kinescope—A moderate quality system for transferring video-to-film using high quality video monitors and a synchronized camera.

Lavaliere—Also called a lav. A small, inconspicuous microphone usually attached to clothes.

Lens—Plastic or glass carefully shaped and crafted to collect and focus reflected light.

Letterbox—A way of displaying film on a television without having to crop portions to compensate for differences in the aspect ratio.

Lighting Ratio—The light level when the key light and fill light are turned on, compared to the light level when only the fill light is turned on.

Linear Editing—Editing performed using videotape decks to assemble projects in a sequential order.

Lockdown Shot—A shot where the camera does not move.

Locked Audio—Audio information is recorded directly synchronized to picture information using a precise timing system.

Locked Picture—The point after which no additional changes will be made to a film's edited visuals.

Log–A listing all of time code and notes for all shots, scenes, and takes on source tapes.

Looping–See Automatic Dialogue Replacement (ADR).

Low Key Lighting–Lighting characterized by high contrast range, particularly with the use of black and white.

LP Mode–Long Play Mode. Increases the amount of information that can be recorded on a videotape, usually at the expense of video quality.

Luminance Keying–Similar to chroma key except video is replaced based upon lightness or darkness as opposed to color.

Luminance–The black and white portion of a video signal that represents the brightness and contrast.

Lux–A measurement of light intensity.

M&E Tracks–Music and Effects tracks. Mixed independently to allow for soundtracks to be easily re-mixed with foreign dialogue tracks.

Magnification Factor–A number representing the range between the widest zoom lens angle and the most telephoto angle. Also called zoom ratio.

Make Movie–A command in Adobe Premiere and other nonlinear editing programs that informs the software to create a file representing the entire project, including any transitions that must be rendered.

Married–Combining and synchronizing individual film and audio elements in preparation of creating a final negative.

Master Shot–A select angle from which the entire scene is recorded prior to recording any additional coverage.

Mastered–The process of creating a final version of a project.

Mbps–Megabits per second.

MBps–Megabytes per second.

Megabytes (megs)–One million bytes of information. One thousand Kilobytes.

MIDI–Musical Instrument Digital Interface. A communication format and protocol for music instruments and notation.

Mini to XLR Adapters–A cable allowing audio equipment with XLR connectors to be used with consumer equipment.

Mini-plug–A small 1/8" connector for consumer audio devices.

Mixdown–The audio combining tracks while adding effects and adjusting their respective levels.

MJPEG–Motion JPEG. The scalable compression format for video, derived from JPEG. Used for most video editing systems, including Avid and Media 100.

Moire–An undesired pattern created by the convergence of lines in a video image that closely match the scan lines.

Monochromatic Image–An image comprised only of white plus one other color, i.e., black and white or sepia tone.

Motherboard–The main computer circuit board onto which other components are added.

MPEG–A video compression format with a limited data rate.

MPEG-2–An advanced version of MPEG compression with a higher data rate. Used primarily for video distribution such as DVD and digital satellite.

Nagra—A high quality reel to reel tape recorder that for years has been the film industry's standard audio recording device.

Negative Cut—Physically cutting the negative film based upon a cut list created from the edited work print.

Net Profits—Profits shown after the deduction of all expenses.

Noise—Any unwanted electrical signal that is not part of the audio or video signals.

Non-Drop Frame Time Code—A type of time code that continuously counts a full thirty frames per second.

Nonlinear Editing—Editing performed with a computer system that allows programs to be completed in a random, non-sequential order.

NTSC—National Television Standards Committee.

NTSC VIDEO—A television standard based on 525 line images recorded and played at thirty frames per second.

Off Frame Sound Effects—Sound effects that have no relationship to events visible on the screen.

Offline Edit—A low-quality edit created to allow for primary editing decisions to be made prior to an online edit session.

On Frame Sound Effects—Sound effects that relate to actions visible on screen.

Online Edit—Assembling the final edit at the highest resolution or using top of the line equipment, based upon the offline edit.

Open Calls—Talent searches open to the public.

Open System—A computer system for which the hardware and software specifications are available for anyone to adopt or utilize when developing equipment or software.

Optical Audio Track—Audio information recorded as visual images running down the side of a film strip.

Optical Printer—A device for shooting individual frames of film under very controlled circumstances.

Optical Stabilization—A use of lenses and motion detectors to reduce the effects of camera movement when recording.

Organic Effects—Computer generated transitions that mimic motion and characteristics of natural elements such as water and fire.

Out Point—The point at which to stop recording a scene.

Overexposure—When more light reaches a CCD or frame of film than is required, resulting in excessive brightness and the loss of details in the recorded image.

Overscan—The edges of an image or areas of a video image that may not be visible on regular monitors or televisions.

Page Turn—A video transition where a current image appears to be pulled from one corner, like the page of a book, to reveal the new image below.

PAL—Phase Alternation by Line. A television standard based on 625 lines recorded and played back at fifty fields per second.

Pan and Scan—The process of selectively cropping film to fit the aspect ratio of television.

Pan—Turning the camera right and left on the horizontal axis.

PCI Bus—Peripheral Component Interconnect. A standard for connecting devices to a computer.

Performance Rights—The rights to publicly exhibit a work.

Pick-Up Shots—Scenes and shots filmed after principal photography, often to fill in elements missing in scenes or the script as a whole.

Pixel—The minimum picture element from which video or computer images are created.

Pixilated—When the pixel elements of an image are very noticeable.

Plug and Play—A feature of an operating system that allows devices to easily be added with minimal manual configuration requirements.

Plug-Ins—A supplemental computer program that operates within another program to add additional features.

Posterization—A computer-generated effect that modifies the color and pixel size of an image.

Pre-Light—To light a set in advance of shooting.

Premastered—Preparing the final DVD file.

Preview—Viewing a video clip, an edit, or an effect prior to recording.

Principal Photography—The period during which the majority of recording or filming occurs.

Production Boards—An organizational tool used when scheduling a shoot.

Program Monitor—The monitor connected to the record device. Used to review the project as it is being assembled.

Program Window—A portion of the computer screen that performs the functions of a program monitor.

Progressive Scan—Capturing video as an entire frame as opposed to interlaced fields.

Pulse Code Modulation (PCM)—A format for digitizing audio information.

QuickTime—An internal computer format for handling video information. Created by Apple Computer is now becoming the standard for Windows computers as well.

Rack Focus—An intentional shift in focus to change the viewer's attention.

RAID—An array of hard drives that operate in sync to provide faster speeds and larger capacities.

RAM—Random Access Memory.

RC Time Code—Rewritable Consumer Time Code. Sony's own version of time code.

RCA Plug—A connector commonly used in video and audio devices.

Record Deck—The video deck on to which the final program is assembled or recorded.

Record In Point—The entry point on the recorder at which recording is to begin.

Record Out Point—The exit point on the recorder at which recording is to end.

Reflected Spotlight Meter—A light meter used at the camera's lens. Measures the amount of light reflected from the subject it is aimed towards.

Rendering—When a computer performs the computations required to create or display video, audio, a graphic, or an effect.

Resolution—The amount of detail in an image.

Reversal Stocks–A positive film stock that can be directly projected after development. Does not require a print to be made.

RGB–Red, Green, Blue. The primary colors from which all other colors can be created.

Room Tone–The ambient sound of any given room.

Rough Cut–A preliminary edit of a project prior to a fine cut.

RPM–Revolutions Per Minute.

SAG–Screen Actors Guild.

Samples–The portions of an analog signal converted to digital.

Scan Lines–The visible lines that are the result of the interlacing of the odd and even fields of video.

Scrim–A lighting tool made from mesh wiring and used to reduce the intensity of a light without diffusing it.

Script Breakdown–Identifying every element of a script that must be accounted for during principal photography.

Scrub Video–Full resolution, full speed video playback while editing.

SCSI–Small Computer System Interface. A high speed computer device controller.

SECAM–System Electronique Pour Colour Avec Memorie. The 625, fifty fields per second television format developed in France.

Sequencer–Computer hardware or software used to compose MIDI music.

Serial Data Interface (SDI)–A high speed digital interface.

Service Bureaus–Companies that perform specialized services.

Shooting Schedule–The timeline in which scenes are to be filmed.

Shooting Script–The final script that will be used for all production planning, budgeting, and scheduling decisions.

Shot Sheet–A listing of shots the director intends to record for a given scene.

Shotgun Microphone–A highly directional mic with the ability to only pickup audio that it is aimed towards.

Shutter–1) A mirrored portion of the lens that controls the duration of exposure for film. 2) An electronic setting that determines how long the CCD of a video camera is exposed to light.

Shutter Speed–The duration of the exposure expressed as a fraction of a second.

Signal-to-Noise Ratio–The relationship between the amount of usable signal and undesirable noise in a signal. The higher the better.

Slip Cover Tape Case–A plastic videotape case with a clear plastic cover that allows a printed paper cover to be securely tucked inside.

SMPTE–Society of Motion Picture Engineers.

SMPTE Time Code–A time code standard for North America.

Software CODEC Cards–IEEE-1394 cards that rely on the computer and the hardware codec of a an attached DV device to compress and decompress DV during editing.

Software Patches–Small computer programs designed to correct minor problems with a software package.

Sound Mixer–The person responsible for microphone selection, placement, and audio level monitoring while recording.

Source Deck—A video player from which tapes are played during editing.

Source Window—An area of an editing program where clips are viewed and editing points are established prior to moving the clips to the timeline.

SP–Standard Play—The normal record speed for videotapes, compared to LP.

Splicing—Cutting film and taping or cementing portions together to assemble a project.

Spotting Session—Reviewing a locked film to establish the points where music and/or sound effects will be added.

Stamping—The physical process of reproducing a DVD from a master.

Steadicam—A camera stabilization device that helps produce smooth shots.

Stingers—Short pieces of music used to accent an event on screen.

Story Boards—Graphic, comic book like representations of important moments in a scene as the director intends to shot it. A communication tool.

Streaming—Data sent over the Internet at a steady enough pace to facilitate smooth playback of audio/video files by the recipient.

Strobing—Video playback or lighting that visibly flickers at a steady rate.

Sub-mixing—Mixing several tracks down to combine them prior to the final mixdown.

Superimposed—The ability to lay a graphic or video over other material.

Sustained Throughput—The minimum, consistent data rate that can be maintained by a computer or device.

Sync Point—A visual and audible point used to match video/film elements and audio elements.

Synchronization Pulses (SYNC)—A timing system used to keep video signals and data properly formatted.

Synchronization Rights—The legal rights to pair a song to your picture.

Talent Release Form—A legal form granting you permission to use a performer's likeness and voice in your production

Telecine Machine—A machine used to transfer film to video.

Temporary Tracks—Temp Tracks. Pre-recorded music tracks that represent the type of music intended for the final production.

Time Code—A system that assigns every frame of video a unique number that can be used for consistent and quick reference to that point.

Timeline—The area in nonlinear editing software where a project is assembled based upon the order of the occurrence of events.

Treatment—A brief summary of a film script.

Trinescope—A variation of the kinescope that films video using three high resolution monitors instead of one.

UDMA—Ultra Direct Memory Access. A high speed hard drive controller.

Unbalanced Line—A lower quality audio cabling system frequently used in consumer products, more susceptible to electrical interference than a balanced line.

Underexposure—When too little light is allowed to reach the film frame or CCD resulting in a dark image lacking contrast and detail.

Underscan—A feature on some professional monitors that reduces a picture to allow the entire image to be seen.

Unlocked Audio—The audio recording method used in DV that does not record audio precisely matched with the video information. Theoretically allowed slippage of +/-1/3 frame, unlike locked audio.

Up Convert—Converting a lower resolution video to the higher resolution of another video format such as high definition.

Upgrades—Software that adds substantial improvements to a computer program.

Value-Added Reseller (VAR)—A retailer that specializes in building and selling computers designed for specific purposes.

Video Sleeves—Cardboard boxes that slip over a videotape.

Viewfinder—The small screen built-in a camera and used to monitor video. May be inside a small eye piece or attached to the side of the camera.

Voltage—The strength of an electronic signal.

VU Meters—A device or software that visually displays the volume of a signal.

VU—Volume Unit. A unit of measurement of average audio level.

Walk Through—Preparing for a scene on set by casually reviewing action and placements with key personnel.

WAV—A Windows audio file format.

Webcasting—The distribution of audio and video over the Internet.

White Balance—Adjusting a camera's light filtering system, based upon current lighting conditions, to ensure that the camera accurately responds and records colors.

Wild Sounds—Audio recorded without images.

Window Dub—A copy of a tape created with time code visually recorded in a portion of the screen.

Windows 95/98—Microsoft's graphic based computer operating system.

Windows NT—The Microsoft operating system based on Windows but originally geared toward computers in a networked environment. Requires much more computing power than Windows 95/98. However, it is a much more stable system. Used by several high end nonlinear programs.

Wipe—A transition between two images, the first shot is replaced by the second shot using a variable, moving pattern.

XLR—A three pin plug used on the balanced audio cables found in professional audio equipment.

Y/C—A component signal format that separates Luminance (Y) and Chrominance (C). The true name of S-VHS cables and connectors.

YUV—The professional component video format that separates video into Luminance (Y) and two chrominance variables, U which is for the red component, and V which is for the blue. Green is calculated from the difference between U and V.

Zoom Lens—A lens assembly that uses adjustable lenses to vary the focal length and size of objects in the frame.

Zoom Range—The distance between the wide angle setting of a lens and the telephoto setting.

Zoom Ratio—See Magnification Factor.

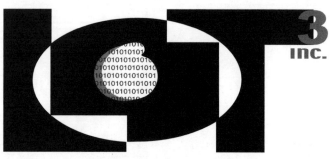

Leading Others Through Tomorrow's Technology

Award Winning DVD
for Independent Film Makers

DVD Creation
featuring
Sonic Solutions DVD Creator

5.1 Dolby Digital Mixing and Encoding • Director's Commentary
Making Of • Multi-Angle • Interactivity • Copy Protection
Internet Connectivity and Controlability
Duplication • Packaging

Long and Short Format Online Finishing
featuring
Discreet Logic and Avid|DS

Editing • Compositing • Paint
Animation • Effects • Audio

Lot^3 • www.lot3.com • (303) 863-9755

HOLLYWOOD
OnSet

your window
on Hollywood

www.hollywoodonset.com